Marvels & Mysteries
of the
Unexplained

Marvels & Mysteries
of the
Unexplained

An imagination-defying exploration of our world's strangest secrets

KAREN FARRINGTON

BARNES & NOBLE

NEW YORK

This book was created for Arcturus Publishing Limited
by Amazon Publishing Limited,
7 Old Lodge Place, St. Margarets,
Twickenham, Middlesex TW1 1RQ

Editor Ella Fern
Designer Stuart Perry
Illustrator Tamasin Boyer

ISBN-13: 978-0-7607-8491-4
ISBN-10: 0-7607-8491-4

Printed and bound in China

10 9 8 7 6 5 4 3 2 1

Contents

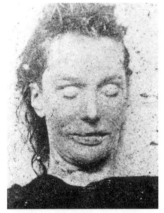

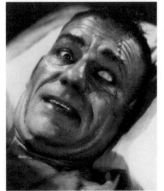

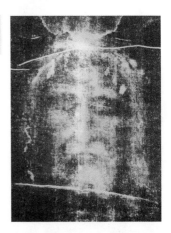

SECRETS OF THE OUTER UNIVERSE

Events that occur in the furthest reaches
of space rarely register on our planet.
Yet occasionally, signs of life in the boundless
universe do impinge on us here on earth, keeping us
guessing about what is really out there. Reports of
alien abductions and UFO sightings have become
increasingly frequent, suggesting that perhaps we are
not the only life form to have broadened our
horizons beyond our own planet. But at the moment
we possess just pinpricks of knowledge that shimmer
enticingly like distant stars in a night sky.

Angel Hair

Angel hair is a rare and perplexing phenomenon that has so far defied explanation. It is a delight to behold, made up of silken threads that rain down on to the earth and look startling against a cloudless blue sky. But reach out to touch it and it will almost certainly vanish before your eyes.

MIRACULOUS MORNING

In September 1741, one corner of Hampshire, England, became remarkable for a blizzard of gossamer that continued for hours. Residents from three small towns – Bradley, Selbourne and Alresford – saw the downpour, which indicates that the fall covered a considerable area. One witness related what he had seen in a letter written four years after the astonishing event:

'As the morning advanced the sun became bright and warm, and the day turned out one of those most lovely ones which no season but the autumn produces; cloudless, calm, serene, and worthy of the South of France itself.

'About nine [in the morning] a very unusual appearance began to demand our attention, a shower of cobwebs falling from very elevated regions, and continuing, without any interruption, till the close of the day. These webs were not single filmy threads, floating in the air in all directions, but perfect flakes or rags; some near an inch broad [2.5cm], and five or six long [13-15cm], which fell with a degree of velocity which showed they were considerably heavier than the atmosphere.

'On every side as the observer turned his eyes might he behold a continual succession of fresh flakes falling into his sight, and twinkling like stars as they turned their sides towards the sun…Neither before nor after was any such fall observed; but on this day the flakes hung in the trees and hedges so thick, that a diligent person sent out might have gathered baskets full.'

WORLDWIDE PHENOMENON

This account is one of the most familiar stories of an angel hair shower, but by no means was it an isolated incident. Since then, there have been reports of this strange occurrence from all over the world, although the greatest number are from North America, Australia, New Zealand and western Europe.

In 1914, soon after the first winter rains arrived in South Australia, there were accounts of angel hair falling in pieces between 15cm and 23cm long, and then swiftly dissolving on the ground. Three weeks later another shower, lasting for an hour, was reported.

According to a 1950 edition of the *Philadelphia Inquirer*, two police officers in South Philadelphia in the United States were on evening patrol when they saw what they thought must be a parachute falling to earth. When the 1.8m-long object finally landed, the officers saw it glow in purple and crystalline colours. As one of the men reached down to touch the substance, 'the mass on which he laid his hands dissolved, leaving nothing but a slight, odourless, sticky residue.' Within 25 minutes it had all disappeared.

Two years later, a school headmaster in Oloron-Sainte-Marie in south-west France saw objects in the sky that he could not identify. In their wake came trails of an unknown substance, which was described as gelatinous at first, but that quickly turned into vapour.

Global reports about angel hair have continued with surprising frequency, sometimes detailing that it arrives in balls rather than flakes. Indeed, descriptions vary from fluorescent filaments, through to flecks and strands and even to jelly and goo. One conclusion is that the substance has come from spiders or perhaps

Angel hair is described as being similar in substance to spiders' web, made of gossamer-like intertwined fibres.

another silk-spinning insect. Spiders do sometimes migrate by flying in wind currents, but there is a marked absence of spiders in the material described as 'angel hair' and, as yet, a link to arachnids has not been proven.

The mystical qualities of this substance are enhanced by the fact that some – although not all – accounts of angel hair are associated with the sighting of an unidentified flying object (UFO).

THE RESEARCH

So far, there has been little orchestrated research into the qualities of angel hair. This is primarily due to a lack of reliable data, as it tends to disappear after coming into contact with human flesh. However, one woman is trying to change this. Analytical scientist Phyllis Budinger, from Ohio, has used the restricted number of angel hair samples available to draw some conclusions about its chemical content.

She investigated four samples, drawn from across North America. Incredibly, the first dated from 1977 and had been stored in two air-tight glass jars for more than twenty years before being analyzed. It fell in Los Gatos, California, and the samples lay forgotten until 1998.

In 1999, a bemused driver who had driven for some 24km through a fall of angel hair near Sacramento, California, collected the second sample. Some strands were just a few centimetres long, while others measured up to 17m long.

The third sample came from Burlington, West Virginia, in 2000, and was discovered after the householder heard a mysterious droning noise lingering

At Oloron in south-west France, a headteacher saw UFOs trailing strands of angel hair. Could this mysterious substance be extraterrestrial exhaust?

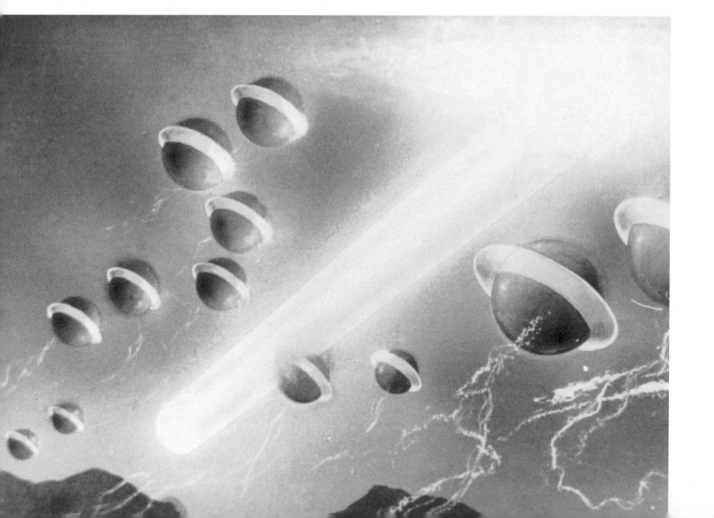

outside her home the previous night. It was only in this case that the substance was described as transforming into a slimy goo. Inexplicably, both the householder and her dog fell ill after finding the angel hair, although it is not known if the events were linked.

Shenandoah in Iowa was the location of the fourth angel hair sample. The fall occurred in 1981 and lasted for nearly six hours. This case was notable for being concurrent with the sighting of a UFO.

Budinger was able to scrutinize the Los Gatos samples through an extremely powerful microscope and saw bundles of fibres rather than single strands. They were even thinner than spiders' silk, and the droplets often seen with arachnid webs were not apparent. However, while it is true that spiders' silk is frequently characterized by the presence of droplets, this may not always be the case. Only further research into the nature of spiders' webs will clarify this.

Some – although not all – accounts of angel hair are associated with sightings of a UFO.

Unfortunately, access to the powerful microscope was no longer available when the other samples reached Budinger's laboratory. Nevertheless, she was able to determine that all four specimens had similar molecular structure. She defined this as 'a polymer containing protein-amide type linkages'. A polymer is formed from repeated units of smaller molecules, while amides are ammonia-based compounds.

WEB OF MYSTERY

Budinger's findings indicate that angel hair originates from a biological source. But to date, she has been unable to identify this source. There are similarities between angel hair and spider or caterpillar silk, but they do not seem to be identical.

Angel hair is not only difficult to collect, but it is also highly sensitive. It is subject to contamination from car exhaust fumes, or even from the human hand, which might skew the chemical results of analysis.

The two most compelling samples of angel hair are those collected at Burlington and Shenandoah, where there is a strong suspicion of UFO activity. Indeed, a different analysis of information about angel hair falls in Australia discovered that in eleven cases there were no reports of UFO sighting, while in eight there were. It is this extraterrestrial aspect of angel hair that both baffles and intrigues investigators today.

Budinger is in no doubt as to what is now needed to resolve the mystery of angel hair. 'Clearly a broader database is required. Most important is the need for angel hair from events coinciding with witnessed UFO activity. More samples are needed from a variety of locations and from falls at different times of the year. Unfortunately, a predominance of data is from falls in the United States and in the month of October…Proper sampling is needed. It should be done as soon as possible after the event…Proper analytical testing is required.'

Until such a thorough scientific approach is adopted, the unusual sight of a fall of angel hair can be valued as one of today's enduring mysteries.

Alien Implants

The notion that extraterrestrials have visited earth and abducted humans for close quarters examination has been around for some fifty years. More recently it has come to light that those who believe they have had close encounters may be marked out forever by an intravenous implant.

CALLING CARD

For over a decade, implants have been reported in the hands, feet, abdomen and nasal cavities of abductees. Only x-ray technology can discern whether aliens have left their extraordinary calling card, as there are no obvious indications remaining on the skin. However, those afflicted are frequently dogged by illness, even before any suggestion of an implant is made.

So why would aliens implant humans in this way? It is a matter for conjecture, but there is one generally accepted opinion – that the implants might act as transmitters or beacons so that when the aliens return they can trace their human subjects. So far, though, hard evidence for implants is in short supply.

Indeed, there is no conclusive proof that humans have ever been inside spaceships. All the evidence is anecdotal, leading the sceptics to claim that the experiences reported by abductees are nothing more than lucid dreams. Yet how can we explain that the accounts of kidnappings by aliens number in their hundreds? Furthermore, the stories all bear a curious similarity.

Stories of abduction usually begin with the sighting of a UFO. The accounts that abductees give of dancing lights in the sky or cigar-shaped craft shooting overhead are sometimes verified by other people in the area.

Alone and helpless, the abductees are reportedly taken to a brightly lit, clinical room on board the spacecraft, where the aliens proceed to examine them.

Abductees then apparently walk, float or fly up into the spacecraft inside a beam of light. Inside, they find the craft brightly lit and clinically clean. They recount how the examination takes place in this surgical setting, with the human subject naked and quivering beneath the eyes of the aliens. It is presumably at this point that an implant is inserted. Afterwards, the human interlopers might be offered a tour of the craft. Attempts to remove a keepsake have always ended in failure, although the aliens are apparently friendly and keen to give advice that will benefit mankind.

A HAZY MEMORY

Returned to their homes or vehicles, the abductees typically discover they have only been missing for a few minutes, although it seems to them that hours have passed by. Immediately, the events inside the craft become a hazy memory, but then return in haunting and vivid dreams. After abduction experiences, people often sense that they are being observed, although they do not generally feel the surveillance has sinister motives.

Hypnosis is one of the methods used to try and understand what has happened to abductees – or experiencers as they are sometimes called – during the time lapse inside the spacecraft. In the absence of film footage or other incontrovertible evidence, this information would otherwise remain hidden in their subconscious. In the 1980s, 270 cases of claimed abduction were analyzed in detail using hypnosis. All accounts showed astonishingly close consistencies, especially given that those involved were from different backgrounds, professions and geographic locations. However, the accuracy of using hypnosis for the purposes of recall is not proven, and it is believed that interviewers' beliefs on the subject may influence the outcome. The results are open to debate.

Accounts of alien abduction usually start with the sighting of mysterious lights in the sky, or an encounter with a UFO.

MYSTERIOUS IMPLANTS

So what about the implants? Surely they must provide hard evidence of abductions. If experiencers submit to a second examination, the implanted particle or device can be analyzed. However, results have proved disappointing. One item believed to be an alien implant was sneezed out, and turned out to be a ball-bearing. Another was proved by chemical scrutiny to be a dental filling. There is no conclusive proof about the nature of implants, although recent accounts allude to small, tear-shaped rocks of an unknown substance.

Perhaps more worryingly, there is an oft-repeated allegation that women are implanted with sperm and become pregnant, only to be robbed of the foetus before giving birth. If the accounts of experiencers are to be believed, the aliens take a special interest in human reproductive organs.

THE ACCOUNTS OF EXPERIENCERS

In September 1961, Betty and Barney Hill were driving along the isolated Interstate Route 3 in New Hampshire when, as they relate, they encountered a spacecraft that looked like 'a big pancake'. Later, they were to reveal the details of their encounter while under hypnosis and their convincing stories became a kind of benchmark in terms of alien experience. They recounted how they ended up aboard the craft, where there were uniformed men with large eyes, flat noses and lipless mouths. Betty, a social worker, was given 'a pregnancy test' by some futuristic machinery through the navel. Meanwhile, mail sorter Barney endured the extraction of his semen.

Betty was given a 'pregnancy test' through the navel by some futuristic machinery.

Although Barney died years later, Betty has always maintained that she was taken by aliens. Yet her approach remains underpinned by common sense. Her experience, she insists, does not reflect any extraordinary personal talents. 'I'm about as psychic as a dead fish,' she jokes.

Likewise Elaine Darlington, a former Royal Air Force servicewoman living in Newquay, Cornwall, enjoyed an ordinary life before her alleged contact with aliens. She recites four different encounters with aliens, and it was during the last of these that she said an 'operation' took place.

ALIEN OP

'They zapped me with a light on the centre of my forehead. They seemed to be able to manipulate matter or body energy,' she said, 'The operation began – I think it was on my stomach. There was no pain but they had some problem with my blood…I came round in my own bedroom with no side effects, apart from one small blotch on my left rib cage. It vanished within 24 hours.'

Because the mark on her body disappeared so quickly, evidence was once again in short supply. However, Elaine's home was hit by power cuts around the time of the visits and she herself suffered electric shocks. Curiously, her local electricity board could find no problems with supply.

On a final alien encounter on Newlyn Downs, Cornwall, Elaine's husband Ian was there to share her experience. Elaine had woken in the early hours, convinced she was to make an excursion to the Downs. On arrival, they recount how they both saw a bright light through the window of their vehicle and watched it shoot up at high speed to the sky.

The lack of hard evidence to prove alien abduction makes it all the harder for experiencers to convince sceptics, but they will not give up. 'My memories of being taken are real,' insists Elaine. 'It isn't like remembering dreams'.

Greys

A spindly body with bulbous, hairless head and large, dark almond eyes. Sound familiar? Probably, since this is the uniform description given of alien life forms spotted here on earth. These beings are known as 'greys', after the colour of their smooth, rubbery skins. In recent years, reports of alien sightings have been relatively frequent, and it is striking how similar most descriptions are.

GREY MATTER

Sceptics do not believe the image of the grey to be the real likeness of alien life-forms, but rather that which appeared in an ABC sci-fi show made in the early 1960s called *The Outer Limits*. They believe this image has somehow seeped into international consciousness as the definitive portrayal of extraterrestrial life, when previously the image was predominantly of 'little green men'. Yet surely this cannot explain that, even under hypnosis, literally scores of people have come up with the same descriptions? The life forms they speak of communicate telepathically, have wasted muscles and closely resemble foetuses.

There has been plenty of speculation about what part of space these extraterrestrials might come from. Among the most frequently cited places is Zeta Reticuli, a binary star, visible in the skies of the southern hemisphere, thirty-nine light years away from earth.

Why would aliens want to visit earth? Perhaps they are on a quest to save their dying race, or maybe they want to clone human beings for an unknown purpose. It is doubtful that they would come here to wonder at our technology,

Greys are described as having spindly bodies, with bulbous, bald heads, and large almond-shaped eyes.

since their own appears to be far superior. Nor does it seem to be their aim to share their knowledge with us, because the recall of abductees is often hazy.

Reports of UFOs began surfacing after the Second World War, when the world was gripped in the paranoia of the Cold War and the fear of the atomic bomb. Rocket technology had advanced during the war years to a point where fast, long-distance flight appeared to be a distinct possibility for the first time. Americans were fearful of a communist invasion and they were sure that, in the event, both nuclear and psychological weapons would be dispatched by the USSR. It was in this climate of fear that pilot Kenneth Arnold saw what he described as 'flying saucers' soaring in formation above the Cascade Mountains in Washington State in June 1947. Arnold's testimony marked the beginning of a flood of UFO sightings in America and around the world.

ROSWELL

On 7 July 1947, these stories reached their climax, with the revelation of the now-notorious Roswell Incident. The wreckage of an odd-looking craft and its equally unusual humanoid crew was apparently discovered on the Foster ranch, near Corona, New Mexico. The following day a press officer for the nearby Roswell Army Air Fields announced that an alien vessel had crash-landed there. But a high-ranking military officer was swift to refute the claim, saying that an experimental balloon had gone down

Many people remained convinced that the US government had evidence of aliens in its grasp.

near Roswell. As he explained it, the bodies at the scene were in fact crash dummies. However, many people did not accept the official explanation, and they remained convinced that the US Government had evidence of aliens in its grasp.

The debate was fuelled in 1995 when a film allegedly showing an alien autopsy following the Roswell incident was unveiled. But there was immediate doubt about the film's authenticity, not least because the creatures which featured in it did not match descriptions given of them at the time.

Since then, theories about what really happened at Roswell have abounded, the latest being that emaciated Japanese prisoners of war were being used as test pilots on an experimental flight. This would certainly explain why the military were keen to have the whole incident hastily covered up.

The entire Roswell episode has been marked by inconsistencies, controversy, claim and counter-claim. It is known that at least two crucial official documents from the era have gone missing. But if some of the original descriptions of the Roswell Army Air Fields crew are to be believed, then this was the first known human contact with greys.

SCINTILLATING FACT OR SCIENCE FICTION?

Since the Roswell incident, large numbers of stories involving contact with greys have circulated, some of which seem convincing, others less so.

In July 1952, Truman Bethurum was sleeping in his truck when he was woken by the voices of eight diminutive figures standing close by. Outside his cab, Truman was astonished to see a 90m-wide spaceship, hovering soundlessly. The beings, he reported, had olive rather than grey skin. According to his account, they told him: 'Our homes are our castles in a faraway land'. Then they allegedly took him aboard the spaceship to meet its captain, Aura Rhanes, who told him they were from the planet Clarion, obscured from earth by the moon.

Linda Cortile announced she was literally beamed up into a spaceship by aliens who were short and grey with round heads and frail bodies.

Ten years after this incident, a UFO that reportedly crashed south of Alamogordo, New Mexico, yielded the bodies of two greys. They have been described as being about 1m tall with large heads, pink-grey skin, large eyes, small noses and mouths and holes for ears. It is said that the bodies were sent to a leading university hospital in America for analysis.

In 1973, student Masaaki Kudou was working as a security guard in a timber yard close to the sea on Hokkaido, Japan, when he apparently saw a space ship taking off from the water. He claims he saw one humanoid figure and another two that were smaller. Other spaceships joined the first before they sped off together, leaving Kudou astounded.

In 1989, mother Linda Cortile announced she was literally beamed up into a spaceship by aliens who were short and grey with round heads and apparently frail bodies. Curiously, the incident happened on Manhattan Island and reportedly had a host of witnesses. Alien appearances are more commonly associated with rural areas rather than metropolitan places like New York. Cortile recalled that during the abduction she was given a medical examination, before abruptly being returned to bed in her twelfth-storey apartment. Scrutiny of Cortile's case continues even today.

ALIEN BLOGS

The internet has enabled the exchange of stories like these to proliferate. There are also many on-line tales from people who claim to have seen spaceships in US air force hangars and spoken to aliens captured from these craft. However, most of these are experiences related by a third person, rather than by first-hand witnesses, and are therefore less reliable.

Sceptics sneer at the stories of contact with aliens, sometimes known as 'close encounters of the third kind'. And some of the stories are so exaggerated that they are hard to believe.

Yet just as the cynics dismiss all claims of alien contact, so ufologists feel able to scoff at many of the earthly explanations given for episodes of this nature. When detailed descriptions of an alien encounter are given by several witnesses, the explanations that those involved mistook a fast-moving mystery disc for Venus in the night sky or for high-flying weather balloons do seem simplistic. To dismiss all reports of extraterrestrial contact is closed-minded, given the size of the universe and possibility of advanced life-forms existing far from earth. And the notion that alien sightings are the product of people's subconscious has yet to be proved to anyone's satisfaction.

Black Holes

In 1927 the pioneer of genetics, J. B. S. Haldane, famously observed that the universe is 'not only queerer than we suppose, it is queerer than we can suppose'. Today, eighty years on, there is little sign of science proving him wrong. Indeed, the more we probe the cosmos, the more baffling it seems.

At the heart of this great debate is the study of theoretical physics, where things happen for no reason and an event in one outpost of space can trigger an instant reaction light years away. Traditionally, theoretical physics has been perceived as a dry and dusty subject, riddled with incomprehensible equations. Yet without it, we can never hope to tease out the secrets of the most mysterious phenomena in the known universe – black holes.

Current theories about what would happen to a manned spacecraft entering a black hole vary greatly. At one end of the argument is the view, held by most physicists, that it would be crushed to oblivion by immense gravitational forces. However, a respected minority believe that the craft could theoretically be spewed backwards or forwards in time, or even into a parallel universe, through distortions in the fabric of space caused by the black hole. These tunnels are known as 'wormholes'.

UNRAVELLING THE MYSTERY

To see what might happen to a spaceship in a black hole, it is important to take a look at our current understanding of how the universe works. Einstein produced huge advances in this area, although his Theory of Gravitation cannot explain the massive forces at work inside a black hole. The idea of black holes first emerged in 1916 when the German astronomer Karl Schwarzschild built on Einstein's work. Schwarzschild calculated the size of a star with a gravitational pull so strong that not even light, the fastest traveller of all, could escape from it. The speed needed to escape from this star, known as its 'escape velocity' was equal to the speed of light. According to Einstein's Theory of Relativity nothing travels faster than light, so such a star will be invisible. Moreover anyone, or anything, which becomes trapped in its gravitational field will be drawn inside and, according to most scientists, obliterated.

Karl Schwarzschild calculated the size of a star with a gravitational pull so strong that not even light, the fastest traveller of all, could escape from it.

These 'stellar' black holes are essentially collapsed stars that have used up all their fuel. They have no material surface, because all their original matter has been shrunk to an infinitely dense point known as a 'singularity'. Recent research led by Hubble space telescope astronomers suggests that there are millions of stellar black holes in our galaxy alone. It is also thought that every galaxy has a 'supermassive' black hole lurking at its centre, a monster whose mass was once millions of times larger than our sun. Supermassives are thought to play a pivotal role in the way a galaxy evolves.

THE FACT OF THE MATTER

However, Hollywood's portrayal of black holes as giant vacuum cleaners sucking up all matter (including planets) across many light years is a myth. If the sun were to become a stellar black hole tomorrow – and such an event is not due for several thousand billion years – the lack of light and heat would certainly destroy

The Hubble telescope has been able to transmit pictures of the whirlpool galaxy M51. The dust nucleus at the centre is thought to hide a massive black hole.

life on earth. However, the change in gravitational pull would be imperceptible. Unlikely as it sounds, you would have to get within a few kilometres of the sun to reach the point of no return.

Mainstream theories suggest that anything approaching a black hole is first torn apart by gravitational forces and then compressed into a flat rotational disc that spirals inside, a phenomenon known as a 'feeding' black hole. When this happens the material heats up (due to friction) and gives off x-rays detectable from earth. If the ring of material around a supermassive black hole contains lots of debris then it can produce an intense light source known as a quasar, one of the most distant objects ever observed. The nearest quasars are hundreds of billions of light years from earth, which gives some idea of the enormous energy they generate.

Anything approaching a black hole is first torn apart by gravitational forces and then compressed into a flat rotational disc that spirals inside...

All this suggests the chances of a manned spacecraft surviving entry into a black hole are nil. Roughly the same odds, in fact, that a nineteenth-century aero-engineer had of landing a craft on the moon and bringing it home. The point is that no one can predict technological advances on the basis of current knowledge. What really matters here is the theory. So what if we assume a spacecraft could get through?

SPACETIME AND WORMHOLES

And this is where things get really tricky. Einstein's Theory of Relativity brought space and time together into a concept known, unsurprisingly, as 'spacetime'. This shows that we exist, in four dimensions – up, down, sideways and through the passing of time. If we can travel upwards, downwards and sideways in space, then why can we not do the same in time?

The best way to visualize spacetime is to imagine a rubber sheet stretched out with marbles rolling across it. Imagine that the marbles are planets, or comets. They travel in straight lines except where they go near a heavy marble (a star) that causes the rubber to dip (a gravitational field). The marbles bend around that dip as they roll, illustrating that everything, including light, follows curved paths in spacetime.

Occasionally they come across a really heavy marble (a black hole). This does not just cause the rubber sheet to dip, it breaks right through it to the other side. Similarly, the sheet itself may contain tiny holes, just as rubber does if viewed under a powerful microscope, allowing a passage through the barrier.

But what is on the other side of these wormholes? It could be the sheet folded back on itself, which would be a location back or forward in time. Or it might be a completely new universe.

THE GRANDFATHER PARADOX

The standard argument against time travel has always been the 'grandfather paradox', the idea that if you travelled back and somehow stopped your grandfather meeting your grandmother then your mother would never have been born…and neither would you! If you never existed, then how come you are wandering around the past?

The notion of breaking into a separate universe altogether solves this conundrum. According to the theoretical model, anyone heading back in time through a wormhole arrives in a parallel universe with a completely new future. The time traveller can now have no effect on the universe he left – he or she simply ceases to exist there – but can shape events in the new one. So there could be an infinite number of universes accommodating an infinite number of time travellers…

A DARK FUTURE?

To readers who have stuck with it this far – and nobody promised this section would be easy – the sad truth is that humankind has barely scratched the surface of cosmology and quantum physics. But scientists are already contemplating the possibility of teleportation, where particles move instantly from one point in space to another. They are also working on quantum computation, which will allow massively complex calculations to be performed in seconds rather than years. One day, they may answer the hardest question of all, namely what is time? It is possible that in the future, Haldane may be proved wrong.

A spacecraft approaching a black hole would almost certainly be destroyed. But if the black hole were a portal to another universe, its fate would be altogether different.

EARTHLY ENERGIES

Our own planet is the source of many unexplained forces and ancient wonders shrouded in mystery. Primitive populations pushed themselves to the limit to achieve such feats as Stonehenge and the Nazca lines, yet in many cases it is impossible to say what purpose they serve. Investigating the powers that lie within the earth, we are struck not by how much we have learned, but by the amount we have yet to find out.

Crop Circles

The inexplicable formation of flattened circles in fields of crops has gripped our imagination since the first recorded evidence in a seventeenth-century woodcut. They range from complex geometric patterns and DNA symbols to simpler versions that look like snowflakes and spiders' webs. While enthusiastic hoaxers may be responsible for many crop circles and patterns, not all can be dismissed so easily.

In the mid-1980s, the crop circle phenomenon gained momentum, as hundreds of patterns began appearing in the fields of southern England. More outlandish explanations – flying saucers, fairies, field sprites and the Devil himself – were quickly laughed off by a sceptical media. But 'natural' explanations, such as rolling hedgehogs, mating foxes, plasma clouds, whirlwinds and changes in the earth's magnetic field hardly seemed more credible. Within a few years, many commentators had agreed that the circles were all just a big hoax.

Soon newspapers were revealing how gangs of tricksters armed with ropes, planks, surveyors' tape, stakes and plastic garden rollers were touring the shires to make their mark in the dead of night. These groups of hoaxers even gained a measure of notoriety and were given names – Merlin & Co, The Snake, Spiderman, The Bill Bailey Gang – but the undisputed grand old men of British 'cereology' were known simply as Doug and Dave. In 1992, Doug Bower and Dave Chorley admitted to devoting more than twenty-five years to crop circle-making. This seemed ample proof for the sceptics that all circles were hoaxes. And yet a couple of successful pranksters working for a few years in southern England could not explain historical and worldwide reports of crop circles. This was certainly not the end of the story…

ANCIENT PHENOMENON

There is nothing new about crop circles. One of the earliest documented reports appeared in 1686, in *The Natural History of Staffordshire* by Robert Plot, a Professor of Chemistry at Oxford University. Professor Plot was seeking to discover a 'higher principle' behind the formation of crop circles. He set out to debunk the then popular theories (rutting deer, urinating cattle and, inevitably, fairies – see page 65) and decided that electrical storms were to blame.

'They must needs be the effects of lightning exploded from the clouds most times in a circular manner,' he wrote. The energy would emerge from the cloud 'so as at due distance to become a circle and in that forme to strike the earth'. Occasionally, he believed, the energy would form rectangular shapes – reflected in the more unusual crop patterns.

AUSTRALIAN ENCOUNTER

While southern England remains a hot-spot for crop circles, they are by no means unique to this corner of the world. Similar markings have been reported in

Japan and North America, and perhaps the most celebrated link between a circle site and a UFO came in 1966 with Australia's 'saucer nest' case at Tully, north Queensland. On 19 January of that year, George Pedley, a 28-year-old banana farmer, was driving his tractor past Horseshoe Lagoon when he saw a dull, blue-grey UFO, roughly 8m × 3m and shaped like 'two saucers face to face'. The UFO apparently rose out of the swamp grass, dipped slightly and accelerated away at extraordinary speed. He could hear a hissing sound above the noise of his engine.

When Pedley ran to look in the lagoon he found a circular area about 9m across where the reeds had been flattened. Three hours later, the reeds had floated back to form a clockwise radial pattern – similar to some 'basic' crop circles. Investigations by the police and Royal Australian Air Force were inconclusive, but the most likely explanation was said to be a 'willy willy' – a peculiar type of tropical whirlwind known to create a hissing sound.

If this was indeed the explanation, then the UFO shape witnessed by Pedley was simply a huge mass of debris sucked up by the twister as it moved off.

Whilst some crop circles are just circular indentations, others appear to show complex mathematical equations and scientific symbols, leading people to believe that an intelligence is at work in their formation.

However it does not fit with Pedley's clear description of the craft (he was standing just 30m away) and fails to account for a distinct lack of debris left on the ground. Neither does it explain why a 'willy willy', which is associated with thunderstorms, should strike Horseshoe Lagoon on a windless, sunny day.

WHIRLWIND VORTEX

Nonetheless, the whirlwind theory is held by many experts to be at least feasible. In 1988, British consultant meteorologist Dr Terence Meaden of the Tornado and Storm Research Organisation, went so far as to claim the mystery had been solved. He told an Oxford conference that most genuine crop circles were formed near hills where wind, gusting on one side, caused a vortex of gyrating air to suddenly spiral downwards.

Three years later, he seemed to have eye-witness confirmation of his theory. Gary and Vivienne Tomlinson of Guildford, Surrey, told how they were caught in the 'eye' of a circle as it was being made in a Hampshire cornfield. Mrs Tomlinson recalled: 'There was a tremendous noise. We looked up to see if it was caused by a helicopter, but there was nothing. We felt a strong wind pushing us from the side and above. It was forcing down on our heads – yet incredibly my husband's hair was standing on end.

'We felt a strong wind pushing us from the side and above. It was forcing down on our heads – yet incredibly my husband's hair was standing on end.'

'Then the whirling air seemed to branch into two and zig-zag off into the distance. We could still see it, like a light mist or fog, shimmering as it moved. As it disappeared we were left standing in a corn circle with the corn flattened all around us. Everything became very still again and we were left with a tingly feeling.'

ELECTRIC ATMOSPHERE

Other scientists believe that electrically super-charged air plays a key role in the formation of crop circles. Professor Yoshihiko Ohtsuki of Tokyo's Waseda University stated: 'The circles are caused by an elastic plasma, which is a very strong form of ionized air. In an experiment…we created a plasma fireball which, if it touched a plate covered in aluminium powder, created beautiful circles and rings just like the ones seen in fields.'

Some years bring more circles than others, and 1991 is regarded as a vintage crop, so to speak, by British cereologists. Apart from the Tomlinsons' bizarre encounter, southern England seemed to be alive with furtive circle-makers, including one formation on farmland next to the Prime Minister's country retreat, Chequers. Presumably the then Premier, John Major, was not at home – and there were no secret service agents around to serve as witnesses.

Further west, near Bristol, Eddie Wise spent four nights in a Wiltshire field which had been the site of previous crop circle activity. He was not disappointed in his vigil, and claimed to have witnessed an enormous alien spaceship land. 'There were no lights but I could see what appeared to be windows,' he said.

'A long object was lowered from the base of the craft and when it touched down in the field everything became quite still.'

Even some of the crop circle hoaxers believe in a UFO link. No less an authority than Doug Bower, the godfather of circle pranksters, swore he had seen UFOs – reminding onlookers that just because some formations are obvious hoaxes, this does not mean that they all are. As Ray Cox, chairman of the UK Centre for Crop Circle Studies, put it in a 2005 interview with The *Guardian*: 'Crop circles are an ongoing enigma unfortunately coloured by people who want to believe extraordinary things, and hoaxers. They make some very beautiful things but I wish they'd leave it alone so that science can get on with trying to evaluate the real thing.'

The fact is that the formation of genuine crop circles remains a mystery to baffle even the world's most advanced scientists. Whether they are formed by the atmospheric conditions on earth, or by extraterrestrials touching down for a visit, the forces at work in our fields lie far beyond human comprehension.

Some experts believe that simple crop circles could be formed by a whirlwind vortex touching down into a crop, flattening it and then moving on.

Stonehenge

The towering, mysterious circle of rocks that rises out of Salisbury Plain has inspired awe in millions of people over the ages. But the reason for its existence baffles archaeologists to this day. Various theories suggest a ritual site, an astronomical observatory, or a focus for some mystical form of 'earth energy'.

ROCKY EVOLUTION

In piecing together the complex Stonehenge jigsaw, we can at least be confident of some basic facts. Using radiocarbon measurements, scientists have dated the earliest work on Salisbury Plain to around 3,100BC. At this time the site was far more primitive, comprising a circular 97.5m diameter ditch, a single entrance and a central wooden 'temple' or sanctuary. Around the edge of the ditch were fifty-six holes, each containing cremated human remains. On the summer and winter solstices the whole structure aligned with rising and setting points of the moon.

By 2,500BC, the wooden sanctuary had been replaced with two circles of the famous bluestones that had been transported 390km from the Preseli mountains of south-west Wales. An entrance avenue of parallel ditches which aligned to the midsummer sunrise was added, together with outlying single megaliths such as the Heel Stone, Slaughter Stone and Station Stones. However, the bluestones were pulled down within a century and recycled for a new design.

The new Stonehenge had a very different emphasis. At its centre was the Altar Stone (now fallen), a large sandstone shipped from the Cleddau Estuary in Pembrokeshire. Over the next 500 years, some of the re-used bluestones were raised around it in a horseshoe shape. Beyond these were placed five massive sarsen trilithons (two uprights bearing a horizontal), a ring of bluestone pillars and an outer ring of sarsen uprights linked by lintels. The bus-sized sarsen blocks are by far Stonehenge's largest, typically weighing 30 tons and at least one as much as 50 tons. Most are thought to have been transported from the chalklands of Marlborough Downs, some 32km west.

HEAVY WORK

According to some estimates these three building phases must together have required more than thirty million hours of labour. For Stone Age people to allocate this amount of time – even over two millenia – seems extraordinary. It suggests a level of co-operation far above what we might expect; a society in which Stonehenge labourers would have had to be fed, watered and sheltered in order to build a seemingly useless monument. How did they do it? More importantly, why did they do it?

The how is comparatively easy to fathom. Many of north-west Europe's neolithic monument builders used large quantities of stone transported from a great distance. The architects of Newgrange in the Irish Midlands, which predates the Stonehenge megaliths by at least 500 years, brought quartz and granodiorite from sites 48km away. It seems likely that Stonehenge's bluestones were brought to Salisbury Plain by a combination of raft-borne river, sea and overland transport. Once the raw materials arrived, the construction of the circle itself would have required a phenomenal amount of manpower, relying on a levering system of wood and rope.

Manpower aside, the thorny question of quite why it was necessary to lug the bluestones 390km is far from clear. A study led by Geoff Wainwright and Timothy Darvill in 2004 suggests that the dolerite crags of the Preseli mountains would have held particular appeal. The stone is naturally fractured into 'ready-made' pillars, so they just needed to be levered off for removal. The stones themselves – strong, durable, and speckled with white feldspar – may have been invested with a symbolic, mythical power.

Which brings us back to the key question, what was Stonehenge for? It may well have had different functions at different times. But the prevailing archaeological view is that Stonehenge was a ritual and burial site, linked to astronomical observations. It was almost certainly not used to predict the agricultural crop cycle. In England the summer solstice occurs long after the start of the growing season and the winter solstice misses the harvest by a good three months.

PIGS AND DRUIDS

In 2005, tests on some neolithic pig bones showed that large numbers were slaughtered in the months of December or January. This lends weight to the idea that a winter solstice festival was held at Stonehenge. It also seems to have been an important burial site. Around the standing stones are a large number of burial mounds, and in 2002 an archer's grave was discovered that contained more than 100 precious items such as gold earrings, copper knives and pottery. Tests have shown that the deceased – dubbed the 'King of Stonehenge' – was born in the

The mammoth bluestones used to construct Stonehenge were transported almost 400km from the Preseli mountains of south-west Wales to Salisbury Plain.

Alps around 2,300BC. This is the richest known burial of the age anywhere in Europe, and the implication is that the 'King' was a settler who played a key role in the constructing the monument.

The link between Stonehenge and the ancient Druid religion has taken a battering in recent years. Experts believe this connection was always tenuous (based as it was on the observations of Julius Caesar) and it is now clear that the heyday of the Druids came a thousand years after work on Stonehenge ended. However, we cannot be certain how early the Druid traditions came into existence, so a link cannot be ruled out.

CELESTIAL CALENDAR

The idea that Stonehenge was used as a celestial calendar is simple to prove. If you stand in the centre of the circle at 5am on a clear Midsummer's Day you can see the sun rise precisely in line with the Heel Stone, 37m beyond the ring. This is the most obvious and impressive of the circle's mysterious alignments. During the 1950s and 60s a further twenty-three alignments were recorded by Oxford University engineer Alexander Thom and the astronomer Gerald Hawkins. Hawkins speculated that Stonehenge was used to predict eclipses, although critics now say

The ancient architects of Stonehenge possessed a level of mathematical and engineering sophistication that defies explanation.

his methodology was flawed and that he overestimated the number of alignments.

What is clear is that the ancient architects of Stonehenge possessed a level of mathematical and engineering sophistication that defies explanation, knowledge that appears to have pre-dated both the Egyptian and Mesopotamian cultures. How can we explain that 2,000 years before Euclid's Pythagorean 'breakthrough', and more than 3,000 years before Arya Bhata 'discovered' the value of Pi, neolithic Britons were using these concepts to construct Stonehenge?

MYSTERIOUS FORCES

Putting aside questions of science, another theory behind the existence of Stonehenge is that it focused some intangible 'earth energy', a natural force field that could be tapped by those in the know. Hard evidence for this theory is lacking, although footage of UFOs in the skies above the circle in October 1977 has never been properly explained. All we can say for certain is that Stonehenge seems to be in a significant place: it stands on a known 35km ley line (see page 33), which also bisects three earthworks and three *tumuli* (burial grounds).

Maybe the greatest barrier to solving the mystery of Stonehenge lies in our own prejudices. Today we live a hectic urban lifestyle that isolates us from the subtle rhythms of nature observed by neolithic societies. Perhaps we are concentrating too much on scientific knowledge, and our problem in unravelling

Ley Lines

In 1921, a mill owner called Alfred Watkins discovered a strange feature of the British landscape — the alignment of ancient sites and natural features across many miles. He called these connections 'ley lines' after the Saxon word ley, meaning 'clearing'. Today the debate over their purpose still rages.

Most open-minded archaeologists accept that ley lines exist. True, it is possible to quibble over detail — a burial mound is bisected at one edge rather than the centre for instance — yet given the effects of agriculture and land management over several thousand years such imprecisions must be expected. The real issue lies not in proving the leys are there, but in interpreting them.

Watkins built up knowledge of his subject over many years travelling the

An ancient trackway typical of the ley lines discovered by Alfred Watkins. The network of trails extends across the whole of the British landscape.

rolling hills of his native Herefordshire. During visits to mills and farms he would note familiar landmarks, photograph them and plot their locations on a map. Combined with his expertise in local history, folklore and place names he soon had an unrivalled insight into the county's geography. When he eventually realized what he had discovered, he likened the feeling to 'a flood of ancestral memory'.

In his first short book, *Early British Trackways*, Watkins describes how the flash of insight occurred one summer's day: 'I had no theory when, out of what appeared to be a tangle, I got hold of the one right end of this string of facts and found to my amazement that it unwound in an orderly fashion and complete logical sequence,' he wrote.

'A visit to Blackwardine led me to note on the map a straight line starting from Croft Ambury, lying on parts of Croft Lane past the Broad, over hill points, through Blackwardine, over Risbury Camp, and through the high ground at Stretton Grandison, where I surmise a Roman station. I followed up the clue of sighting from hilltop, unhampered by other theories, found it yielding astounding results in all districts, the straight lines to my amazement passing over and over again through the same class of objects…'

LEY LOGIC

In his main book on the subject, *The Old Straight Track* – published in 1925 and still the definitive work on leys – Watkins explains his theory in depth. He believed he had uncovered an ancient system of trackways, initially laid out as far back as the Stone Age. These would then have been adopted by subsequent cultures and preserved, some of them right up to the present day. The tracks were marked by obvious reference points to assist travellers, and they might bisect man-made landmarks such as castles, churches, burial mounds, standing stones and stone circles, as well as natural features like hilltops, 'notches' on a ridge, ponds and even prominent groups of trees.

There were some obvious flaws in Watkins' argument, not least that many castles and churches were constructed long after the neolithic period when he believed leys were created. However it is generally accepted by historians that these structures were often built on significant sites. It follows that certain ley markers are original and others evolved from their predecessors. As for trees, while it is true that a few British species date back thousands of years, it is also quite possible for their descendants to occupy the same spot. Very often, clumps of trees are found atop the sites of their forebears.

How would the ancient inhabitants of Britain have planned straight tracks, without modern methods of measurement and navigation?

As mentioned earlier, some sceptics accuse ley hunters of being too 'flexible' in their enthusiasm to plot lines through map landmarks. They argue that a ley is either straight or not, and that a few metres out is not good enough. Watkins himself was more relaxed about these measurements, noting that 'ancient methods of alignment…tended to pass through the edges of circles, not taking their centres as is now the case.'

But how would the ancient inhabitants of Britain have planned straight tracks, without modern methods of measurement and navigation? Watkins believed the 'straight-sighted track' would have been planned using fire beacons at strategic points and a team of men with staves. (He even suspected that these surveyors were the inspiration for the chalk figure of the Long Man of Wilmington in Sussex.) Once the ley was plotted, scrub and woodland along the line would be cleared and additional markers added.

COLOUR DETECTIVE

Place names formed a key component of Watkin's theory. He pinpointed fields called ley or lea as possible sites. Place names containing references to the colours red and white suggested pottery or salt trade routes respectively. It followed that a place name referring to the colour gold was linked to the transport of precious metals, but Watkins later discovered that the answer was more mystical: a 'gold ley' was aligned to the midsummer sunrise.

Black was harder to explain, until Watkins realized that in Anglo-Saxon times the word meant something quite different. Black could mean shining, white or pale – perhaps a reference either to the signal fires or reflective ponds. Watkins decoded many ley names, tracing their symbolism back into the mists of the past.

THE DOUBTERS

But however mysterious and captivating this might be, a key question remained. What was the motivation for constructing leys? To our knowledge, there were

The Long Man of Wilmington in Sussex. Could this be a depiction of one of the ancient surveyors who plotted the ley lines?

almost no straight roads and paths in the ancient British landscape, apart from the Roman legacy. Are we expected to believe that a tradition of straight track-building simply died out, and that ley lines are all that remain? Isn't it just as likely that landmarks form purely chance alignments and that ley followers are all wishful thinkers? Over the years, leading mathematicians have attempted to illustrate this, with varying degrees of success.

Watkins answered his critics with a crude, though intriguing, experiment using a map of the Andover district. He noted the positioning of fifty-one churches on the map and counted the number of alignments between them. He found that there were thirty-eight alignments of three churches, eight alignments of four churches and one of five churches. He then marked fifty-one random crosses on an identically-sized piece of plain paper. This produced thirty-four three-cross alignments, one of four crosses and none of five crosses. Watkins concluded that the number of four-church alignments in Andover was 'exceedingly strong evidence of deliberate alignment'.

If this sounds unscientific, remember that dozens of known leys bisect considerably more than four landmarks. For example, at Glastonbury there are at least seven landmarks aligned over 34km, at Stonehenge there are eight over 35.5km, and one ley line bisecting Cambridge has ten landmarks aligned across just 22km. Nor are 'old straight tracks' unique to the British Isles. In the western Cordillera of the Andes one track stretches for 32km across a hilly landscape at a height of 3,960m.

In the busy, urbanized world of today, we generally prefer to take the easiest path between two points, avoiding hills and obstacles.

MYSTERIOUS PURPOSE

The question of what leys were for remains a tantalizing mystery. It could be they were simply a neolithic version of motorways, allowing travellers to take the straightest, clearest, safest route irrespective of whether this meant climbing a hill or traversing a river. In the busy, urbanized world of today, we generally prefer to take the easiest path between two points, avoiding hills and obstacles even if it is longer as the crow flies. But it does not follow that Stone Age humans would have done the same. Given their active, outdoor lifestyle, striding up a hill or two would hardly have counted as strenuous.

Leys may have had other practical or religious purposes – perhaps they were used for astronomical alignment (see Stonehenge on page 30). Inevitably they have taken their place in New Age thinking, and some pagans believe they were intended to channel an undefined 'earth energy' between sacred sites. Others claim they are linked to UFOs, perhaps functioning as ground markers for alien visitors coming in to land.

Our landscape is criss-crossed with these mysterious lines, but the truth is, we still do not know why they are there. More than eighty years after Watkins' breakthrough discovery, their presence in the British countryside remains as enigmatic as ever.

The Nazca Lines

Across a 434km² stretch of Peru's Nazca desert, archaeologists have identified 13,000 lines and pictures etched into the sun-baked surface. That these images were produced by an ancient civilization is beyond doubt. But their purpose is far harder to explain.

The designs were first noticed in the 1920s, as manned flights began to venture into South America. Pilots reported seeing straight lines which ran for miles, traversing mountains and occasionally ending on cliff edges. Geometric shapes included triangles, rectangles, spirals, wavy lines and concentric circles. Animal geoglyphs included birds, whales, a dog and lizard. Some images were drawn on a truly vast scale: a 305m pelican, a 285m bird with a curiously zig-zag shaped neck and a monkey complete with 100m spiral tail.

There were also more surreal pictures – specifically an 'astronaut' figure and a bizarre creature with two colossal hands, one of which had only four digits. Was this, as some have claimed, an attempt to record contact between prehistoric humans and alien beings?

WHAT WE KNOW

Before considering this and other interpretations of Nazca, it is worth setting out areas of agreement among experts. Firstly, it is obvious that the lines were made by removing the desert's top layer of iron-oxide-coated stones to reveal lighter-coloured soil underneath. Secondly, it is accepted that this must have been a colossal effort, perhaps lasting a thousand years, and that because of the scale of the work the artists could never have seen the full fruits of their labours from the ground. The lines are so unobtrusive that during the last century the pan-American highway was built straight through them without anyone noticing. Thirdly, it seems likely that the patterns were made by ancient Nazca Indians sometime between 400BC-600AD. This estimate is based on radiocarbon analysis of Nazca fire and ceramic debris, although it is not conclusive, since the lines themselves cannot be radiocarbon-dated.

It is possible that an even older civilization did some of the hard work, perhaps evolving from the Paracas culture which blossomed in southern Peru between 1100-200BC. The Paracas people are thought to have constructed the giant El Candelabro geoglyph. Also known as the Tres Cruces or the Trident, this form stretches to more than 120m wide. It is situated on a slope overlooking the Bay of Paracas, together with some fifty figures – humans, birds, cats and monkeys – near the Peruvian city of Palpa.

> *The lines are so unobtrusive that during the last century the pan-American highway was built straight through them without anyone noticing.*

SOUTH AMERICAN STONEHENGE?

The first academic to make a proper study of Nazca was Paul Kosok, an American who stumbled across the site in the late 1930s while researching prehistoric irrigation systems. He suspected that the lines were linked to astronomical alignments, a theory reinforced when in the late afternoon of the southern hemisphere's winter solstice (22 June) he and his wife witnessed the sun set precisely at the end of one line. Kosok enlisted the help of a German astronomer, Maria Reiche, and together they developed the idea that some Nazca shapes were used as a calendar to help farmers calculate crop planting times. The animals, they believed, represented major constellations.

Another American scientist, Gerald Hawkins (see Stonehenge on page 30) used a specialist computer program to calculate the number of significant solar alignments produced by the Nazca lines. He decided that alignments would have to point consistently to a specific celestial event, such as the rising or setting of stars, sun and moon. Neither was it enough merely for some lines to fulfil the criteria. If the astronomical link were to be proved, then it had to account for all the lines.

Hawkins instructed his computer to show how many were aligned on extreme positions of the sun or moon. The answer was thirty-nine out of 136, barely better than would be expected by chance. Worse, only a few of these thirty-nine alignments could be linked to significant solar or lunar positions. Hawkins tried a similar experiment with the stars, inputting a catalogue of their positions dating back to 10,001 BC. Again, the alignments were statistically insignificant.

An aerial view of the Nazca lines criss-crossing the Peruvian desert. Could these really be some kind of communication for extraterrestrial visitors?

ALIEN SPACEPORT

In 1968, as Hawkins published his results, the Swiss writer Erich von Daniken inflamed the Nazca debate by claiming that the lines marked out a giant alien spaceport. His book *Chariots of the Gods* essentially argued that it was impossible for ancient people, incapable of flight, to have produced the drawings themselves and that they must have been taught by visiting aliens.

Critics accused von Daniken of making the facts fit his theory. His cause was not helped by a television investigation into pottery fragments which, he claimed, dated from biblical times and depicted flying saucers. Unfortunately, von Daniken's fragments proved to be of more recent vintage, after television journalists found and interviewed the potter who made them.

As if to rub salt into his wounds, a flamboyant American publisher and adventurer called Jim Woodman set out to prove that Nazca people could, in any case, have known how to fly. Using

One of the more bizarre geoglyphs has few recognizable features other than two huge hands, one of which has only four digits.

cloth and rope based on samples found in Indian graves, and reeds cut from Lake Titicaca on the Bolivian border, he constructed a 2,260m³ hot-air balloon, powered by heat from a bonfire on the ground. Together with the British balloonist Julian Nott, Woodman ascended to a height of 90m, neatly illustrating that Nazca designers could well have had the technology to fly and monitor progress of their work. This theory may sound far-fetched, but archaeologists have already shown that at least 500 years earlier, Paracas doctors were performing brain surgery through trephination – the removal of skull sections with a cylindrical saw.

WHY BOTHER?

Yet even if the ancient inhabitants of South America had the means to make the lines, this still does not explain what they were for. Few archaeological sites have spawned quite so many theories, and in recent years Nazca has been cast as a giant map of subterranean water sources, a focus for earth energies (rather like Stonehenge), a cathedral plan, an athletes' racetrack and even a giant loom on which vast teams of weavers produced cloths or nets. Even harder to grasp is the idea that the Nazca lines are located on a global 'Code Matrix' in which the world's significant ancient sites correlate precisely to the Great Pyramid at Giza. Evidence for this is reportedly found in the geometry of Nazca's layout.

The most likely explanation is that the lines were linked to religious or magical ceremonies. Nazca was an agricultural society skilled in planting, irrigation, harvesting, storage and distribution, but it was also vulnerable to natural disasters and disease. Could the lines have been communal sites for appeasing or worshipping specific gods? Perhaps they served as a gentle reminder of the needs of the Nazca people, and a prompt for regular help from on high. The truth is that, even discounting the role of alien architects, the purpose of the lines remains frustratingly elusive.

The Arthur Stone

The legend of King Arthur is one we are all familiar with, but we are not so sure of the historical facts concerning his life. On 4 July 1998, an archaeologist working at Tintagel Castle in Cornwall unearthed an inscribed chunk of slate. It bore the name Arthnou — an early version of Arthur — re-opening a furious academic controversy about where the 'Once and Future King' of the Britons resided.

TINTAGEL FINDS

The discovery of what became known as 'The Arthur Stone' caused a sensation in archaeological circles. The chief archaeologist of English Heritage, the government-backed body which manages the castle site in North Cornwall, declared it 'the find of a lifetime'. Dr Geoffrey Wainwright added: 'It is remarkable that a stone has been discovered with the name "Arthnou" inscribed on it at Tintagel, a place with which the mythical King Arthur has long been associated.'

What so excited Dark Age historians was that the stone emerged from a proven 'sealed context', meaning it had lain undisturbed since at least the seventh century AD. Measuring 20cm x 35cm, and 1cm in depth, it was originally a plaque of some kind, and bore the Latin words: *Pater coli avi ficit artognov* – 'Arthnou, father of a descendant of Coll, has had (this) made/built/constructed'.

> *What so excited Dark Age historians was that the stone emerged from a proven 'sealed context'...*

Quite what he had constructed remains unclear, because the slate had been broken and re-cycled as a seventh-century drain cover. However 'Arthnou' was clearly once a leader of means and stature. In Britain of the Dark Ages, literacy was the preserve of monks and the educated nobility.

Previous excavations at Tintagel had produced fragments of wine and oil pots imported from the Mediterranean, suggesting that the castle was a high-status, secular site, possibly the royal court of a chieftain of Dumnonia (the ancient kingdom of southwest Britain). The slate's significance was that it proved people here were reading and writing Latin, and living a Romanized way of life, 200 years after the Romans left in 410AD, which is exactly the period when King Arthur was supposed to have been in power.

THE LEGEND

In unravelling the mystery of the Arthur Stone, it is important to separate the legendary story of the King from the historical version (such as it is). Few other areas of ancient British history produce quite so much disagreement among scholars and given that there at least nine competing claims for 'ownership' of Arthur – Brittany, Cornwall, Cumbria, Scotland, Somerset, three areas of Wales, Wiltshire, Warwickshire and Yorkshire – it is hard to see a consensus emerging.

What is clear is that Arthurian legend has been much reproduced and embellished over the years. Fantasies such as Malory's fifteenth-century tome

Le Morte D'Arthur, Tennyson's *Idylls of the King* and T. H. White's *The Once and Future King* have all contributed to Arthur's legendary status. In these books we learn how Arthur founds his court on the principle of 'might for right', valiantly defending his kingdom against the invading Saxons. He thrives under the counsel of the wizard Merlin but is eventually betrayed by the adultery of his best friend, Sir Lancelot, with his Queen, Guinevere, and dies a hero's death in the 'last battle' against evil forces led by his nephew Mordred. Despite this, according to the old stories, he lies buried in a secret tomb and will return to aid his people in their hour of need.

The Arthur legend is loosely based on the writings of the twelfth-century canon Geoffrey of Monmouth, whose *History of the Kings of Britain* was widely read in Europe. Geoffrey's declared aim was to promote patriotism by extolling the glories of the early Britons, but unfortunately the distinction between fact and myth is lost in his work. When Geoffrey wrote of Arthur's birthplace as Tintagel, he was mis-translating an earlier text which used the term 'din-dagol', an old Welsh word meaning 'double-banked hillfort'. He also wrongly believed the Cornovii tribe, supposed ancestors of the King, were based in Cornwall, although they actually controlled what is now the West Midlands. In fact some historians argue that Cornwall has the weakest claim of all to an Arthurian link.

The ruins of Tintagel dominate the dramatic Cornish coastline. Could this have been the home of the legendary Arthur?

WORD OF MOUTH

However, just because the written history of sixth and seventh-century Britain is unreliable, this does not mean that traditional folk tales and oral records should be discounted. An oral system worked pretty well for the Vikings, who relied on it for centuries in matters of law and governance. In Iceland there was even an elected Lawspeaker whose job was to hold the law in his memory and recite a third of it each year, for three years, at the main annual assembly. The problem of course is that oral history is easier to manipulate.

The story of Arthur's quest for the Holy Grail (see page 195) is a case in point. Portraying the king as a defender of Christianity against pagan Britain was nothing more than skilful spin-doctoring by missionary monks keen to claim converts. Just as they built churches on sacred pagan sites, so they adapted traditional stories to suit their religious agenda. Arthur, if he ever existed, was almost certainly a pagan.

And yet the legend of the Holy Grail may be an oral allegory for actual events. It draws heavily on the concept of a freezing wasteland where no crops grow, where famine is rife and plague stalks the countryside. Climatologists now believe that the Arthurian period may have seen just such a scenario, perhaps caused by a mass of debris from comets in the atmosphere which partially blocked light from the sun. Contemporary records from elsewhere in Europe bear this out – the Mediterranean writer Zachariah for instance talks of 'fire from heaven' – and an analysis of oak tree rings suggests growth was severely curtailed between 539 and 541AD.

It is likely that the name 'Arthnou' (which originally meant 'known as a bear, known to be a bear') was common amongst ancient Britons.

SEARCHING FOR THE KING

So was there ever a 'real' Arthur figure? Many Dark Age historians now believe that a militarily successful and charismatic leader did emerge in Britain after the fall of the Roman Empire and that his name lived on in folk memory well before any meaningful written accounts. The ninth-century historian Nennius tells us that Arthur was a former Roman General, but offers little by way of explanation. To confuse matters further, it is likely that the name 'Arthnou' (which originally meant 'known as a bear, known to be a bear') was common among the ancient Britons.

Could Arthur's court have at been Tintagel? There are certainly plenty of legends linking the King to Cornwall, among them a stone slab at Slaughterbridge, near Camelford, which is said to mark his grave. Other stories claim his magical sword Excalibur lies at the bottom of either Dozmary Pool on Bodmin Moor, or Loe Pool near Helston, where it was thrown by St Bedivere as Arthur lay dying. The waterfall at St Nectan's Kieve, near Tintagel, is supposedly the place where Arthur baptized his knights before they embarked on their search for the Grail.

English Heritage has been careful to play down any clear, evidential link between the Arthur Stone and either the historical or the legendary king. However as Dr Wainwright puts it: 'Tintagel has presented us with evidence of a court of the Arthurian period with buildings, high-status finds and the name of a person, Arthnou. Arthnou was here, that is his name on a piece of stone.'

Shrouded in mystery and yet somehow familiar, the Arthur stone is a unique archaeological find where, as Dr Wainwright put it, 'myth meets history.'

Dowsing – the Sixth Sense?

Dowsing, or 'rhabdomancy' as it was originally called, is a technique that has been used to find water or minerals underground for thousands of years. Dowsers believe that anyone can acquire this ability – once as natural as sight, but long forgotten by a technology-obsessed society.

Contemporary texts and drawings show that the Ancient Egyptians, Babylonians, Greeks, Romans and Jews all used simple dowsing tools such as split water reeds. The Old Testament tells how Moses and Aaron used a rod to bring forth water from a rock, while among China's royal dynasties the Emperor Kwang Sung of the late third millennium BC was an enthusiastic dowser. Many believe the oriental art of feng shui, which governs building design and layout, emerged from a combination of dowsing and so-called 'sacred geometry'.

DEVIL'S WORK

However by the Middle Ages, and particularly in continental Europe, dowsers were keeping a low profile. The practice was also known as 'water-witching' and anything which smacked of witchcraft tended to attract worrying levels of interest from the Spanish Inquisition. As late as 1853, the Roman Catholic Church was warning that 'it was the devil his very self that pulled and twisted the dowsing rod to give the accurate results.'

Despite this claim (or perhaps because of it) Anglican Britain became something of a dowsing centre of excellence, producing some charismatic characters in the process. A Bristol stonemason, W. S. Lawrence, earned a useful second income during the nineteenth century by using a hazel twig to find water and horseshoe-shaped wire to find mineral deposits. By all accounts he was very successful, and enthralled clients would watch him gripped by impressive muscular spasms as he closed in on his target.

Another celebrated exponent was John Mullins of Wiltshire, who turned professional in 1882 with a confident 'no-find-no-fee' promise to clients. His task would be to pinpoint reliable sources of underground water which were crucial to remote farmsteads and houses. Judging by the way his business expanded, he must have convinced many a hard-headed farmer of his abilities.

By the last century, the technique of dowsing was being applied to a range of new challenges. A French Catholic priest, Abbé Mermet, reasoned that if you could find water underground, then that same skill could perhaps be used to diagnose illnesses linked to the human bloodstream. His 'radiesthesia' pendulum technique achieved some recognition among physicians, and later evolved into a discipline known as 'radionics', in which a dowser attempts to tap into the energy field of a patient.

John Mullins of Wiltshire turned professional with a confident 'no-find-no-fee' promise to clients.

WARTIME TACTIC

Sceptics were quick to poke fun at all this, and yet dowsing has never been the preserve of New Age eccentrics. During the Second World War, the British Army's Royal Electrical and Mechanical Engineers regiment – the Sappers – trained soldiers to use rods to find water. They reasoned that it did not matter how dowsing worked as long as it did work. The US Army took a similarly pragmatic view, and during the Vietnam war, front-line troops were taught to dowse their way through minefields where no conventional detector was available.

HOW DOES IT WORK?

Common dowsing tools today include a hand-held Y-shaped hazel twig (which dips or rises when the user walks across an underground source), L-shaped metal rods (which cross or separate) and a pendulum. Water and mineral deposits are by no means the only targets, and dowsers also specialize in soil testing, locating archaeological remains, and tracking down lost possessions.

Exactly how and why the technique works is unknown, but according to the International Society of Dowsing Research, one popular theory is that a psychic or telepathic link synchronizes a dowser to the 'living field' which emanates from all people, animals and things. A dowser is said to tune into this energy network by focusing on a clear mental image of what he or she seeks. Subtle or unconscious responses in the nervous system then cause the dowsing tool to move.

Dowsers usually hold a Y-shaped hazel twig, which dips or rises when he or she crosses an underground source of water or a mineral deposit.

Some investigators have cited so-called 'E-Rays' (from the German word *erdestrahlen* or earth-ray) as a possible explanation. The idea is that these E-Rays originate deep beneath the earth's crust, rising to form an invisible pattern at the surface. Where the pattern is distorted (by, for instance, an underground stream) the dowser makes a subliminal nervous response which is visually amplified by the

During the Vietnam war, front-line troops were taught to dowse their way through minefields where no conventional detector was available.

chosen tool of his trade. Over the years researchers have given E-Rays various names – electromagnetism, biogravitation, electro-kinetic currents, infra-red light sources, neutron radiation, microwaves, ionizing fields – but the jury is still out on whether these perceived forces can be explained by the current laws of physics.

Similarly, enthusiasts of Curry and Hartmann lines (named after the physicians Manfred Curry, of Switzerland, and Ernst Hartmann, of Germany) are convinced that an energy latticework embraces the entire planet. The precise width between the lines is said to vary according to the position of the sun and moon but is of the order of 20-40cm.

PIONEERING PHYSICS

Academics such as Nils-Axel Morner, head of Paleogeophysics and Geodynamics at Stockholm University, claim they can actually measure E-ray frequencies. Morner uses something called a 'common electrical tone generator' which effectively establishes a line between the source of an E-ray and the generator speaker in his lab. He calculates that Curry lines are at a frequency of 202Hz, Hartmann lines at 142Hz and underground streams at 440Hz.

Morner may be dismissed by many as a maverick, but it is much harder for mainstream science to swat away the beliefs of their most eminent theoreticians, such as Albert Einstein himself. On 4 February 1946, a man called Herman E. Peisach of South Norwalk, Connecticut, wrote to Einstein seeking an opinion on whether dowsing was a genuine phenomenon. Mr Peisach's father, a German doctor, had apparently tried it as a diagnostic aid, and believed there was a link between human health and radiation links from water and mineral sources. Eleven days later, Einstein replied.

'I know very well,' he wrote, 'that many scientists consider dowsing as they do astrology, as a type of ancient superstition. According to my conviction this is, however, unjustified. The dowsing rod is a simple instrument which shows the reaction of the human nervous system to certain factors which are unknown to us at this time.'

With typical humility, Einstein was stating the painfully obvious. The laws of physics, as any student of quantum theory knows, are incomplete. Dowsing may yet come in from the cold.

EARTHBOUND BEASTS

Could there really be supernatural or malevolent beasts roaming the furthest reaches of the planet, occasionally emerging to terrify witnesses? Without photos, film footage or a corpse, there is no firm proof that such creatures exist. But anecdotal evidence is compelling and cryptozoology – the study of unknown species – is a burgeoning branch of science. Perhaps it is only a matter of time before we will be forced to change our minds.

The Jersey Devil

Could a corner of North America really be haunted by a devilish beast from a species unknown to mankind? It certainly seems unlikely, yet, in the early years of the twentieth century, a cluster of appearances by a grotesque winged creature paralyzed villages across the state of New Jersey.

A string of sightings of this mysterious beast, which came to be known as the Jersey Devil, led to panic amongst local people. Schools were closed and factories barricaded. Small town streets were deserted as residents retreated behind closed doors for fear of meeting the monster.

SATANIC SIGHT

Policemen, postmasters, trappers and vicars were among those who reported sightings of the devil in and around New Jersey during January 1909. Although the descriptions sometimes differed in detail, the beast was unquestionably one and the same. After spotting it outside his Gloucester house on 19 January, Nelson Evans gave the following detailed description:

'It was about 3½ft [1m] high, with a head like a collie dog and a face like a horse. It had a long neck, wings about 2ft [60cm] long, and its back legs were like those of a crane, and it had horse's hooves. It walked on its back legs and held up two short front legs with paws on them. It didn't use the front legs at all while we were watching. My wife and I were scared, I tell you, but I managed to open the window and say, "Shoo", and it turned around, barked at me, and flew away.'

During the month-long episode, witnesses of the Jersey Devil numbered in the hundreds. Could they all have been subject to some manner of mass hallucination? The creature has frequently been described as being similar to a traditional horned Satan, and perhaps the news of an extraordinary beast at large infected the fertile imaginations of local people and led them to believe the devil was roaming in their midst. Yet the communities where sightings occurred were scattered far and wide, so it was highly unlikely that the panic and rumours rife in one village should spread to the next.

If it did exist, the Jersey Devil made its home in the Jersey Pine Barrens, some 5,180km² of forested wilderness once inhabited by gangs of thieves. The area had a fearsome reputation for being dangerous and lawless, so the devil might well feel at home there.

When a local woman fell in love with a British soldier during the American Revolutionary War, people cursed her, swearing that her offspring would be a devil.

SPAWN OF THE DEVIL

Over time, various explanations have been proffered for the Devil's existence in New Jersey. One of these holds that a local woman, frustrated at falling pregnant again, cried out that the devil should take her next child away. Although it was born normally, her baby then sprouted wings and flew away up the chimney. Another version of the story maintains that when a local woman fell in love with a British soldier during the American Revolutionary War, people cursed her, swearing that her offspring would be a devil.

Other explanations are that the Jersey Devil is the product of a local liaison between a witch and Satan, or that a devil was installed in the region to punish a community after they mistreated a minister.

Mysteriously, the people involved in the mythology often have the surname Leeds or live at Leeds Point. For this reason, the beast is sometimes alternatively known as the Leeds devil.

BAD OMEN?

Sometimes the appearance of the Jersey Devil is taken as a sign that things are about to take a turn for the worse, although there is no immediate evidence to back up this theory. Sightings have been an occasional feature of the region for several hundred years. Among the most notable witnesses are Commodore Stephen Decatur (1779-1820), who allegedly shot at the beast although failed to harm it, and Joseph Bonaparte (1768-1844), one-time king of Spain and brother of the French emperor Napoleon Bonaparte, when he was living in America.

Is this the image of the devilish creature that has haunted New Jersey for centuries?

But the number of accounts that came pouring forth in during one week in January 1909 was unprecedented. The Jersey Devil was seen in flight and on the

ground. The fire department of West Collingwood allegedly trained its hoses on the beast, but it escaped uninjured. Its bizarre tracks were to be found everywhere – even on rooftops – in the snow that blanketed the district. Two trappers who tried to follow a trail discovered the owner of the prints leapt over fences 1.5m high – and also squeezed through 20cm gaps. Many people, although they did not see it in the flesh, heard its barks and piercing screams. It left behind a trail of farm animal corpses and even attacked pet dogs.

HOAXERS

With good reason, the small communities scattered around the Pine Barrens were riveted by the stories and limp with fear. No one could explain the oddities surrounding the Jersey Devil. Some hoaxers took advantage of the fevered atmosphere to play tricks on the public, including planting tracks with a stuffed bear's paw. Two men, Jacob Hope and Norman Jefferies, even claimed they had captured it. They covered a kangaroo with green paint and feathers, placed deer antlers on its head and charged gullible punters a fee for a peek. However, even when the pranksters had been discovered, there was still plenty of evidence that defied explanation.

Hoaxers covered a kangaroo in green paint and feathers, placed deer antlers on its head and charged gullible punters a fee for a peek.

ELUSIVE IDENTITY

Clearly it has not been a kangaroo causing a stir in New Jersey, but the precise identity of the flying fiend remains unknown. Some people think it is a prehistoric relic that has lived – and may still be living – hidden in a subterranean cavern. The evidence for this theory is based on the proportions of the footprints, recorded in 1909 and at other times, that are similar to those of a pterodactyl.

Others are convinced that a large bird, such as a crane, is to blame, and another alternative is that the creature is of supernatural origin. Since 1909 sightings have diminished in number, although they do still occur. Some locals believe the advent of street lighting, wide roads and fast cars is keeping the creature at bay.

In 1957 the Department of Conservation is believed to have discovered a corpse of an unknown beast, with prominent hind legs and feathers. Could this have been the remains of the Jersey Devil? If so, could it be that the beast has finally been laid to rest, or will he continue to haunt the residents of New Jersey? At the moment there is little to indicate exactly what struck terror into the hearts of witnesses almost a century ago. It is hard to believe that their collective imagination was only thing fuelling the whole episode. Yet until another body is discovered and undergoes analysis, imagination is all that underpins the story of the Jersey Devil.

Chupacabras

In the 1990s the world was gripped by a crytozoological mystery that has yet to be solved. Across the Americas, attacks in the dead of night left farm animals dead, their bodies drained of blood. But just who or what was responsible for the vampyric assaults, no one could say.

At first the attacks occurred solely in Puerto Rico, a Caribbean island lying some 1,600km off the Florida coast. Then the focus switched to Mexico, where a cluster of similar events made the news headlines. Before long there were reports of farm animals with single puncture wounds in their lifeless necks or chests in countries as diverse as Brazil, the Dominican Republic, Argentina, Bolivia, Chile, Columbia, El Salvador, Panama, Peru and the United States. Conspicuously, the flesh of the dead animal was left intact.

SUSPECT LINE-UP

A suspect came to the fore, dubbed El Chupacabras which, translated from Spanish, means 'goat-sucker'. There were numerous sightings of it, and these appear to fall into three different categories.

The first is an upright lizard standing some 1.25-1.75m, with scaly green-grey skin and sharp spines on its back. The horrific picture is completed with a forked tongue and fangs. Alternatively, the chupacabras has been described as a wallaby or kangaroo-style creature with a dog's face covered by coarse fur. The last of the trio of descriptions is a hairless dog with a pronounced spinal ridge.

Could the attacks on farm animals have been carried out by starving vampire bats, desperate for food?

The gargoyles that adorn
historic buildings such as
Notre Dame in Paris bear
a marked resemblance to
descriptions of chupacabras.

All of the above have in common red eyes, three-toed tracks and a distinctive screeching or hissing sound. Sometimes witnesses detected a sulphurous odour in the vicinity of a chupacabras. More tantalizing still are the reports that the goat-suckers have been seen at the same time that UFOs were spotted cruising in an area.

VIOLENT HISTORY

The first chupacabras attack is generally recognized as being in Orocovis in Puerto Rico in 1995 when eight sheep were found dead. Allegedly, their bodies were entirely drained of blood. In August the same year at least 150 barnyard animals were slaughtered in the same ghoulish manner. Three months later came another spate of deaths and the first sightings of the creature deemed responsible.

A hairy, crimson-eyed beast came through the window of an urban home to rip a child's teddy bear to pieces. In its wake there was a slime puddle and a piece of rancid meat.

A hairy, crimson-eyed beast came through the window of an urban home to rip a child's teddy bear to pieces. In its wake there was a slime puddle and a piece of rancid meat. Another witness claimed the chupacabras disappeared before his eyes, while a third decided it was a member of the monkey family.

Unsurprisingly, the population of Puerto Rico was terrified by events. Mobs several hundred strong roamed the countryside at night on the trail of the monster but failed to capture it.

In the early months of 1996 there was a lull in the killings, coinciding with some unseasonably cold weather. Observers came to the conclusion that the goat-sucker had hibernated to escape the chill. In March he was back, though, having killed thirty cocks and hens belonging to farmer Arturo Rodriguez. Shortly afterwards a strange creature walking on two legs, with red eyes, pointy ears, fangs and claws was spotted by a boy called Ovidio Mendez. The creature made no threatening moves towards young Ovidio before it finally bolted. Police were called to the scene, but they failed to find any further clues about the beast's identity. Scientists on the island stuck to their theory that dogs or perhaps even rhesus monkeys were to blame.

By 1996, when chupacabras activity was focused on the United States, the response from the population was similarly fearful. In Florida, a police department spokesman commented: 'People here are hysterical'. Meanwhile in San Salvador, attacks of the same nature were firmly blamed on vampire bats. The bats were starving, the government minister elaborated, for vampire bats are parasitic and rarely, if ever, kill their food source. By the end of 1996, one Mexican newspaper reported that there had been forty-six domestic attacks involving more than 300 animals and four people.

Since then, chupacabras killings have diminished, but are certainly still in evidence. Farming folk in affected areas remain cautious or even terrified. Different national authorities are united in their dismissal of events as being the work of wild animals or the product of fertile imaginations, fatally combined with sensationalism in the press.

LIVING GARGOYLE?

Were chupacabras around before the 1990s? There are sporadic reports of bizarre animal slayings in the Americas before this date, which some observers now believe fit the *modus operandi* of the beast. Cattle deaths in one area of the United States in the 1970s were thought to have been the work of a rogue condor, but perhaps the truth was more sinister.

Speculation that chupacabras existed years ago is mainly based on their apparent facial likeness to the gargoyles that adorn old European buildings. If we accept that this string of farm animal killings is more than a bizarre co-incidence that can be blamed on various starving predators, then what is the explanation? The hypotheses are fascinating, even if some are barely credible.

ALIEN PREDATORS

Biblical scholars pointed to the fact that demonic creatures of this type were forecast as a precursor to the apocalypse in the book of Revelation. Elsewhere, a clairvoyant monk claimed the chupacabras were representative of a race of vampires that could only be countered with a laser beam or silver bullet. Another group decided these were creatures from space almost certainly infected with deadly diseases, whose intention was to cripple the human race. Failing that, they could be alien pets given some freedom on the planet after a long space voyage, with the mother ship hovering nearby.

A clairovoyant monk claimed the chupacabras were representative of a race of vampires that could only be countered with a laser beam or silver bullet...

GENETIC MISFIT

Thinking along similar though not identical lines, there were those who felt the chupacabras were the horrible results of a genetic experiment that had gone badly awry. Humans or aliens could have carried out such experiments, and then let loose the hideous spawn of their research. This would explain why the governments of afflicted countries were slow with a response at times of crisis, unwilling to admit to clandestine or unethical experimentation.

There is, of course, the suggestion that chupacabras is a supernatural beast. The paranormal argument is given credence by the few examples of animals attacked by the beast and killed within cages that have remained intact. As in the case of the child whose teddy was ripped to pieces by an unknown beast, there are often traces of slime among the animal corpses. There is no firm evidence yet as to what this substance might be.

The mysterious chupacabras looms large for those faced with the consequences of its actions, but there is no consensus about what it actually is. For now its activities provoke more questions than answers. The prospect of this cryptozoo-conundrum being resolved in the near future appears remote.

The African Dinosaur

Conventional wisdom holds that dinosaurs became extinct 65 million years ago. However, there is another school of thought that says at least one variety of these mighty beasts is alive and well, living in the dense and impenetrable jungle of equatorial Africa.

From an urban or Western perspective it seems inconceivable that there is a corner of the planet that remains obscure. Yet the part of the African continent most closely associated with dinosaur sightings is so remote and dense with undergrowth that it is impossible to explore it thoroughly.

Lake Tele is in the People's Republic of Congo, a country recently torn by conflict and all too often rife with disease. It is fed by numerous tributaries, and it lies at the heart of some 142,450km^2 of swampland, only an estimated 80 per cent of which has been explored. Even in the twenty-first century, the number of visitors to the shores of the lake is startlingly few. If dinosaurs had survived largely unseen anywhere on earth, then it would be here.

MOK'ELE-MBEME

The evidence for the existence of a dinosaur is mostly anecdotal. However, these are stories that have persisted for centuries and are particularly potent among the indigenous population.

As long ago as 1776, before the existence of dinosaurs was even known about, the French missionary Abbé Proyart wrote a description of the clawed tracks he saw embedded in African mud. Their dimensions were 90cm in width with about 2m between steps.

In 1913, a German explorer revealed the name given to the mysterious creature by locals, 'mok'ele-mbeme'. It was, he claimed, 'of a brownish-grey colour with a smooth skin, approximately the size of an elephant, at least that of a hippopotamus. It is said to have a long and very flexible neck and only one tooth but a very long one, some described it as a horn. A few spoke about a long muscular tail like that of an alligator'.

In 1932, a British scientist roaming in the region, heard some unidentifiable sounds and recorded gigantic tracks.

The waters were muddied in the years following the Second World War by a hoax and by claims that creatures of similar dimensions were residing in the Congo River, the swamps of Gabon and also Lake Bangweulu in Zambia.

Nevertheless, a series of expeditions to the Congo from the UK, America and Japan was dispatched between 1972 and 1992 – with largely disappointing results. Most had difficulty breaching the shores of Lake Tele or even of the Congo river. Those that did often claimed that they heard noises that they presumed belonged to mok'ele-mbeme. Two men saw the monster but in both cases film taken of the momentous event failed to come out.

CAMERA SHY

In 1981 Herman Regusters took a number of pictures of a swamp beast but the film was apparently damaged by the extreme climatic conditions of the jungle. Two years later Congolese zoologist Dr Marcellin Agnagna was so awestruck when the creature reared up in front of him that he neglected to take the lens cap off his movie camera. The resulting footage was useless.

In 1992 the most convincing film was shot as a Japanese documentary crew flew over Lake Tele, not on the trail of the elusive monster, but in search of panoramic views of the region. As the plane sped over the lake the cameraman noticed a disturbance in the water. He struggled to maintain a focus on the object, which was creating a noticeable wake. By the time the plane banked around and returned the thing had vanished, although ripples in the surface of the water were still visible.

A Congolese zoologist was so awestruck when the creature reared up in front of him that he neglected to take the lens cap off his camera.

The film is indistinct. It could be the first genuine footage of mok'ele-mbeme or it might be an elephant on the move. The blurred shape in the frame mostly resembles two people travelling in a motorized canoe, although it is said that no people travel across this part of the lake. One inexplicably strange aspect of the film is that whatever is in the water ends up entirely submerged – unlikely for either an elephant or a canoe.

LOCAL CHARACTER

But the most irresistible evidence to date has come from people living in the vicinity. The swamp inhabitants are various pygmy tribes, all of whom appear to have some knowledge of mok'ele-mbeme. Shown pictures of gorillas, hippopotamuses and elephants they have quickly registered recognition and put a name to them all. When shown a picture of a sauropod – the dinosaur that best fits the description of what lives in the lake – a consensus has also swiftly been reached. It is mok'ele-mbeme.

One hunter, Nicolas Mondongo, was a teenager when he encountered the monster. He said it had a head and neck some 2m long, crowned by a frill like that of a cockerel. Its four legs were stout and its tail was greater in length than its neck.

Another persuasive tale was recorded among the people of the river villages who remembered when a monster was attacked and killed by fishermen. The corpse was cooked and eaten by selected tribespeople. All those who tasted the flesh died soon afterwards, although no one as yet knows why. The event apparently occurred in the later 1950s and there is still the hope that explorers will discover the bones discarded after the fatal feast.

From the villagers of the swamp, expedition members have discovered that mok'ele-mbeme is vegetarian but nonetheless ferocious, using its tail to lash out at anyone who gets too close. Tribespeople are also convinced there is enmity between mok'ele-mbeme and hippopotamuses as they do not cohabit the same stretches of water.

ON THE TRAIL

In November 2000, Adam Davies undertook one of the most recent expeditions to this inhospitable region and the following year he reported his findings in the *Fortean Times*, a journal that specializes in cryptozoology.

Although Davies did not see or hear mok'ele-mbeme himself, he picked up two vital pieces of information. The first was a description from a village elder who claimed to have seen it many times.

'It has feet like an elephant and a neck like a giraffe. It does not live on the lake but in the forest. It travels across the lake for food'.

The second fact that he gathered was from Dr Agnagna, who told him not to concentrate his search on Lake Tele but on other lakes close by that were even more remote.

At the end of this examination, the facts are maddeningly few. Something has been seen in the vicinity of Lake Tele – and at other locations – that has led a significant number of people to believe that dinosaurs still exist in the heart of Africa. A series of expeditions has brought various pieces of evidence to light, but these are mostly anecdotal and a definitive photograph has not yet been produced. Rather than an unknown beast, there is a possibility that the sightings were of unexpected activity by elephants – although local people well acquainted with wildlife might be expected to distinguish between elephants and other creatures. Testimony from local tribes might be coloured by superstition or imagination.

The density of the jungle works both for and against sceptics. While hostile terrain makes the dinosaur idea difficult to prove, it likewise means the notion is perhaps feasible, as this is uncharted territory and no one can say with certainty what does, or does not, reside there.

Africa was once home to hundreds of thousands of dinosaurs. Could one have survived the passage of time, hidden deep in the jungles of the Congo?

The Lizard People

The idea that a race of Lizard people could live covertly in North America sounds risible. Yet over the last century, frequent and credible eye-witness accounts of such creatures have attracted huge interest from cryptozoologists. Still more sinister is the claim that a serpent race is controlling leaders and infiltrating governments around the world.

Reports of giant lizards roaming free are nothing new in the American Midwest. A traditional Shawnee Indian story tells of a Shawnahooc, or 'River Demon', living in the Little Miami River area of Ohio. As late as the 1950s, residents of the Ohio Valley related ancestral accounts of pink lizards up to 2.4m long. Dozens of these reports were collected by the folklorist David K. Webb and re-printed in the *Columbus Despatch* in August 1954.

Webb disguised the precise location of the Ohio lizard stronghold by using the invented name 'Catlick Creek' (researchers have since identified this as Scippio Creek). He claimed to have logged hundreds of reports and wrote that '…all the old families I contacted were God-fearing folks. Some were rich and some were poor but there was no reason to doubt their word.'

ECCENTRIC ENCOUNTERS

Despite this entreaty, there was clearly a good deal of doubt amongst the wider American public. In May 1955, an unidentified man driving home at 3.30am near Loveland, Ohio – close to the Little Miami – told police he had seen three bipedal lizard-like creatures standing by the roadside. He claimed to have pulled over and watched them for three minutes, recalling how one held a stick which spewed out sparks. The cops did a cursory search, found nothing, filed a report and quietly forgot the whole incident.

Three months later, a woman called Darwin Johnson was swimming in the Ohio River at Evansville, Indiana, 193km southwest of Loveland, when a 'claw-like hand' grabbed her knee. Mrs Johnson's attacker twice tried to drag her underwater but she fought back, hitting it with an inflatable rubber ring. News reports later claimed that scratches and a green palm print were left on her knee.

When these stories emerged, most people regarded both the driver and the swimmer as eccentrics with an active imagination. It took another eighteen years for their accounts to be viewed in a new light with the case of the Loveland Frog, perhaps the best documented of all lizard-race sightings. This time the credibility of the witnesses was beyond question. Both were Loveland police officers.

THE LOVELAND FROG

In the freezing early hours of 3 March 1972 the first, unidentified, Loveland officer was driving alone along Riverside Road when he spotted what looked like a large dog in the glare of his headlamps. As he got closer he saw a creature about 1m

long with leathery skin and the head of a lizard or frog. It stared back for a few seconds, then jumped a fence and escaped down to the river. Later that day, the officer returned with a colleague and found what appeared to be slide marks on the embankment.

Two weeks later while driving on the same highway another policeman, later named as Mark Matthews, spotted an animal lying motionless in the middle of the road. He assumed it had been struck by a car and pulled over to drag it clear, but as he approached it ran off. Realizing that it was a lizard, and anxious to prove his colleague had not fabricated the earlier sighting, Matthews squeezed off a shot. Although he believed he hit the animal, it managed to flee the scene and its body was never found.

Neither officer filed an official report of their experience, but word of their encounters inevitably leaked to the press. When the story broke, a Loveland farmer came forward to say that he too had seen a frog-like creature in March 1972. Sceptics suggested the creature was either a Nile monitor lizard or a large iguana, although neither species is native to the area and exotic pets were very rare locally.

In some parts of the world, adult iguanas can reach gigantic proportions. The unaccustomed sight of a lizard such as this might well lead to speculation.

LAKE LIZARD

In the same year, further lizard-man sightings were reported in America. On 19 August 1972, the Royal Canadian Mounted Police received reports that a 1.5m silver-coloured creature had emerged from Lake Thetis, near Cottonwood, British Columbia and attacked two young men. The location is close to Vancouver Island and Cadboro Bay, haunt of a legendary local sea monster nicknamed 'Cadborosaurus' (see Lake Monsters on page 70) by the media.

According to the men, Robin Flewellyn and Gordon Pike, the lizard appeared on the surface of the lake and chased them from the beach. Flewellyn claimed he had been cut on the hand by six razor-like spikes on its head and, to their credit, the RCMP took him seriously. 'The boys seem sincere,' said a spokesman.

'...A scaled, man-like creature appears at dusk from the red, algae-ridden waters to forage among the fern and moss-covered uplands.'

Just four days later, the lake monster revealed itself again – this time to two different male eye-witnesses, Mike Gold and Russell Van Nice. Both men ran as it emerged from the water, but Gold saw enough to give a detailed description. It was 'like a human being body but it had a monster face and it was all scaly [with] a point sticking out of its head [and] great big ears,' he said.

In 1973, it was the turn of the eastern states to experience a clutch of sightings. Residents of the Newton-Lafayette district of New Jersey told of a 'man-like alligator' on the loose, echoing old Indian tales of a giant fish-like creature which could never be caught. A 'lizardman' trapped in the headlights of a car near Wayne, New Jersey, in November 1974 was described by the driver as a tall, scaly, green humanoid with a reptilian face and bulging frog-like eyes. And in New York State's Southern Tier, residents were aghast to learn from a respected naturalist, Alfred Hulstruck, of a sinister neighbour in their midst. '...A scaled, man-like creature appears at dusk from the red, algae-ridden waters to forage among the fern and moss-covered uplands,' said Hulstruck.

Back in the Ohio Valley, giant lizards were spotted in the Canip Creek area of Milton, Kentucky, where in 1975, junkyard owner Clarence Cable described a creature 4.5m long with black and white markings, bulging eyes and a foot-long forked tongue. Isolated, single-witness sightings such as this were hard to corroborate, but in 1988 lizard-man investigators received a series of highly credible reports from the Scape Ore Swamp area of Bishopville, South Carolina. A 17-year-old called Chris Davis told how he fought off a reptilian creature trying to drag him from his car. Soon the local Sherriff was inundated with reports of encounters with a mysterious lizard-man.

According to one state trooper, Mike Hodge, officers checking the swamp area discovered 'humongous footprints' measuring 35cm x 18cm. He and Lee County deputy sherriff Wayne Atkinson followed these prints for 400m. They realized how close on the trail of the elusive beast they must have been, because when they returned they found fresh prints in their car tyre tracks. Analysis by biologists indicated that the prints matched no known species.

REPTILIAN CONSPIRACY

So what is the explanation? Even accounting for exaggeration, hoaxes, and over-active imaginations, it is hard to see how so many solid eye-witnesses could be so wrong. In a country as vast as North America, is it possible that some unknown species survives in remote strongholds, occasionally venturing into urban regions for food? Or is there, as some reptilian theorists believe, a more sinister interpretation?

However bizarre it might sound, a substantial body of alternative authors and researchers believes that an alien serpent race has occupied earth since prehistoric times, using technological superiority to manipulate human bodies and minds. Some say its leaders abduct people and surgically implant control devices into their brains, maintaining a covert existence through 'shape-shifting'. According to the author and former BBC broadcaster David Icke, the reptilian race have set their sights on global government and have infiltrated our political and religious hierarchies. If he is right, then the lizard sightings, together with literally thousands of alien abduction accounts, suggest the masterplan is well under way in North America.

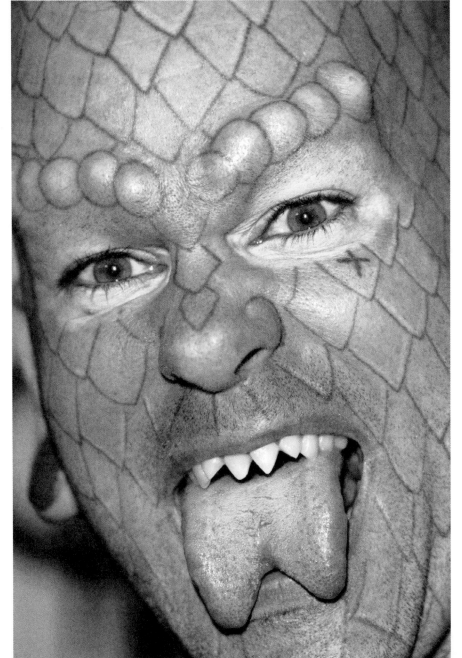

Some fanatics go to great lengths to turn themselves into human versions of animals, including lizards. Could such people be at the root of the lizard-men sightings?

The Venezuelan Apeman

It is among the most notorious images in the annals of natural history. Seated on a gasoline crate, and propped up grotesquely by a stick, the dead ape had been photographed in a mountainous forest district of Venezuela. The problem for early twentieth-century zoologists was that such no such animal was believed to exist in the continent of the Americas.

The photograph was taken around 1920 by François de Loys, a Swiss geologist on a three-year expedition to explore rivers and swamps southwest of Lake Maracaibo. Their aim was to identify lucrative oil reserves, but it was a mission that extracted a heavy price from de Loys and his men. Of the original twenty-strong party only four survived; the others were all victims of disease or attacks by hostile local tribes.

APE ATTACK

During the last year of the survey, the beleaguered group was camped beside the Tarra River when two red-haired creatures around 1.5m tall emerged from the forest in an excitable state. De Loys thought at first they were bears, but as they moved closer he realized they were apes, probably male and female. The animals screamed, waved their arms, broke off branches (seemingly to use as weapons), defecated into their hands and threw their faeces at the camp.

The animals screamed, waved their arms, broke off branches, defecated into their hands and threw their faeces at the camp.

This type of behaviour is a common aggressive response among spider monkeys and some apes and it suggested an attack was imminent. De Loys did what any self-respecting European explorer would do under the circumstances and shot them, to defend himself and his party. The female was killed and the injured male ran off into the jungle.

CURIOUS CARCASS

Gathering around the carcass, everyone in the party agreed that the species was extremely unusual. Native guides said they had never seen anything quite like it and de Loys, although not a zoologist, realized it might be of interest. Unfortunately, given the circumstances, the chances of getting the body back to Europe in a recognizable state were non-existent. De Loys decided to take a photograph as documentary evidence, and the picture was taken from a distance of about 3m away.

What happened next is not clear. Some reports suggest the flesh was cooked and eaten by de Loys' men; others that the remains were partly preserved and later lost in a battle with Motilones Indians. Either way, when de Loys finally returned home, his only evidence was the photo.

THE INVESTIGATION

Curiously, it was nine years before this emerged. Even then, it was not de Loys who presented it to the scientific establishment but one of his close friends, George Montandon, a Swiss anthropologist, who apparently chanced on the picture while inspecting some of de Loys' ageing files. Montandon published it in the *Illustrated London News*, naming the creature *Ameranthropides Loysi*, in honour of its intrepid discoverer.

Soon after this, the Academy of Science in Paris met to discuss the implications of the find. The cornerstone of primate evolution theory was that apes and humans emerged only in the Old World, and specifically Africa. If, after all, they were present in the Americas, then long-established rules would have to be re-written. It would be a leap in the dark and, unsurprisingly, the Academy did not take it.

The scientists concluded that the animal was a sapajou, a fairly common New World monkey. The only evidence to the contrary, they argued, was its size and lack of a tail. Assessment of size was dependent on de Loys' word and the tail could have been either cut off or tucked out of shot.

The ape theory was further undermined when sceptics waded into the debate. Sir Arthur Keith implied that the animal was a spider monkey, while others went further, accusing de Loys of blatantly fabricating a crude hoax. Throughout the twentieth century the same questions were asked: Why did de Loys not photograph a man beside the ape to provide size context? Why such an odd pose? Why wait nine years before allowing a friend to reveal such a major discovery? And so on.

The notorious photograph taken by de Loys shows the dead ape sitting on a crate, propped up by a stick.

RACIST HOAX?

As late as 1996, cryptozoologist Loren Coleman, writing in the *Anomalist Magazine*, argued that George Montandon had been working to a secret racist agenda. This theory held that different races were descended from different apes and consequently some were superior to others. Until the Venezuelan apeman appeared, Montandon had struggled to explain which ape was the ancestor of native American Indians.

In fact, the hoax argument is itself hardly watertight. For one thing why would de Loys, a serious geologist, wish to risk the wrath of the scientific establishment by pulling a silly stunt in an area outside his expertise? Secondly, in an expedition dogged by disease and violent deaths, he surely had more urgent priorities – such as getting home alive. And as for the nine-year delay, isn't it possible that de Loys did not appreciate the significance of what he had seen?

Supporters point out that an analysis of the gasoline crate seat revealed it was 50cm high, putting the de Loys creature at 1.55m, almost exactly the height he claimed in his report. If so this would certainly rule out a spider monkey, which has an average height of between 38-68cm. Other researchers say that while there are some likenesses to a spider monkey – the round ridges surrounding the eyes, the long hair and long fingers and toes – there are also several contradictory features. These include the shape of the face (oval rather than triangular) the lack of a prognathism (a protruding lower jaw) and a highly prominent forehead.

Why would de Loys, a serious geologist, wish to risk the wrath of the scientific establishment by pulling a silly stunt in an area outside his

NOT ALONE

If Montandon had been alone in reporting a mysterious ape-like animal in the Americas, his claim would be easier to dismiss. But in fact there are many accounts. A chronicle written in 1533 by the conquistador Pedro de Cieza refers to a Spaniard finding one dead in the woods. In the eighteenth century Edward Bancroft, doctor, naturalist and British spy, recounted Indian legends of a 1.5m-tall creature which walked upright and was covered in hair.

Nineteenth century science writer Philip Gosse, in his *Essay on the Natural History of Guyana*, suggests the existence of 'a large anthropoid ape not yet recognized by zoologists', and in 1876 explorer Charles Barrington Brown wrote of a beast dubbed 'Didi' by Guyanese Indians – 'a powerful wild man whose body is covered in hair and who lives in the forest.' More recently, in 1987, an American mycologist called Gary Samuels was working in Guyana, courtesy of a grant from the New York Botanical Gardens. Hearing footsteps, he looked up from his inspection of fungi to see a 1.5m-tall, bipedal, ape-like animal which bellowed at him before running away.

It is easy to dismiss the de Loys photograph as a hoax, perhaps because we are uncomfortable with the idea that such a significant species could exist without our knowledge. Yet natural history is littered with similar examples – the okapi, the Komodo dragon and the coelacanth (see Lake Monsters on page 70) were all twentieth century finds – and there remain surprisingly large swathes of the planet that have not been properly explored. De Loys may be a charlatan…but the jury is still out.

Fairies

Fairies have been a feature of folklore in many cultures through the centuries. Disney would have us believe they are all well-meaning, although other story tellers insist that they possess a malignant streak, stealing babies and blinding those who spy on them. One enduring question remains, do fairies really exist outside the realms of fantasy?

For centuries, the idea that humans shared the planet with small, shiny folk was beyond question. But with the spread of Christianity in the West, faith in fairies fell into decline, their existence being construed as Satanic, although interest in them stirred once again in Victorian Britain.

Even today, there are numerous parts of the world where talk of the 'little people' and their activities would not raise an eyebrow. The sceptical West mostly does not fall in this bracket, although there does seem to be a long-held desire for proof in their existence.

FAIRIES IN THE FRAME

So when in November 1920 a London magazine proclaimed: 'An epoch-making event – fairies photographed', eager readers were fascinated. The writer was Sir Arthur Conan Doyle, creator of the archly logical detective Sherlock Holmes and – at the same time – a staunch proponent of the paranormal. He illustrated the feature with photographs taken in Cottingley, Yorkshire, by two young girls, Elsie Wright and Frances Griffiths, purporting to show fairies by a beck that they alone could see.

Professional photographers failed to find evidence of a hoax when they inspected the negatives. To Conan Doyle's eye, it was the proof the world needed to endorse at last a widespread belief in fairies, especially as the girls initially refused the trappings of fame and fortune they might easily have seized upon in such extraordinary circumstances. Indeed, the photographs had lain undisturbed in a drawer at Elsie Wright's home for three years until her mother attended a Theosophy meeting in Harrogate, Yorkshire, where the subject of fairy folk was raised. Whenever Elsie wrote or spoke about seeing fairies, it was done so in passing and without any sense of drama. She seemed, to Conan Doyle's mind, a most convincing witness.

The Evidence for Fairies by A. CONAN DOYLE

WITH MORE FAIRY PHOTOGRAPHS

This article was written by Sir A. Conan Doyle before actual photographs of fairies were known to exist. His departure for Australia prevented him from revising the article in the new light which has so strikingly strengthened his case. We are glad to be able to set before our readers two new fairy photographs, taken by the same girls, but of more recent date than those which created so much discussion when they were published in our Christmas number, and of even greater interest and importance. They speak for themselves.

WE are accustomed to the idea of amphibious creatures who may dwell unseen and unknown in the depths of the waters, and then some day be spied sunning themselves upon a sandbank, whence they slip into the unseen once more. If such appearances were rare, and if it should so happen that some saw them more clearly than others, then a very pretty controversy would arise, for the sceptics would say, with every show of reason, "Our experience is that only land creatures live on the land, and we utterly refuse to believe in things which slip in and out of the water; if you will demonstrate them to us we will begin to consider the question." Faced by so reasonable an opposition, the others could only mutter that they had seen them with their own eyes, but that they could not command their movements. The sceptics would hold the field.

Something of the sort may exist in our psychic arrangements. One can well imagine that there is a dividing line, like the water edge, this line depending upon what we vaguely call a higher rate of vibrations. Taking the vibration theory as a working hypothesis, one could conceive that by raising or lowering them, creatures could move from one side to the other of this line of material visibility, as the tortoise moves from the water to the land, returning for refuge to invisibility as the reptile scuttles back to the surf. This, of course, is supposition, but intelligent supposition based on the available evidence is the pioneer of science, and it may be that the actual solution will be found in this direction. I am alluding now, not to spirit return, where seventy years of close observation has given us some sort of certain and definite laws, but rather to those fairy and phantom phenomena which have been endorsed by so many ages, and still even in these material days seem to break into some lives in the most unexpected fashion.

Victorian science would have left the world hard and clean and bare, like a landscape in the moon; but this science is in truth but a little light in the darkness, and outside that limited circle of definite knowledge we see the loom and shadow of gigantic and fantastic possibilities around us, throwing themselves continually across our consciousness in such ways that it is difficult to ignore them.

Copyright, 1921, by A. Conan Doyle.

Arthur Conan Doyle was a firm believer in the existence of fairies and was a vocal supporter of the Cottingley photographs.

After seventy years of mockery, both went to their graves at great ages, still firmly believing in fairies.

Not everyone was convinced, though, not least Elsie's father and the owner of the 'Midg' quarter-plate camera used in the episode. Critics were quick to point out the photographed fairies were wearing contemporary fashions and that there was no sign of motion in the photographs, despite the fact that they were airborne.

CONAN DOYLE'S BATTLE

Like many others, Conan Doyle invested greatly in the potency of the paranormal after losing a son and other close family members to the brutal fighting of the First World War. By this time he was considered ageing and eccentric by many. Mediums he had championed were being exposed as fakes by campaigners like the eminent escapologist Houdini. (Intriguingly, Houdini was sometimes thought to have falsified evidence in order to unveil those he believed to be phonies.) Soon the photographs were widely accepted as being fraudulent. Decades later a fabrication was confirmed, although the belated confession left plenty of wriggle-room for believers.

Shortly before Elsie and Frances died, they confessed to forging some photographs using cut-outs held in place by hat-pins. However, Elsie implied that she and Frances had only tried to reproduce what they had actually seen. The last photograph of five, called *The Fairy Bower*, was, they insisted, genuine. After seventy years of mockery, both went to their graves at great ages, still firmly believing in fairies.

FAIRY FEVER

Even if the girls had constructed the fairy scenes themselves, the publicity surrounding the Cottingley photographs brought forth numerous testimonies from other witnesses.

From the Isle of Man, Rev. Arnold J Holmes wrote: '…my horse suddenly stopped dead and, looking ahead, I saw amid the obscure light and misty moonbeams what appeared to be a small army of indistinct figures – very small, clad in gossamer garments.'

On the other side of the world, in New Zealand, one Mrs Hardy saw 'eight or ten tiny figures on tiny ponies like dwarf Shetlands… The faces were quite brown, also the ponies were brown…They were like tiny dwarfs or children of about two years old.'

These mysterious figures became popularly known as 'elementals', although debate about whether they are the souls of unbaptized children, ancestral ghosts, fallen angels or spirits of nature has made little headway.

Fairy talk has continued since the Cottingley fairy era, and has gained momentum since the advent of the internet. But belief in fairies is still far from being considered 'the norm'. People like Sheila Jeffries in south-west England have become used to being mocked for maintaining an unflinching conviction in the existence of fairies.

CORNISH MAGIC

A patch of ancient woodland on her Cornish smallholding – a place called Hallowglen on old maps – is, says Sheila Jeffries, among the last outposts of the fairy kingdom in Britain. She thinks they have fled to secret strongholds like this one in the face of environmental destruction wreaked by humans on the countryside.

'If you wish to see them you must throw away your reasoning, sit very quietly and get rid of any resentment, stress or anger in your thoughts,' she says. 'They are very sensitive to people's vibes. You need to be totally relaxed.'

Mrs Jeffries has few explanations for her experiences. She thinks the fairies live 'in a separate dimension; not holes in trees'; that they were once regularly seen and accepted by country people and that advances in agriculture have driven them from all but Britain's wildest places. She flinches at the idea of photographing them and insists she would not even try. In the absence of such proof, she knows she will always be regarded as a crank.

She is not, however, alone. In 2005 in Scotland a developer was forced to re-think his plans when neighbours objected to him moving a rock widely believed to shelter fairies. The rock lies at St Fillans in Perthshire, on the banks of Loch Earn, and when builders moved in a local man was swiftly on the scene, shouting: 'Don't move that rock, you'll kill the fairies'.

Belief in fairies is interwoven with a strong superstition that moving ancient upstanding rocks like that at St Fillans will bring bad luck. In the face of the protest, the developer re-located his scheme to a nearby site. It was a small but significant victory for the minority that believes in the existence of fairy folk. They wholeheartedly share the sentiments once penned by Conan Doyle, that have a poignant appeal even for the sceptics:

'The recognition of [the fairies] existence will jolt the material twentieth century mind out of its heavy ruts in the mud and will make it admit that there is a glamour and a mystery to life.'

Little folk, whether well-meaning or spiteful, have been a part of folklore for hundreds of years.

MONSTERS OF THE DEEP

Reaching to great depths, oceans and great lakes cover the vast majority of the surface of our planet, a mysterious watery world that remains largely unexplored. Reports of colossal serpentine creatures and prehistoric monsters have traditionally been dismissed as folklore and fantasy. Recently however, conjecture about the mind-boggling life forms that lie beneath the waves is at last getting scientific confirmation.

Lake Monsters

Gazing across a glassy Scottish Loch framed by rugged, stunning scenery, it is impossible to believe that such a tranquil scene could be shattered by the antics of a massive, possibly prehistoric, monster lurking in the depths of the lake. Yet this is precisely what has happened on numerous occasions, if hundreds of people who claim to have seen a serpent-style creature are to be believed.

This monster-mania is not solely centred on Loch Ness, where the region's most famous extraordinary inhabitant apparently resides. Curious beasts have been spotted in various lochs in Scotland and in other deep lakes around the world, and the testimony from witnesses about them has been as persuasive as accounts about Nessie, the Loch Ness monster.

MORAG

One venue for several famous sightings has been Loch Morar, where the monster is known as 'Morag'. Fishermen Duncan McDonnell and William Simpson were afloat on 16 August 1969, when they had a close-quarters experience with this being of gigantic proportions.

It was 9pm and the fishermens' boat was travelling at a speed of about seven knots when a splash in the loch nearby caught the men's attention. Natural curiosity soon turned to terror as the thing churning the water made a bee-line straight for them. As McDonnell recounted: 'I looked up and saw about twenty yards [18m] behind us this creature coming directly after us in our wake. It only took a matter of seconds to catch up with us. It grazed the side of the boat, I am quite certain this was unintentional. When it struck, the boat seemed to come to a halt or at least slow down. I

'I looked up and saw this creature coming directly after us in our wake. It only took a matter of seconds to catch up with us...'

grabbed the oar and was attempting to fend it off, my one fear being that if it got under the boat it might capsize it.'

Later, Simpson wrote of the terrible experience: 'We watched it catch us up then bump into the side of the boat, the impact sent a kettle of water I was heating onto the floor. I ran into the cabin to turn the gas off as the water had put the flame out. Then I came out of the cabin to see my mate trying to fend the beast off with an oar, to me he was wasting his time. Then when I seen the oar break I grabbed my rifle and quickly putting a bullet in it fired in the direction of the beast.'

The shot was enough to see off the marauder, although neither of the men believed the bullet had wounded it. They estimated that the creature measured about 9m in length and had a snake-like head extending some 0.5m above the water. Its skin was rough and brown.

With a depth of 305m, Loch Morar is deeper than Loch Ness and its waters run clearer. If this were the home of a beast it would remain a private one, as there are no roads running around the loch. One rumour is that Morag is the ghost of a long-extinct dinosaur.

IN THE PUBLIC EYE

Meanwhile, in Loch Ness, a creature has been oft seen and sometimes even photographed. The first recorded witness to Nessie's exploits was St Columba, who allegedly saved a man from its attack. Sightings have escalated since 1933, when John McKay reported seeing 'an enormous animal rolling and plunging on the surface'. There have been photographs in abundance, most famously one taken in 1934, which made international headlines. However, most of the photos, including that one, have since been branded as fakes. Other sightings are usually assumed to be uprooted trees drifting in the wind.

In 2003 a BBC 'Nessie hunt' decided to test the waters using scientific expertise. The team sent 600 sonar beams into the loch without finding evidence of a deep-water creature. This result has fuelled the sceptics' cause, which assumes that Nessie has more to do with a buoyant tourist trade than any underwater phenomenon. There is insufficient food in the loch to support an animal of Nessie's dimensions and the sceptics claim that the sightings are more likely to be of giant eels, catfish or sturgeons. However, they do not explain how the loch would provide enough food for these fish. (One sturgeon was found to be 3.75m long, weighed 400 kilos and achieved an age of eighty years.)

If the Loch Ness monster does exist, then perhaps it is rearing young in the depths of the loch, so the legend will continue into the future...

A LONG WAY FROM THE DESERT

The latest attempt to debunk the Nessie story insists that the creatures spotted by witnesses were in fact elephants. During the 1930s, a travelling circus owned by Bertram Mills frequently fetched up on the banks of the loch and its elephants took a dip. The saga was stepped up by the sharp-witted impressario Mills, who offered a vast reward for capture of the Loch Ness monster, having realized his elephants were the root cause of a rash of sightings.

Yet still there are regular reports that Nessie has surfaced from people who are neither tourist trade operators nor circus proprietors, who appear to have no vested interest in proving her existence.

MONSTERS AROUND THE WORLD

The coelacanth fish was thought to have become extinct at around the same time as the dinosaurs, until it was discovered alive and well in 1938.

Although Nessie is the most well-known, there are monsters reported in other freshwater lakes in different parts of the globe. The creature that allegedly resides in Lake Champlain, lying between Vermont and New York in North America, has become fondly known as 'Champ'. A French explorer by the name of Samuel de Champlain recorded the first sighting of the creature in 1609, and since then, reports have numbered in the hundreds. Native Americans in the region firmly believed in its existence and in 1873, circus owner PT Barnum offered a $50,000 reward for its hide.

In 1977, a photograph purportedly of 'Champ' stoked up the rumours and, as yet, the validity of the picture has not been entirely refuted. In 1979, sonar experiments on the lake apparently picked up evidence of a 5m-long moving object beneath the surface but even this failed to convince sceptics of a monster-type existence.

LAW OF THE DEEP

Meanwhile Canada, with its expansive wild terrain and deep lakes. has at least a trio of monsters to its name. In Lake Pohenegamook, Quebec, the reported resident is Ponik, a 12m-long beast with a horse's head, humps and two flippers. Over in British Columbia, in lake Okanagan, a creature called Ogopogo has been sighted on several occasions since 1850. The notion that something lives in the

The notion that something lives in the lake is so much ingrained into Canadian culture that it is against British Columbian law to harm it.

lake is so much ingrained into Canadian culture that, should the monster surface, it would be against British Columbian law to harm it. In Newfoundland, the Crescent Lake is reputedly the home of Cressie, a snake-like creature with a fishy head. Alleged appearances by all three in recent times have made headlines around the world.

The hunt continues for Selma, resident in Lake Seljordsvatnet in Norway. Also reportedly possessing a horse's head, Selma is said to be black, have flippers and measure somewhere between 3-12m in length. Locals have reported sightings of their elusive neighbour since 1750.

NOT SO EXTINCT

So can these really be supernatural beings or creatures isolated from a bygone age? The jury is still out on the exact identification of the creatures that reside in the lochs and lakes. Yet we do know that some things have survived in the deep for centuries, unknown to mankind. The most prominent example is the coelacanth, the so-called 'fossil fish' thought to pre-date the dinosaurs by millions of years, that was assumed to have become extinct at around the same time. Then, in 1938, it was discovered alive and well and living in South African waters. Because of the extreme sensitivity of its eyes, the coelacanth is rarely caught by fishermen during the daytime or on nights with a full moon. If the coelacanth remained hidden from man for many millions of years, then it is more than likely that other species elude us too.

Indeed, for all our technological advances, there are plenty of things about life in the murky depths of the world's vast inland waters that remain a mystery. It is tempting to believe that the Morag, Nessie and the rest of the world's lake monsters are among them.

Sea Serpents

Lake-residing creatures are not the only outsized serpents at large in the planet's waters. Given the size of the oceans, it is not surprising that unfamiliar creatures lurk in their depths. Heads, humps and tails of indeterminate origin have been spotted in the open waters off almost every continent.

One popular theory is that monster-like creatures spotted in our open waters might in fact be plesiosaurs, relatives of dinosaurs that were thought to be extinct...

MORGAWR

Off the coast of Cornwall, in England, a creature named Morgawr has been seen by several generations and is accepted by locals as an occasional part of the seascape. In two dramatic episodes, fishermen netted large and mysterious creatures that they could not name. The first occurred in 1876 and the second fifty years later, when the catch was described as 6.5m long with a beaked head, scaly legs and hairy back. Unfortunately, the beasts were released, rather than being brought back to shore for investigation.

From the 1970s onwards, there have been a flurry of sightings and, intriguingly, witnesses were frequently in pairs. When more than one person is present at a sighting, the possibility that it was an imagined experience is eliminated. Several were also strangers to the area and probably unaware of local legends that might have influenced their interpretation of events. In 1975, one couple walking along the coast saw a 'hideous hump-backed creature with stumpy horns and bristles

down the back of its long neck.' Another pair in a motorboat saw two large, grey humps in the water before they submerged. The following year, a woman took photographs of an unknown beast which were published in a local newspaper. Although poor quality, the outline of a serpent is distinct. Choosing to remain anonymous, she nevertheless gave this account: 'It looked like an elephant waving its trunk, but the trunk was a long neck with a small head on the end, like a snake's head. It had humps on the back that moved in a funny way. The colour was black or very dark brown, and the skin seemed to be like a sea lion's…the animal frightened me. I would not like to see it any closer.' When her description was published, the response from readers was astonishing, and scores more sightings were submitted by local people.

A LIVING FOSSIL

Following this, a fisherman who encountered Morgawr estimated it was twice the size of a horse. In 1999, John Holmes, who used to work at the British Museum's natural history unit, filmed a mysterious sea-borne creature in Gerrans Bay. Its head was raised a metre above the water and it swam some 200m from the shore. He kept the film under wraps for several years for fear of being ridiculed, but at least one expert has since examined the tape and found it to be genuine.

Later Mr Holmes told the BBC: 'I have gone through all the text books to try and work out what this may have been and my theory is that it could be a living fossil…It appeared bird-like at times but was very uncharacteristic of any diving birds. I really do think there is some sort of zoological discovery around the coast of Cornwall.'

The legend of Morgawr was sufficiently strong to attract the interest of a television company. Documentary film-maker Tony White spoke to eight Morgawr witnesses. 'One of the people we spoke with was an elderly lady who saw the monster in the Helford River. And the most recent sighting was by some people out fishing…who said Morgawr reared up out of the water in front of their boat.

'Descriptions of the creature vary but many people describe it as looking a bit like the Loch Ness Monster, although an expert we consulted for the documentary believes that Morgawr could be some sort of primitive, prehistoric ancestor of a whale.' Morgawr differs from the Loch Ness monster, as one inhabits salt water while the other lives in fresh. There has been speculation that Morgawr is in fact some new species of seal.

The stretch of coastline where most sightings occur is now locally known as 'Morgawr's Mile'.

The stretch of coastline where most sightings occur is now known locally as 'Morgawr's mile'.

FISHY CHARACTERS

Meanwhile, thousands of miles away, folk around Vancouver Island insisted that something strange dwelt in the nearby seas. Their case was at least partly proven in 1937, at a whaling station, when a 3m creature was discovered within a whale, with a serpent-head, fins and a tail. It has since been named as a Cadborsaurus and is known as Caddy for short.

Speculation about Caddy's existence began in the 1930s, after a couple boating near Victoria Island went public about their sighting. A greenish-brown creature coiled on the water surface before heading for the depths, close to the boat containing Mr and Mrs Langley. 'It took my fancy that it wasn't anything I had seen before,' Mrs Langley told reporters. After this encounter, more accounts came flooding in, and sightings have continued to the present day.

On the south Georgia coast where the sea meets the land, there are creeks, inlets, marshes and rivers which, claim local residents, provide a home for Altamaha-Ha, named after the river Altamaha. This creature is said to look like a cross between an alligator and an eel, with dark skin and protruding eyes. Using its flat, horizontal tail, it reportedly undulates through the water, churning it up when it surfaces. Sightings in the vicinity have occurred with consistency.

PLESIOSAURS

The single suggestion continually surfacing about the freshwater loch and lake monsters and their salt-water cousins is that they are plesiosaurs – or a close relative. Plesiosaurs are cousins of the dinosaurs with broad bodies and short tails, and are distinguished by their flipper limbs.

In 1977, a Japanese trawler dredged a rotting corpse from New Zealand waters that bore all the hallmarks of a prehistoric creature.

In 2002, the fossilized remains of a plesiosaur were discovered in Mexico. Dubbed the 'Monster of Aramberri', it was a staggering 15m long and would have weighed in at an estimated 150,000kg. Two years later, one of the best-preserved remains of a juvenile plesiosaur were found in Bridgwater Bay, off England's Somerset coast. It measured 1.5m.

The notion that plesiosaurs still lurk unseen in the oceans was reinforced in 1977, when a Japanese trawler dredged a bizarre rotting corpse from New Zealand waters that bore all the hallmarks of a prehistoric creature. The rotting corpse was dumped back in the sea, so precise evaluation was not possible. However, samples taken from it were analyzed and it seemed the odd body belonged to a basking shark.

At the moment, the existence of sea serpents is still in doubt. There have been plenty of sightings across the world – sometimes accompanied by photos – but these accounts are not conclusive. A corpse or skeleton would excite both believers and sceptics alike. Presumably, though, when water-borne creatures like this perish, their bodies sink to the ocean floor, out of sight and beyond reach.

Sea serpents and lake monsters bear a likeness that encourages everyone with an interest in natural oddities to believe they are related. For the time being, all we can say with certainty is that they are cryptids, an animal species not recognized by scientists through insufficient evidence.

Kraken

Sailors have long believed that gruesome beasts with a taste for blood lurk beneath the waves, occasionally surfacing to attack a passing ship and its unfortunate crew. On land, people have been swift to dismiss their tales as ludicrous exaggeration. But the latest scientific evidence says that they were right to be fearful of mighty creatures from the deep.

The monster most feared by sailors down the centuries was known as the Kraken. Its flailing arms reached as high as the lookout nests in the masts of sailing ships, it had eyes the size of footballs and it was commonly depicted with the dimensions of a small island. Probably seen over 2,000 years ago in classical times, the Kraken has been variously described as a squid, an octopus, a whale, a crab and a lobster.

Persuasive records of the Kraken exist in the *Speculum Reglae*, or *King's Mirror*, a Scandinavian text in the form of a conversation between a father and son dating from 1250. 'I can say nothing definite as to its length…for on those occasions when men have seen it, it has appeared more like an island than a fish. Nor have I heard that one has ever been caught or found dead. It seems likely that there are but two in all the ocean and that these beget no offspring, for I believe it is always the same ones that appear.'

The Kraken was said to have flailing arms or tentacles that could reach as high as the top of a ship's mast.

When Erik Pontoppidan made records of the natural world in Norway in the eighteenth century, he also referred to the Kraken. And in 1802, an illustration of the monster by Pierre Denys de Montfort was circulated, who based his drawing on the recollections of sailors from a French vessel apparently attacked by the Kraken off the shores of Angola in Africa.

WASHED UP

Speculation about a hitherto unidentified underwater beast was fuelled when a partly decayed body was discovered on a Florida beach in 1896. The body was 5.5m long and some 3m wide. Detached tentacles were in the order of 11m in length. Local naturalist De Witt Webb was sure it was an octopus, although other experts believed it could have been the remains of a whale.

But an octopus, even one of gigantic proportions, tends to be a shy creature and would be unlikely to attack ships. His cephalopod cousin the squid, with ten rather than eight tentacles, is far more aggressive and seems a more convincing candidate for Kraken. Two particular types of squid are in the frame but, until a short time ago, evidence for both was in short supply.

It is believed that giant squid can reach up to 187m in length and that their daily diet typically consists of 50 kilos of fish.

Until recently, mystery cloaked the activities of the giant squid (*Architeutis dux*), thanks to its secretive nature. The best indicator scientists had of its existence was the presence of a few tentacles in the stomach of predator whales. In 2001 a body was discovered off the coast of Spain, spurring scientists on to make fresh calculations about its lifestyle. It is believed that giant squid can reach up to 18m in length and that their daily diet typically consists of 50 kilos of fish.

YEAR OF THE SQUID

2003 proved a pivotal year for squid-watchers. In January of that year, a French yacht taking part in the round-the-world race for the Jules Verne Trophy became enveloped in the arms of a giant squid. Yachtsman Olivier De Kersauson realized the creature was clamped to his boat's hull when he caught sight of a tentacle through a porthole.

'It was thicker than my leg and it was really pulling the boat hard,' said De Kersauson, who was close to the Portuguese island of Madeira when the incident happened. The squid, measuring an estimated 8.5m in length, was jamming the rudder of the boat, effectively putting the vessel out of action. Giant squid can exert an amazing amount of strength by using the visible flaps of muscle at the top of their tentacles. The suckers that help them to cling onto boats and other surfaces are the size of dinner plates. Fortunately for De Kerauson and his crew, the squid released its grip when the vessel stopped. 'We didn't have anything to scare off this beast, so I don't know what we would have done if it hadn't let go,' Mr De Kersauson said. 'We weren't going to attack it with our penknives. I've never seen anything like it in forty years of sailing.'

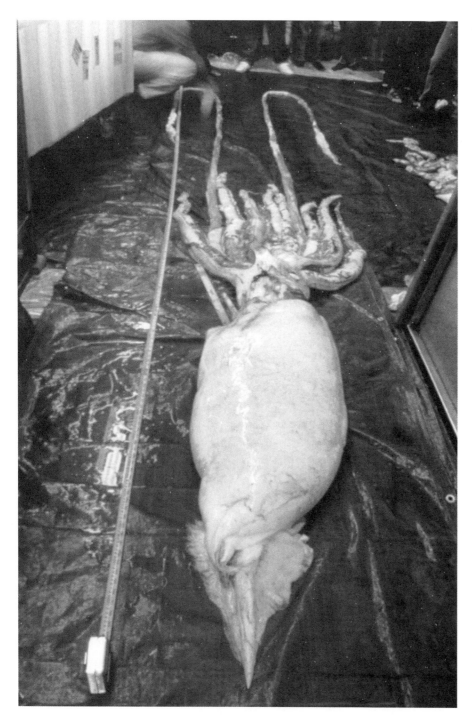

A giant squid has an extremely long, strong beak, and can exert a huge amount of strength using the flaps of muscle at the end of its tentacles.

De Kerauson was one step ahead of marine scientists, who have never yet seen a giant squid alive. But, more significantly still, in April that year a colossal squid (*Mesonychoteuthis hamiltoni*) was retrieved almost intact from the Ross Sea in the Antarctic. Although it was dead, it gave scientists their first opportunity to study the species, which was first officially identified in 1925.

Its overall length could not be calculated due to tentacle damage, but its mantle (body) measured 2.3m, already exceeding the maximum body length of the giant squid. Startlingly, scientists believed it was not yet fully grown. One feature that set it apart from other squid were swivelling hooks on the clubs at the end of its barbed tentacles. It also has the largest beak of all known squid.

Both the giant and colossal squid stay well away from mankind at depths of between 60m and 300m in cold waters. Evidence of their sinister strength has been found on the washed up bodies of mighty sperm whales that appear to have sustained deep cuts following squid attacks. A famous battle between these two ocean-going titans featured in Herman Melville's *Moby Dick*, and it seems that this is the stuff not just of fiction, but of reality.

Scientists now believe that the colossal squid is not only the biggest invertebrate known to mankind but also one of the most aggressive predators on earth. Unexpectedly, their assertions have given credence to the stories of sailors from a by-gone age.

Wedging itself on to the bow of the Kuranda, the weight of the enormous jellyfish began to push the vessel down.

THE KURANDA

Just as stories of enormous squid were once treated with disdain, so tales of giant jellyfish are also cautiously received. Jellyfish have been around for 650 million years, and are believed to pre-date even the dinosaurs. They comprise 95 per cent water and have no heart, blood or brain. And they are even rarer and harder to come by than the elusive squid. Yet there is conclusive evidence that at least one large, rogue jellyfish haunts the oceans.

In 1973, a ship called the *Kuranda*, travelling between Australia and the Fiji Islands, literally hooked up with a gigantic jellyfish. It is assumed that the jellyfish mistook the ship for prey before it latched on to the craft. One unfortunate seaman who came into contact with the jellyfish's stinging cells (nematocysts) experienced severely burned skin and later died from his injuries. The captain of the *Kuranda*, Langley Smith, said the tentacles of the lethal stinger measured some 60m long.

Wedging itself on to the bow of the *Kuranda*, the weight of the enormous jellyfish began to push the vessel down. A swiftly-issued SOS brought another ship, the *Hercules*, to the extraordinary scene, whose crew managed to dislodge the jellyfish by using a high pressure hose. Later, when the slime from the jellyfish was analyzed, it turned out to be from a species called Arctic Lion's Mane. The largest known Arctic Lion's Mane was washed up on a beach in Massachusetts in 1865, measuring 2.3m across with tentacles of 37m long.

In 1969, two divers reported seeing a jellyfish measuring upwards of 46m. However, swimming at great depths in the remotest corners of the world's oceans have helped the jellyfish retain its largely obscure existence.

Safe on land, we tend to forget that two-thirds of the surface of the earth is taken up by the oceans, vast and mysterious watery territories that plummet to depths of several kilometres. Much of this ocean world remains unexplored by humans, and we have much to learn about the life forms that exist there. What does seem clear is that the stories of seafarers, so often dismissed over the centuries, in fact provide a glimpse of sea monsters that are all too real...

Monster Waves

The notion of giant waves higher than ten storey buildings looming up from the earth's oceans was once dismissed as the fantasy of melodramatic sailors. Now science has stepped in to prove that not only do rogue waves like this actually occur, they are even fairly commonplace.

The sight of a voluminous wall of water inspires awe and terror. Mighty ships that seem invincible on shore look miniature and vulnerable when dwarfed by such a vast amount of water, rearing into the air. Many have simply been swamped and sunk, leaving little trace of their existence.

In 1995 the luxury liner *Queen Elizabeth II* encountered a 30m wave during a voyage across the North Atlantic. Captain Ronald Warwick said: 'It looked as if we were going into the white cliffs of Dover.' Waves like these are not tsunamis, the wave surges caused by underwater earthquakes. No one knows why the rogue waves, measuring some 25-30m, happen or where they are going to occur next.

OFFICIAL INVESTIGATION

Film footage of the phenomenon is rare and sailors' stories were generally thought to be subject to exaggeration. But in 2000, when it was calculated that severe weather had sent 200 supertankers and container ships exceeding 200m in length to the sea floor over a period of just two decades, an official investigation into major wave activity was launched, orchestrated by the European Commission.

The investigators used satellite information from the European Space Agency about the state of the oceans during three weeks spanning February and March 2001. They proved that during that short snapshot of time, there were more than ten giant waves around the globe measuring over 23m.

'Two large ships sink every week on average, but the cause is never studied to the same detail as an air crash. It simply gets put down to "bad weather"', explained senior scientist Wolfgang Rosenthal, of GKSS Forschungszentrum in Germany, one of the major partners of the probe. 'Having proved they [rogue waves] existed in higher numbers than anyone expected, the next step is to analyze if they can be forecasted.'

Of course, it is not only ships that are at risk. Oil platforms are also vulnerable to these giant waves and in twelve years, no fewer than 466 were recorded to have unleashed their power over the North Sea's Goma oilfield.

With broad acceptance of rogue waves in the scientific community, it now seems likely that at least one enduring ship mystery has been solved. But one dramatic episode has gained a place in history for the bizarre circumstances surrounding the disappearance of a ship.

Satellite information proved that over three weeks, there were more than ten giant waves around the globe measuring over 23m.

THE SS *WARATAH*

In 1909, the SS *Waratah*, flagship of the Blue Anchor Line, vanished in broad daylight after setting sail from Durban, heading for Cape Town, taking with her 211 passengers and crew.

Subsequent generations have been fascinated by this sudden disappearance, not least since several passengers displayed a strong sense of foreboding about the ship's fate.

In 1910, the Board of Trade carried out an inquiry into the disaster in London, where company director Claude Sawyer, a first class passenger travelling on the *Waratah*, related his lucky escape. Together with fears about the ship's listing, he suffered from troubling dreams. 'I saw a man with a long sword in a peculiar dress. He was holding the sword in his right hand and it was covered with blood. I saw this vision three times.

'The second time it came I thought "I will know it again" and the third time I looked at it so intently that I could almost design it, sword and all, even now.

'Next day I mentioned the dream to a gentleman and he said: "It's a warning." Then I began to think why I should be warned and I was anxious to leave the ship.' The fortunate Sawyer took heed of his warning dreams and decided to remain in Durban, while his fellow passengers boarded the ship again.

On the night the 3-year-old *Waratah* disappeared, Sawyer was once again subject to a vision. 'That night I had another dream. I saw the *Waratah* in big waves, one went over her bows and pressed her down. She rolled over on her starboard side and disappeared.'

Rogue waves of up to 30m can rear up out of relatively calm seas, dwarfing even large ships.

ALL TOO AWARE

He was not the only passenger to have qualms. But he was luckier than one girl,
simply known as Evelyn, who confided to a friend that on three consecutive
nights before embarking she had dreamt the *Waratah* would sink. In the
aftermath of the disaster, this friend wrote to a British newspaper saying that the
last time she saw 15-year-old Evelyn she had been 'frantically clutching the
handrail as she was led weeping up the gangway'.

Another passenger, Nicholas Sharp, declared the life-saving apparatus on
board was inadequate. The ship's chief officer had advised him to secure passage
on another vessel as 'this one will be a coffin for somebody'.

...the last time she saw 15-year-old Evelyn she had been 'frantically

clutching the handrail as she was led weeping up the gangway.'

The *Waratah* was sighted in the morning of 27 July by another steamship.
Only when she failed to turn up in Cape Town was the alarm raised. Despite a
widespread search, no wreckage or bodies were found.

It was known that bad weather swept across the ship's route on 28 July. That
same day a mounted rifleman on shore reported a ship foundering at the mouth
of the Xora River. Nearly a month later crew from a steamer called the
Tottenham may have spotted wreckage and corpses in the water, but the captain
refused to deviate from his course. The Board of Trade inquiry did not conclude
that either of these sightings positively related to the missing vessel. A lifebelt
belonging to the ill-starred ship finally washed up on the shores of New Zealand
in 1912, a poignant symbol of the fate of those on board.

SEANCE WITH THE DROWNED

Speculation about the *Waratah* caught the attention of Sir Arthur Conan Doyle,
author and spiritualist, who decided to hold a seance to determine what had
happened to the doomed ship. Spirits of the passengers told him the *Waratah*
had been hit by a giant wave, which sent it immediately to the ocean floor.

Ninety years after the *Waratah* vanished, marine historian Emlyn Brown
thought that he had located its wreckage using sonar and filmed it with closed-
circuit television cameras during a deep-water dive. He had been financed by
Adrian White, whose grandfather, a ship's steward, perished in the tragedy. The
ship in fact turned out to be the *Nailsea Meadow*, a cargo ship carrying British
Honey tanks torpedoed in the Second World War by a German U-Boat.

The *Waratah* may well be one of the untold thousands of ships to be claimed
by rogue waves, its loss remains remarkable for the psychic sub-text now firmly
attached to the story. For those embarking on subsequent voyages, it is spine-
chilling to think that the incredible sight of a rogue wave was the last thing those
unfortunate passengers ever witnessed.

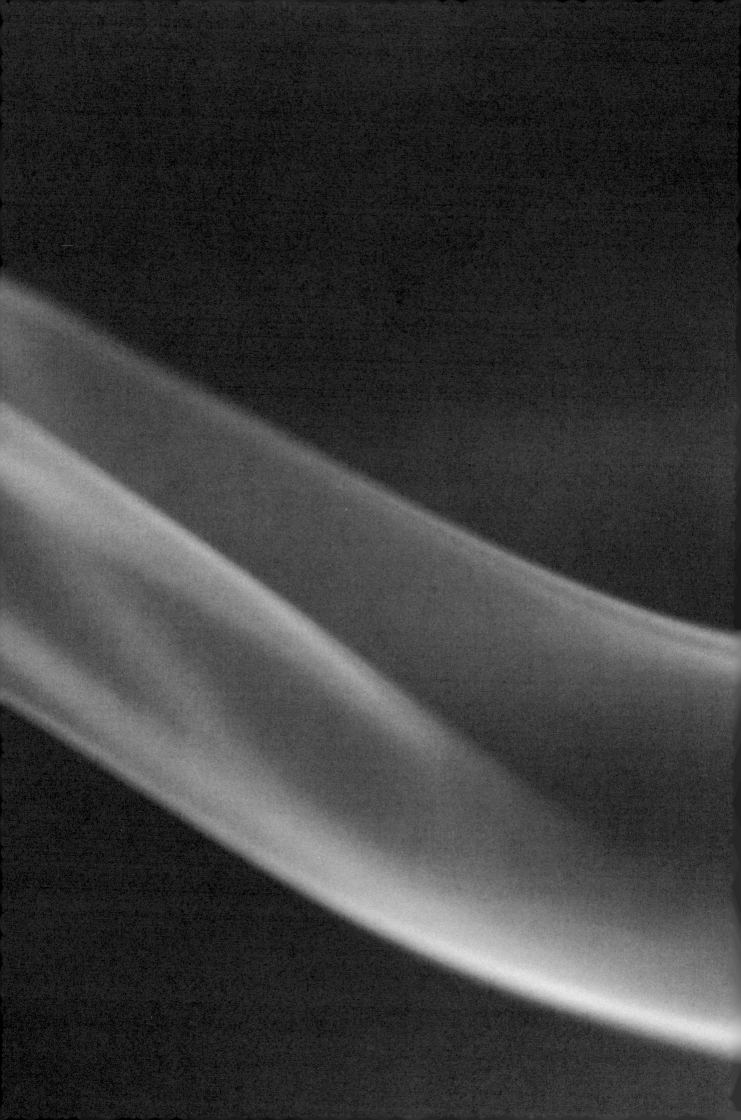

PARANORMAL POWERS

While the human body is no longer a medical mystery, the mind and its powers remain largely unknown. Psychics are able to tap into events that happened in the past, involving people they don't know, and prophets are able to predict how the future will unfold. Intriguing tales of curious ability – that can apparently be channelled at will – have led us into uncharted territory, and they raise more questions than answers.

R. J. Lees

While the horrific murders of Jack the Ripper were bloodying the neighbourhood of Whitechapel, Victorian London was paralyzed with fear. The police force was under intense pressure to arrest the perpetrator and bring him to justice, but they had few clues to go on. One man believed he held the key to the gruesome outrages. The age of the 'psychic sleuth' had dawned.

In this case, it was an unexpected 'psychic detective' that put himself forward to aid police in their investigations. Robert James Lees was born in 1849 in Leicestershire, England. He was a discreet and devout man, not at all the type to seek the limelight or newspaper headlines. In many ways he was the last person to seek the kind of controversy that is attached to serial killers. Yet his conviction about the existence of a powerful spiritual world never wavered, and was closely linked to his intense religious beliefs.

A killer stalked the deprived back streets of east London, securing the services of prostitutes and then butchering them.

GRUESOME KILLINGS

Debate about the Ripper killings still rages today. What is known for sure is that a killer stalked the deprived back streets of east London, securing the services of prostitutes and then butchering them. His crimes were typified by his cut-throat methods and the horrific practice of disembowelling his victims, often decorating the vicinity with inner organs. Five deaths were put down to the Ripper, although there may have been more. (One killing that took place in New York has even been attributed to him.)

His confirmed victims were Mary Ann Nichols, Annie Chapman, Elizabeth Stride, Catherine Eddowes and Mary Jane Kelly, who were all killed between 31 August and 9 November 1888. Stride and Eddowes were killed on the same night, an occasion that became known as the 'double event'.

The police were baffled by the murders. Lacking the scientific know-how that we use today in criminal investigations, they were nevertheless subject to fierce scrutiny by the press, and under real pressure to solve the case. A sense of melodrama surrounded the manhunt, as the perpetrator stole away from the scenes of carnage like a phantom. Later, he apparently went so far as to send taunting letters and body parts to the police.

NO ORDINARY BUS RIDE

The facts surrounding Lees' involvement in the Ripper case are by no means certain. It seems that one day, soon after the 'double event', Lees had a sudden vision whilst travelling with his wife on a London bus. He became sure that one of the other passengers was the Ripper himself. Despite his wife's desperate objections, Lees followed the man and made a note of his home address.

When he took his information to the police, he was greeted with derision. In October 1888 he wrote the following in his diary: 'offered services to police to follow up East End murders, called a fool and a lunatic.' The police refused to listen to him until he apparently quoted the contents of one of the letters sent in the name of the Ripper. There was, of course, no way that he could have known what was in the communication, and the police began to take note. They already knew that the address pinpointed by Lees, 74 Brook Street, belonged to an eminent doctor, Sir William Withey Gull. The respected professional seemed at first to be beyond suspicion. Yet Dr Gull's wife told the police that recently he had been subject to violent rages and had even disappeared at the time when the notorious murders were taking place.

It emerged that the doctor was already ill, and he progressed to an asylum where he later died. Following his incarceration the murders halted.

Robert James Lees was a studious and devout character, not at all the type to seek the limelight by claiming to have identified Jack the Ripper.

CASE CLOSED?

It is this explanation that has earned Lees the reputation of being the man who captured the Ripper. But although the killer clearly had some anatomical interest or knowledge that might link him to the medical profession, there is actually scant evidence to endorse the tale. Lees barely spoke about the incident. Nor did he include details of the experience in his copious diaries, although it was highly sensitive information and he may have omitted it as a matter of discretion. Much later Lees' daughter revealed that her father had known something of the Ripper case, but she would say no more than that. Observers have both verified and denounced the story of the psychic vision on the bus, and ultimately the police refused to give him official credit for solving the case.

So why was there so much doubt about the outcome of case? In the year preceding the murders, Dr Gull had suffered a stroke. Although it left him in a weakened physical state, one supposition is that the stroke might have altered the balance of his mind, perhaps rendering him capable of heinous acts. However, there is another, even more sensational theory. Gull was a loyal royal physician and there has been considerable speculation that the killer was royalty, specifically Prince Albert Victor, Duke of Clarence. He was son of the Prince of Wales,

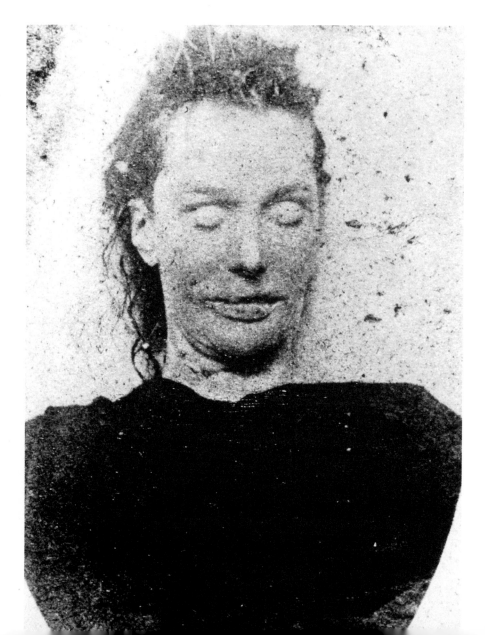

Jack the Ripper victim Elizabeth Stride, photographed after her death in September 1888. Unlike the other victims, Stride had not been mutilated, and her only wound was her slit throat.

grandson to Queen Victoria. He was a self-indulgent, wayward young man, and certainly bi-sexual. Could it be that the prince himself was the real Ripper, and Gull's obvious anxiety was caused by the duty of protection he felt towards him?

A WEB OF SUSPICION

Of course, Dr Gull and the Duke of Clarence were not the only two suspects in the case. Barrister Montague John Druitt was in the frame, especially since he committed suicide shortly after the final Ripper murder. However, there was nothing to suggest that he had the medical know-how to carve up the corpses.

Crime writer Patricia Cornwell believes that artist Walter Sickert was the Ripper, not least for his offensively detailed pictures of mutilated prostitutes.

Aaron Kosminski, a Polish Jew who lived in Whitechapel, was also of interest to the police. They noted that the killings stopped when he was committed to an asylum, where he died in 1919. Being poor and Jewish, Kosminski would have been a convenient scapegoat.

The case against two other doctors has been examined. Dr Francis Tumblety, who collected women's uteruses in jars, fled to America where he was popularly believed to be the Ripper. He died of old age in 1923. Dr Thomas Neil Cream had been convicted for two other killings, and implicated himself as he stood on the gallows with the noose around his neck. As the trap doors opened he cried: 'I am Jack the…!' However, he failed to finish the sentence and is widely believed to have been (belatedly) playing for time. Crime writer Patricia Cornwell strongly believes that the artist Walter Sickert was the Ripper, not least for his offensively detailed pictures of mutilated prostitutes. Yet others theorize about a Masonic link.

RESPECTED SPIRITUALIST AND HEALER

So what became of Robert Lees? Quite apart from the furore surrounding the Ripper case, he was a well-respected spiritualist in an age when mediums were often exposed as fraudulent. He is even believed to have held seances with Queen Victoria so that she could contact her late and beloved husband Prince Albert. There are claims that he helped police identify the Fenians, an Irish patriotic group who were plotting to blow up the Houses of Parliament.

As a healer, he is credited with curing Leona Petherbridge of South Devon, who was suffering from a mental affliction linked to an eating disorder. The case was widely reported, and his reputation spread.

Perhaps Lees' most remarkable psychic feat was a trilogy of books revealing the secrets of life after death. Bizarrely, Lees claimed no literary credit for these books, which he claimed were dictated to him over years by 'Fred' in the next world. When he died in 1931, Lees was a psychic of great reputation, but he left

Noreen Renier

Clutching a single shoe to her breast, Noreen Renier summons up a picture of the appalling tragedy that befell its owner. She spills details of the disturbing scenes that fill her head into a nearby tape recorder, hoping that her words will bring about a breakthrough in a deadlocked investigation.

Noreen is a psychic sleuth, one of very few psychics who are recognized by some members of the police force as an asset in a tricky inquiry. The technique she uses is called psychometry, which allows her to sense the radio waves emanating from an object after it has been put aside by its owner. As she puts it: 'We all possess unseen energy fields. When we touch an object, we leave behind an invisible fingerprint.' And, according to Noreen, psychometry is something we would all be capable of doing, if only we used the whole and not just part of our brains.

FROM SCEPTIC TO PSYCHIC

Noreen speaks as a former sceptic. She was so convinced that paranormal claims were fake that she wanted to ban a psychic convention from the Hyatt Hotel in Orlando where she was public relations director.

However, her view changed when a friend persuaded her to be more open-minded. She met with a psychic called Ann Gehman who was able to describe her daughters, her hidden surgical scar, and the new chair in her office. This was compelling evidence that the supernatural world really existed. 'Slowly, this "psychic stuff" began to take root in my life,' Renier writes in her book, *A Mind for Murder*. 'I didn't understand it, but I couldn't deny it, either. I was completely captivated by the amazing new world that had opened in my mind. I started neglecting my job. All I wanted to do was practice what other people claimed they could do in the books I was reading.'

Eventually she lost her job, admitting with good humour that this was something she didn't predict. She began a fortune-telling business in hotel foyers, clad in gypsy garb. Corny though this sounds, it gave her ample opportunity to hone her talents. As she grew in confidence, she put herself forward for scientific tests to measure her psychic skills. Since 1980, as a fully-fledged psychic, she has been helping the police with their investigations, either at their request, or of the families involved.

> 'It would be too much to be psychic all the time. So I've found a wrecked plane a thousand miles away, but sometimes I can't find my car keys.'

REMOTE VIEWING

In addition to psychometry, Noreen uses remote viewing. That means that she is able to see, hear and feel the world through the senses of another. She can place herself as an eyewitness at the scene of a murder or amid the panic of a fugitive. In investigations, it is vital to take down all the details whilst she attempts to describe the events she is experiencing. Ideally, a forensic artist is standing by as she talks to sketch the face of the killer or rapist, and tape recorder is running to capture her psychic advice.

Afterwards, the memories of her 'flashbacks' are erased from her mind and she returns to normality, sometimes for weeks at a time.

As Noreen describes: 'It would be too much to be psychic all the time. So I've found a wrecked plane a thousand miles away, but sometimes I can't find my car keys.' She finds the experience very draining and limits herself to two cases a week. By and large, her work is carried out in the comfort of her own home. Relaxation is key to her success.

THE FIRST CASE

The first case that Noreen was involved in occurred when a small town was being terrorized by a rapist, and the local women asked for help. After visiting the homes of two victims, Noreen saw a man in a green uniform with a scar on his knee who drove a mystery vehicle that, for some reason, continued to turn around constantly. Although her intervention did not directly secure an arrest, her

Mayhem ensued after an assassination attempt on President Reagan as he was leaving the Washington Hilton in 1981. Could events like these have been predicted, and maybe even prevented?

information was proven correct when the culprit was finally caught some months later. He did work in uniform, he was scarred and he drove a cement lorry, all of which Noreen had described.

ATTEMPT ON THE PRESIDENT

One of her most impressive and high-profile predictions was that of an assassination attempt on US President Ronald Reagan. Speaking in January 1981 at the FBI academy, she said that in spring the President would suffer piercing chest pains. It was not a heart attack, she was sure, but a gunshot wound from which he would recover. Amazingly, on 30 March that year John Hinkley attacked Reagan, who did make a good recovery.

Since then Noreen has worked on hundreds of cases across America and internationally. The tributes paid to her are a persuasive testament:

'You definitely opened many eyes to the potential investigative tool of the psychic. Obviously, many a doubting Thomas had to revise his ideas concerning this somewhat esoteric area,' said Daniel Grinnan Jr. from the Bureau of Forensic Science in the Commonwealth of Virginia.

'Noreen never could have known this stuff beforehand and she was so accurate it was chilling,' retired Lt. Commander R. Krolak told The *Times Union* on 11 February 1992.

'It was kind of scary when we did find [the body], and it was almost exactly as she described it. I wouldn't say I'm a total believer, but I don't throw out anything they say.' So said Lt. Robert Miller in the *Port St. Lucie Tribune* on 19 May 1991.

KEEPING IT REAL

Sceptics point out that much of the information revealed by psychics is vague, so that it can be applied to a host of outcomes. Futhermore, they claim that the practice of psychometry can seriously damage vital evidence. Although the police accept more psychic advice now than ever before, they are generally sceptical of information provided by psychics. Their reluctance is understandable, especially since in the wake of any high profile homicide, they are deluged with calls from people claiming to be psychic.

Noreen is well used to a measure of scepticism, especially since she herself used to be a sceptic. Even now, she maintains that her skills are not foolproof and

'Noreen could never have known this stuff beforehand and she was so accurate it was chilling.'

admits she thinks that psychic detectives should only be used as a last resort. Her aim is for a success rate of about 80 per cent. Often she does not know herself if the information she gives the police will be of immediate interest to an inquiry or whether it might help solve a crime at some point in the future. Psychic detection is an elusive skill, but sometimes an invaluable one.

Annette Martin

A blood-curdling scream splits the night. A weapon falls to the ground and a killer goes on the run. When psychic detective Annette Martin slips into a trance she is able to experience a re-run of these terrible events in minute detail. Hopefully her second-sight will provide police with fresh clues.

This is a world away from the life Annette Martin thought she would lead. 'My intention was to become a famous movie star or opera singer. It certainly wasn't my goal to be looking inside people's bodies and finding murderers,' laughs Annette at her California home.

EARLY STARTER

But she was just a child growing up in San Francisco when her psychic skills first became evident. She relates the turning point with trepidation even now. 'I was seven years old, I was playing with my friends, when all of a sudden I looked up to the sky and I saw this huge picture. In it was myself and my friends and they were rushing towards me with rocks and sticks, intent on killing me.' Moments later, her neighbourhood playmates did indeed attack her, and she rushed home screaming and crying, forgetting that her parents were out.

Psychic detection is a world away from the kind of life Annette thought she would lead. But perhaps her musical abilities are linked to her psychic gifts...

'I ran up the steps to my home. I turned around and faced my tormentors when I heard this male voice saying "pick up that stick". I thought it was my father but when I turned towards the door there was no one there. The voice spoke to me again, saying "pick up the stick and throw it." Annette did as the voice told her and threw the stick, breaking the nose of the gang leader.

Happily for all involved, the fracas was forgotten within days. However, for Annette it was just the beginning, and the fight was hotly followed by another strange occurrence. 'I was out shopping with my mother when I saw inside this woman's stomach. I saw all these bugs running around and I told my mother that woman should see a doctor. I came into the world being a very dramatic person so my mother thought I was dramatizing.' It was only when the young Annette accurately predicted the medical condition of a family friend that her parents began to take her claims seriously.

Although still a child, Annette had to learn to turn her special powers on and off like a light switch. 'I was seeing inside children's bodies at school, who liked me and who didn't. It was

'My guide Cama told me that when I learned to control my emotions the information would come through much clearer and easier.'

exhausting and mostly it was simply none of my business. Everybody has to lead their own life.' It is this ability to stop her second sight at will that has allowed Annette to enjoy a normal existence, despite her astonishing career.

CAMA AND CAYCE

The voice she had heard that day on the steps of her house belonged to Cama, a spirit guide who has remained with her ever since. 'I started seeing him when I was aged ten or eleven. He was once a yogi. He is tall and very well built. If I'm doing something and he wants to talk he hollers to me in a very loud voice in his distinctive Middle Eastern tones.' Cama has helped her develop her psychic awareness. 'In the beginning I was just too emotional. My guide Cama kept telling me that when I really learned to control my emotions the information would come through much clearer and easier.'

More than thirty years ago a second 'other worldly' guide made his presence felt. This time it was Edgar Cayce (1877-1945), a famous twentieth-century psychic who carried out thousands of readings during his lifetime and was a renowned healer. Cayce makes himself felt during Annette's own healing sessions, although he does not get involved in her police work.

MUSICAL INTUITION

Annette maintains that the love of music she fostered as a child has helped with her career. 'Music provides a great link into a person's intuition or extra-sensory perception,' she says. 'During radio work I'm hearing the sound waves. I'm getting the electromagnetic waves that are coming from a person's aura. When someone is sitting across from me they are sending radio signals. I tune into that sound. The information is carried on the sound.'

To enter a trance or altered state Annette simply takes three deep breaths, breathing in through the nose and exhaling through the mouth. When she does police work the trance is deeper and she is in it for longer, sometimes several hours. She works in partnership with Richard Keaton, a private investigator and former police detective. They met after Annette experienced a frightening vision of a murder and rushed into a sheriff's office to share the information. Keaton, the officer in charge, was initially sceptical, but he soon put aside his doubts as Annette quoted unpublished details of the case, known only to police officers.

PARTNERS IN CRIME

Working together, they combine his aptitude for criminal investigation with her psychic insight. While Annette is in a trance, Keaton questions her closely about details that might seem inconsequential to the onlooker, but which are crucial to those with a detective's mindset. In a trance state, she can revisit the scene of a crime, visualize the victim and even describe an attacker. Together they can discover minute details from the crime scenes she 'visits'. As Annette describes it,

'I see scars, moles, diseases that they have, medication that they are taking, which has been extremely helpful because then the police have much more to go on… I also get conversations. I pick up conversations between the victim and assailant.'

She is able to assume three personalities while she is 'under' (in a trance): that of the victim, the perpetrator and an observer. Keaton identifies these switches in character as her voice, face and body movements change. When the trance is at an end, Keaton has pages of notes to study.

Of course, the word of a psychic counts for nothing in court. Police may use the detail and information offered by a psychic to capture assailants, but they still have to provide hard evidence to make a case against them. 'I don't believe psychic detectives solve the case. We give the police the pieces of a puzzle. We are just a tool for them', says Annette.

The scepticism surrounding the use of psychics in criminal investigations does not unduly worry Annette, who has succeeded in persuading some hard-bitten police detectives of her talents simply by results.

UNCOVERING THE TRUTH

When 71-year-old Dennis Prado went missing, Pacifica detectives drew a blank, despite an exhaustive investigation lasting two months. His family asked that Annette should be brought in on the case and, although the investigating sergeant was doubtful, the police had nothing to lose. Using a photo and map of Mr Prado's apartment complex, Annette 'saw' that Mr Prado had hiked into the County Park for a stroll and veered off the main path towards a small hill, perhaps to rest and look at the scenery. Along the way he suffered a stroke and dropped dead. Annette marked the location of the body on the map. The County Park covers an area of 8,000km², but Annette's pointer was precise. Two rescue volunteers headed for the fateful spot and found Mr Prado's body using a dog, as she had predicted they would.

Annette sat meditating on the ground for two hours, describing the grisly event and giving police a full description of the assailant.

Following one murder in Marin County, California, Annette used her intuitive skills to divine the exact spot where the victim had been killed. She sat meditating on the ground for two hours, describing the grisly event and giving police a full description of the assailant. Afterwards, they knew how he had left the crime scene and where he was. They even had a full description of his house.

DAY AT THE OFFICE…

Today, in addition to cracking murder cases and continuing with her healing sessions, Annette locates missing people and finds stolen goods. She has even tracked down thoroughbred horses before. She also conducts psychic readings, usually remotely with the use of psychometry, which involves picking up messages from an original photograph. Annette, who gained a degree in psychology aged 40, has even branched out into ghostbusting.

The Girl with X-ray Eyes

'New Light Sees Through Flesh to Bones' was the headline in one newspaper when, in 1896, Wilhelm Conrad Roentgen (1845-1923) unveiled his new x-ray machine. His discovery was to change the course of modern medicine. But in 1997, some 100 years later, a young Russian girl claimed to see inside human bodies without the benefit of technology, using her eyes alone.

As a young girl growing up in Saransk, the capital of Mordovia some 480km east of Moscow, there was little to mark Natasha Demkina out from her playmates. But all that changed when, aged ten, she confessed to her mother that she could 'see' beneath her skin, inside her body. Under Natasha's penetrating gaze, her mum's bones, sinews and blood-pumping veins were all startlingly apparent.

'At first I was disgusted,' Natasha later admitted. 'Then I became used to it. It seems normal now and, if I don't see anyone for a while, I miss the experience.'

Natasha began to use her unexpected talents to diagnose ailments among friends and family. Her startling success rate soon led people to call her 'the girl with x-ray eyes'. As her reputation spread, Natasha was confronted with more 'patients' than ever. She returned from school each day to discover a line of people outside her house, hoping that she would identify health problems undetected by doctors. She began to charge people a small fee. Natasha dreamed of going to medical school, and when her family realized how expensive this would be, the cost went up again. Some Natasha enthusiasts claimed she had offered her diagnostic opinion to 10,000 people.

Her bizarre visual surgery finally attracted the interest of an international television company, who asked her to appear on air and expose her skills to camera scrutiny. Ringing in the ears of the television producer were the words of her proud mother Tatyana, 'She has never been wrong in six years.'

> *'At first I was disgusted,' Natasha later admitted. 'Then I became used to it. It seems normal now and, if I don't see anyone for a while, I miss the experience.'*

PUT TO THE TEST

In May 2004, the show arranged for Natasha to be put to the test. Unfortunately for Natasha, the notoriously sceptical Committee for the Scientific Investigation of Claims of the Paranormal was involved in drawing up the conditions of the test.

Seven people were selected as subjects for the experiment. Six had different but specific medical issues that would show up on an x-ray, for example, one had an artificial hip while another had internal metal staples. The seventh was, medically speaking, intact. Natasha was given cards with illustrations of the conditions she was expected to identify. Descriptions of them were written in both Russian and English. All seven were expected to remain seated during the test, although Natasha generally saw patients while they were on their feet.

The authors of the test decided Natasha would be deemed successful if she got five out of seven diagnoses correct. The result of the test would not provide definitive evidence that Natasha possessed supernatural powers, the authors decided, but would only determine whether her 'gift' warranted further study. The experiment was to take place in New York, a long way from home for 17-year-old Natasha.

The test was expected to be over in just over an hour, but in the event it lasted four hours. This was unusual, since up until then Natasha had completed most consultations within 10 minutes. Furthermore, she was thought to have chatted to friends and family on her mobile phone, when the rules stated she was to talk to no one.

THE RESULT

At the end of the test Natasha was found to have made four correct diagnoses rather than the necessary five. It proved, said Andrew Skolnick, one of the authors of the test, that her gift as a 'medical intuitive' should be called into question. Natasha had contravened the rules of the test, he said, and taken hours to produce a result that simply was not very impressive. Among the medical conditions she had missed was a man with a metal plate in his skull that was reportedly visible to the naked eye.

CRITICAL EYE

Assertions that she could make cellular diagnoses were disputed by those who organized the test, who said a drawing she submitted of a particular rogue cell was in fact nothing like the real thing.

The test organizers suspected Natasha of making 'cold readings', a technique honed by fortune tellers of old. It entails the psychic or healer bombarding their subject with questions and alighting on minute clues to draw sweeping conclusions about the state of their health. In the face of such questioning, subjects tend to focus on the correct statements while disregarding the flurry of false information offered beforehand, especially if they are eager to believe. Furthermore, they said she was operating from a position of strength, since it was almost impossible to prove her wrong. In many instances it would take an autopsy to determine whether her medical diagnoses were correct or not.

As far as the test organizers were concerned, all these factors meant that Natasha was no longer of interest.

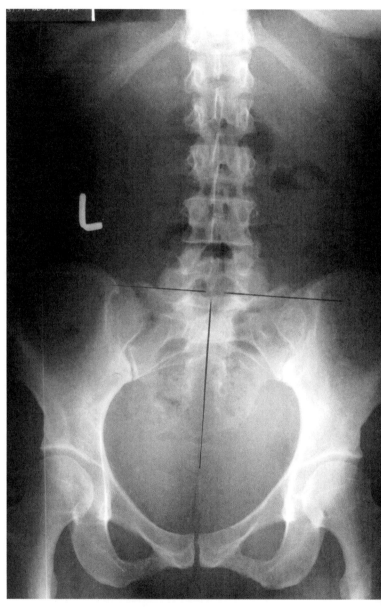

An x-ray showing the lower spine and pelvis of a female patient. Could Natasha really see into people as clearly as this?

SUPPORT AT HAND

But Natasha's supporters took issue with the results of the test. Her figures, although not up to the required standards of the panel, were nevertheless statistically significant. There was only a one in fifty chance of achieving such a result, which surely put it beyond mere chance. 'Why is it that if I get five out of seven I pass but if I get four I'm a total failure?' asked a dejected Natasha.

Furthermore, Natasha was operating under stressful, unsupportive conditions when all psychics work better in a relaxed atmosphere. Her sympathizers felt that she had been ambushed by sophisticated sceptics with a vested interest in branding her claims as false. Their reputations were, at the end of the day, rooted in disproving paranormal events rather than endorsing them. This was the same crowd who had decided Uri Geller, a famous spoon-bending psychic with armies of devotees, did not have sufficient skill to warrant further investigation either.

In the meantime, Natasha's talents had come under scrutiny elsewhere. She was judged to be entirely convincing by a variety of different audiences, not least the *Sun* newspaper in Britain. Nor is she the only person in the world today to apparently possess x-ray vision. There are a number of psychic healers who make similar claims and offer a list of success stories to back their case.

DOCTOR IN THE MAKING

Afterwards Natasha sank from the limelight, concentrating on her studies at medical school. She was following the ambition she had as a child, to become a doctor, before she attracted so much international notoriety. As she put it, 'The dream is, if I preserve my gift, to use it but on the basis of proper medical knowledge.' With medical training behind her, Natasha may yet return to confound her critics.

No ordinary eyes: after undergoing international scrutiny of her abilities, Natasha is now concentrating on her medical studies at university in Moscow.

Matthew Manning

Matthew Manning's life story might resemble a strange combination of Harry Potter *and* The X Files, *but there is nothing fictional about the scientific data on his extraordinary powers. For almost three decades, this remarkable British healer and psychic has worked with some of the world's leading academics as they try to explain the inexplicable.*

Manning first came to public prominence in 1974, following his appearance on a BBC prime-time show *The Frost Interview*. He caused a national sensation with a display of automatic writing – apparently transcribing messages from the dead – which accurately diagnosed health problems suffered by members of the audience. However, for his family, friends and former schoolmates, this feat was unsurprising compared to some of the extraordinary displays of Manning's past.

THERE'S NO PLACE LIKE HOME

In his autobiography, *One Foot in the Stars*, Manning tells how his family first experienced poltergeist activity in February 1967, at their 1950s-style home in Shelford, near Cambridge. Events began unremarkably when a silver tankard threw itself off a wooden shelf overnight, and progressed to the daily movement of everything from ashtrays to armchairs. Eventually, Manning's father contacted George Owen, Professor of Genetics at Trinity College, Cambridge, and the world's leading authority on poltergeist activity.

Professor Owen assured the family that they were experiencing a natural, though unexplained, phenomenon that would eventually pass, and for a time it seemed he was right. But in the autumn of 1968, when 12-year-old Manning and his family moved to Queens House, an eighteenth-century home in nearby Linton, the poltergeist returned with a vengeance. In one incident, which Manning describes as 'worthy of a horror film', he watched a bedroom wardrobe inching towards him – then he felt the bed itself vibrate, hover about 15cm above the ground and then reposition itself.

The following morning, the family went downstairs to find that the kitchen, sitting room and lounge had all been completely ransacked. Over the next few months, dozens of similarly bizarre events occurred, which included random scrawling on walls inside the house and water appearing out of nowhere. At one point, Manning's mother suggested they leave a paper and pen in a locked, empty room to see what happened. A few minutes later they returned to find the words 'Matthew Beware' alongside a Leo sign.

Three years later, the extraordinary goings-on at Queens House had increased yet further in intensity. In a single week, no fewer than 503 signatures,

> *In a single week, no fewer than 503 signatures, including the names of deceased locals, appeared on the walls of the house.*

Manning is a renowned healer, and has treated tens of thousands of patients for everything from toothache to secondary cancer.

including the names of deceased locals and the dates of their deaths, appeared on the walls of the house.

At first Manning's father, a particularly level-headed architect, tried to find rational explanations for what was going on. But after witnessing so many paranormal events, he grudgingly accepted them as fact. When his son started boarding at Oakham School in Rutland, Manning Senior warned the headmaster, John Buchanan, about what might happen. It was just as well he did.

EXTRACURRICULAR ACTIVITY

In his book, Manning recounts some of the weird, wonderful and frightening incidents witnessed by pupils and teachers at Oakham school – many of which easily compare with Harry Potter's supernatural experiences at Hogwarts. Beds moved around as their occupants tried to sleep. Nails, glass and bone-handled knives materialized and flew about. Wire coat hangers squashed themselves into small balls and glowing lights appeared on dormitory walls.

In desperation, Manning's house tutor took him to see an occultist to learn a 'banishing ritual'. Unfortunately this did not work, and within two weeks terrified pupils were massing in their matron's sitting room. Later that night, she watched wood chippings, pebbles and shards of glass falling from nowhere into her lap. Incidents such as these became a feature of Manning's school life, although with time, more 'sophisticated' psychic skills began to emerge.

Despite general agreement among staff that Manning was hopeless at art, he began producing outstanding 'automatic drawings' in a variety of styles. Among them were pictures supposedly originating from dead masters such as Paul Klee, Thomas Rowlandson and W. Keble Martin. Later, Manning produced work resembling that of Picasso, Goya, Beardsley and Durer, and sometimes his feats were witnessed by teachers from beginning to end. His housemaster Roger Blackmore later told how he had watched Manning at work and questioned him. 'He could answer quite happily', recalled Mr Blackmore, 'He would talk about the period in which the drawing was based. He didn't appear to be in a trance. He was working as a normal artist of considerable talent.'

Throughout this period, Manning was also producing messages from apparently dead people in widely differing handwriting styles. During the summer holidays of 1971, one of his most regular otherworldly correspondents was a certain Robert Webbe, who seemed to be a previous owner of Queens House (and spoke as though he still was). The following year Manning, concerned about his sick grandmother, established a dialogue with a physician called Thomas Penn, whom he found could be summoned at will. It was Penn whose diagnoses later captivated David Frost's audience in 1974.

DEVELOPING TALENT

The media frenzy that followed *The Frost Interview* turned Manning into an international celebrity overnight. He wrote a bestselling book entitled *The Link* and travelled the world promoting it. But he also tried to satisfy the curiosity of mainstream science, by submitting to a seemingly endless series of tests under laboratory conditions. From late 1976, he toured university campuses in the United States, starting at the University of California and the Washington Research Institute in San Francisco.

His experimental successes were many and varied. They included the ability to influence an electrical impulse on the skin of a frog, sedating or rousing a subject sitting in a separate room, influencing a coin to land heads or tails, and predicting which of ten canisters held water or ball bearings. In this last ESP (extra-sensory perception) test, Manning was correct eight times out of ten in each of three separate runs – far beyond the realms of chance. One experiment in California even showed that he could improve the yield of commercial grass seeds by holding a vial-full in his hand and concentrating.

HEALING POWER

Perhaps Manning's most astounding result came the following year at the Mind Science Foundation in San Antonio, Texas. Here, a team led by psychologist William Braud sought to establish whether psychokinesis (using psychic power to make things move) could influence human biological systems. His experiments with Manning on slowing the abnormal degeneration of red blood cells suggested that it could.

Braud later observed Manning attempting to destroy cancer cells. Manning operated under strict laboratory conditions and a control subject mimicked his every move. The control failed to have an impact on any of the cells. Manning succeeded in twenty-seven out of thirty attempts, increasing the number of dead cancer cells by anything between 200 and 1,200 per cent. This was a ground-breaking result. Braud concluded: 'What Matthew has demonstrated is that he can influence cancer cells. There may be para-psychological factors involved that could be used to heal oneself or heal others.'

The rest, as they say, is history. These days Manning focuses his powers on healing, and since the 1980s he has been consulted by tens of thousands of patients, including the likes of Prince Philip and Pope Paul VI. Despite many documented successes – from back pain to secondary cancer – Manning rejects any suggestion that he is special and describes himself as 'proudly irreligious'. He does not claim to understand how his powers work, only that they do.

Manning has come a long way since the first poltergeist visits in the 1960s. He has collaborated with the world's leading scientists to try and discover how healing power works.

Nostradamus

In the sixteenth century Nostradamus gained a measure of notoriety for making uncannily accurate prophecies. But even he could not foresee that his words would have such a long-lasting effect, remaining pivotal in the beliefs of many people up to five centuries after his death.

The words penned by Nostradamus during his many years as a seer have been translated, pored over and debated. Still, no one is sure how much weight to lend them. While some of his predictions appear wildly speculative and never came to pass, others seem to have neatly summed up events with spine-chilling clarity.

Nostradamus was born Michel de Nostradame in St Rémy de Provence on 14 December 1503. He was from a prosperous middle-class family and his father is generally described either as a lawyer or grain merchant. Young Michel proved to be a brilliant young scholar, showing particular skill for languages and the sciences. He also read voraciously. The family had recently converted from Judaism to the more prevalent Roman Catholic faith, so Michel grew up with a thorough knowledge of both belief systems.

THE BLACK DEATH

However, Nostradamus' first passion was medicine, and at the age of 18 he entered the University of Montpelier to train as a physician. He was able to put his new-found expertise to good use, since the bubonic plague, or the 'Black Death' was ravaging medieval Europe, and doctors were in great demand At the time his approach to patients was

His medical skills were not sufficient to save his young family from the clutches of the Black Death.

radical. Donning the protection of a rudimentary mask, he treated people using good hygiene and herbal poultices rather than the barbaric practice of 'bleeding' patients that brought them to the brink of death.

Nostradamus married and fathered two children, but his medical skills were not sufficient to save his young family from the clutches of the Black Death. After the death of his wife and children, the bereft Nostradamus became a wandering scholar, travelling throughout southern France and Italy.

POPES AND PROPHECY

It was while he was in Italy that the first sign of his future career became apparent. He came across a group of Franciscan monks herding cattle and had a strong premonition of the future, which led him to kneel down and address one of the monks as 'your holiness'. Years later the monk, Felice Peretti, became Pope Sextus V (1520-1590).

When Nostradamus reached the age of 44, he ended his itinerant lifestyle and settled in the Provencal town of Salon. He married a wealthy widow and began his career in prophecy in earnest. His aim was nothing less than to prophesy the future of mankind, and eight years later he produced the first of a more than a dozen books of predictions. The books are called *Centuries* because each is made up of a hundred verses, or quatrains.

Nostradamus was a devout man, but he saw no conflict between his religion and his prophecies. However, he knew that others would not share this open-minded attitude. This was the age of the Inquisition, and anyone suspected of anti-Catholic sentiment was mercilessly punished. The art of peering ahead in time would certainly not sit well with the cruel monks who led the Inquisition. So he set about disguising his predictions by couching them in a mysterious combination of French, Latin, Greek and Italian. Furthermore, he used metaphors and anagrams to produce baffling and impenetrable riddles. He did this, so he told his son, so that the enlightened folk of the future could decipher his messages. But as yet, the generation he was pinning his hopes on has not emerged.

Nostradamus (1503-1566) couched his prophecies in a mysterious combination of French, Latin, Greek and Italian, in order to avoid condemnation by the Catholic Inquisition.

MICHEL NOSTRADAMUS.

THE PREDICTIONS

Despite the mysterious nature of the predictions, Nostradamus' *Centuries* became popular reading material, particularly amongst nobility and royalty, and his reputation grew ever greater. During his lifetime, he came to prominence for one prediction in particular, which gained him both friends and enemies.

> *The Young Lion will overcome the older one on the field of combat*
> *in a single battle,*
> *Inside a cage of gold his eyes will be put out,*
> *Two wounds made one,*
> *He dies a cruel death.*
> *(Century 1, Quatrain 35)*

Just four years after this prophecy, King Henry II died during a joust when a lance pierced his gilded visor and caused two mortal injuries. Many believed that Nostradamus had caused the death of the King, and demanded that the prophet be tried for heresy. Fortunately for Nostradamus, the king's widow, Catherine de Medici, did not share their view. She was so impressed by his powers that she hired him as physician to her son and heir.

But Nostradamus was not only adept at predicting events during his own lifetime. After his death in 1566, one prophecy in particular appears to have pinpoint accuracy:

> *The blood of the just will be demanded of London,*
> *Burnt by the fire in the year 66,*
> *The ancient Lady will fall from her high place,*
> *And many of the same sect will be killed.*
> *(Century 2, Quatrain 51)*

This seems to refer to an event that was to rock Europe exactly a hundred years after the death of the seer. In 1666, the great fire of London destroyed much of the city, including St Paul's cathedral. This prediction is particularly striking because it includes a date. Unfortunately, many of the others do not, but in translation they do seem to jigsaw with history.

> *That which neither weapon nor flame could accomplish will be achieved,*
> *By a sweet-speaking tongue in a council,*
> *Sleeping, in a dream, the king will see the enemy not in war,*
> *Or of military blood.*
> *(Century 1, Quatrain 97)*

This prediction seems to have a particular resonance with the fate of King Henri III of France. The king, who was on the throne during Nostradamus' lifetime, survived wars and jousts, but in the end he fell victim to a treacherous monk. Just three days prior to his death, he had a premonition about what would happen in a dream.

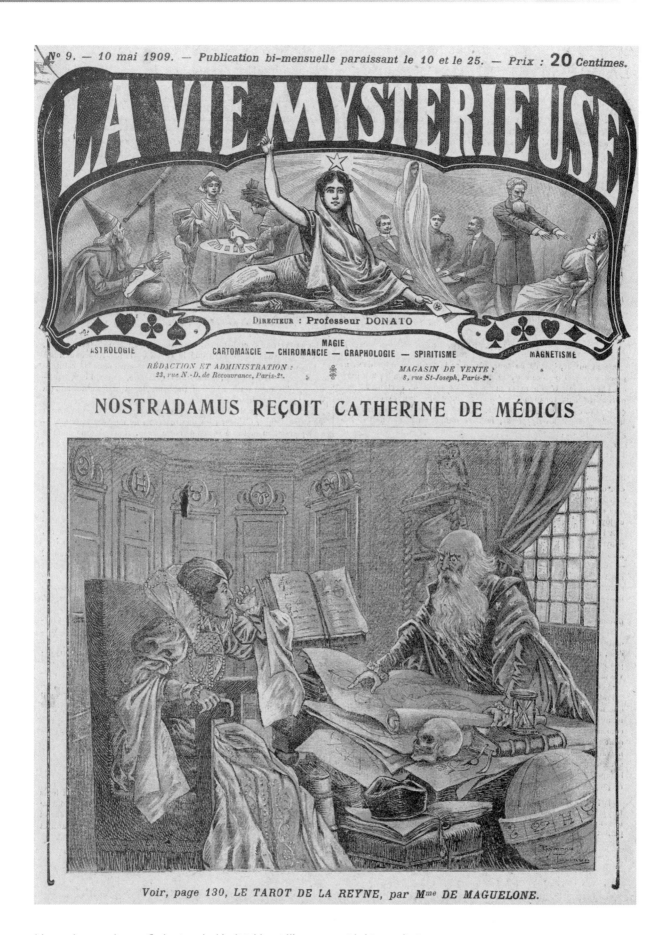

Nostradamus alarms Catherine de Medici, Henri II's queen, with his predictions.

> *The rejected one shall at last reach the throne,*
> *Her enemies found to have been traitors,*
> *More than ever shall her period be triumphant,*
> *At seventy she shall go assuredly to death, in the third year of the century.*
> *(Century VI, Quatrain 74)*

Surely this refers to Queen Elizabeth I of England, who was the least favoured of her father's children. But when she finally ascended the throne in 1558, in the face of Catholic opposition, her reign was indisputably glorious. She did indeed die aged 70, and the year was 1603.

Although many of Nostradamus' predictions tally with historical events to a startling degree, others are tantalizingly vague and they are not in chronological order. Sceptics have drawn attention to the prophet's ambiguous language, and the fact that he is thought to have copied other prophecies current in his era. The subject matter he chooses is invariably war or natural disasters, and these will always be a feature of history. The critics claim that if the cryptic messages of Nostradamus can be applied to real events, then it is nothing more than co-incidence. Take, for example, the quatrain thought by many to refer to the coming of Hitler:

> *Beasts wild with hunger will cross the rivers,*
> *The greater part of the battlefield will be against Hister,*
> *He will drag the leader in a cage of iron,*
> *When the child of Germany observes no law.*
> *(Century II, Quatrain 24)*

Incredibly, this quatrain does at first seem to sum up the events of the Second World War during Hitler's dictatorship and to allude to the savage Nazi troops swamping Europe and humiliating conquered leaders. However, Hister is also the exact name of an area close to the Danube. So the prediction can be read with two meanings, although with historical hindsight, it makes better sense when Hister is read as Hitler.

A PROPHETIC LEGACY

Some of Nostradamus' prophecies have been wrong, most spectacularly the one that implied a catastrophic war would break out in July 1999. Yet despite the ambiguity that surrounds his predictions, thousands of people give due respect to Nostradamus, believing his case has been proven at least in part. With long grey hair and a beard, he certainly must have looked the part of an accomplished seer. Whilst other prophets of a similar kind have been forgotten, the reputation of Nostradamus has flourished through the centuries since his death. And since his predictions continue until 3797, he still has plenty of time to be proved right.

One premonition that he got exactly right was his own death. 'You will not see me alive at sunrise,' he told his assistant on the evening of 1 July 1566. True to his word, by the following morning he was dead.

WITCHCRAFT

Sorcery is an age-old obsession. Humans seem irresistibly drawn to using supernatural powers against each other – whether it be in the form of issuing curses against places or people, or brewing up poisonous concoctions to seal the fate of another. The prospect that someone can manipulate natural or supernatural forces to their own ends is a frightening one, but when the practice of such ritual magic has been condemned, it has led to cruel and unjust punishment that seems to be the work of the Devil himself.

Haitian Zombies

We think of zombies as the dreadful, decomposing creatures with a taste for human flesh that we see in films. These are, of course, the products of fertile imaginations and talented make-up artists in the film studios. Yet there is evidence to show that zombies really do exist. Sapped of their personalities, probably by a cocktail of drugs, they are lowly slaves rendered incapable of independent action.

THE STORY OF CLAIRVIUS NARCISSE

The phenomenon of zombies is associated with the voodoo faith in Haiti, and there are several well-documented examples, including that of Clairvius Narcisse.

Clairvius Narcisse died at the Albert Schweitzer Hospital in Haiti in 1962. After his death had been certified, he was buried. Eighteen years later, Clairvius himself turned up at his sister's house, very much alive, and able to recount stories from their childhood that only he could know. He told how his brothers had been angry about his refusal to sell family land, and how they had sought revenge by ordering his zombification.

After his burial, during which he lay conscious but inert in his coffin, Clairvius was taken from the graveyard and became the subject of spells by a voodoo witch doctor (known as a bokor) that turned him into an 'empty vessel'. He was able to move, but he could not communicate properly and had lost his free will. Voodoo worshippers see a zombie as a body without a soul, and this is what he seemed to have become. For two years he worked in the fields alongside other zombies. After the death of his master he lived rough for eighteen years, returning home only when he was sure that the brothers who engineered his zombification were themselves dead.

Clairius' story matched with the hospital records. His cheek bore a scar that, he said, was inflicted when a nail was driven into his coffin. So just what happened to him after his 'death' in hospital?

A POISONED EXISTENCE

For years the assumption was that zombies – if they existed – were literally raised from the dead through the supernatural powers of the bokor. Today it seems more likely that a poison is administered to a living victim. This poison slows down bodily functions so much that they become imperceptible and the body seems corpse-like. Following burial, the barely-breathing body is then retrieved and further drugs are given that bring about a controlled recovery. So while the victim might regain physical strength, his mind remains feeble, his memory is all but erased and he is effectively powerless.

Much of the mystery was revealed by anthropologist Dr E. Wade Davis, who, following extensive research, assured the world: 'Zombiism actually exists. There are Haitians who have been raised from their graves and returned to life.'

Davis analysed some of the poisons used by bokors and found toad skin and

Felicia Felix-Mentor from Haiti, who died and was buried in 1907. She was found wandering about the countryside in a zombified state in 1937.

puffer fish were two of the most significant ingredients in the poison used to induce a coma. Toad venom is known as a potent painkiller, while the puffer fish contains tetrodotoxin that affects the nervous system. Thereafter, different drugs, including Jimson's Weed (a poisonous type of nightshade plant), are used to keep the victims of zombification stupefied.

Davis paid tribute to the macabre talents of the voodoo bokors: 'A Witch doctor in Haiti is very skilled in administering just the right dose of poison. Too much poison will kill the victim completely and resuscitation will not be possible. Too little and the victim will not be a convincing corpse.'

VOODOO RITUAL

Davis acknowledges that the deep religious beliefs prevailing in Haiti are vital to the process carried out by the bokor. Because people believe in zombiism, it is more likely to become a reality. The voodoo religion is intense and ritualistic, although not inevitably sinister. Broadly speaking, voodoo is a cross between native African beliefs and the Catholic faith once forced upon slaves when they were transported to destinations like Haiti. Davis believes that zombiism is carried out as a punishment and the mindset of the Haitian people permits bokors to do their worst.

Certainly this unquestioning and fearful faith would explain how the dictator Francois 'Papa Doc' Duvalier (1907-71) maintained his grip on the reins of power in Haiti. After coming to power in 1957, Duvalier posed as a witch doctor to encourage the belief that he possessed unearthly powers. His henchmen were called the Tonton Macoute, taking their name from the Haitian word for

The toxins in puffer fish are a significant ingredient in the poisons used by bokors. A delicacy in Japan, where it is enjoyed for making taste-buds tingle, the fish has induced coma and even death in some diners.

'bogeymen'. The implication that transgressors would be turned into zombies – or that the Tonton Macoute were themselves zombies – loomed large. Political opponents were murdered and poverty became endemic as Duvalier inflated his personal bank account. Only long after his death did the population realize they had been duped. But Duvalier's death did not rid them of their folk superstition, and they hauled his corpse from its grave and ritually beat it.

THE ZOMBIE LEGEND

Some commentators remain unconvinced, and question whether zombies exist at all. One piece of research found that the vast majority of Haitians said they knew of a zombie. On further examination, however, it was always a distant cousin or friend of a friend that was the zombie rather than someone they knew well. This is also a feature of 'urban legends' in Western society, when outrageous events occur to someone known only by reputation to the storyteller.

Another theory is that the zombies are in fact people suffering from mental illness who, in the absence of an effective healthcare system, are compelled to wander the countryside begging or undertaking menial labouring jobs to survive. Bereaved relatives identify the so-called zombies as family members through the distortion of grief and because of a desire to see the dead person once more.

But the existence of zombies among Haitians is beyond question, and there is even legislation on the issue. According to the penal code it is illegal to induce a lethargic coma in another person. If proved, the perpetrator is treated in the same way as a murderer.

The Salem Witchcraft Trials

In 1692, seventy years after the arrival of the pilgrim fathers, Salem village in Massachusetts became the focus of a feverish witch-hunt that resulted in the death sentence for twenty residents and the imprisonment of dozens more. Salem remains a by-word for Satanic hysteria to this day.

THE TRIALS OF YOUTH

It all began as child's play. The young people of Salem, constricted by overbearing Puritanism, were agog to hear vivid stories woven by Tituba, a Carib slave brought to the community from the West Indies. The tribal ritual and magic recounted by Tituba must have seemed a world away from the existence of grinding toil led by Salem residents.

But when 9-year-old Betty Parris fell ill and could not be cured by orthodox methods, the doctor said she was bewitched. The affliction quickly spread to her friends, who writhed and groaned and uttered fanciful accusations against adults.

The childrens' imagination was fired not only by the tales told by Tituba, but also by the words of self-appointed Satan expert Cotton Mather, author of a recently published tome relating to the symptoms of witchcraft. Furthermore, they had been experimenting with fortune telling, and they knew their curiosity had led them into forbidden realms. The guilty children believed themselves to be bitten and pinched by devilish creatures or spectres and were soon seeing witches flying through the air.

The zealous village dignitaries led a witch-hunt, convinced that the Devil's agents were lurking in their midst.

Perhaps unsurprisingly, Tituba was swiftly arrested and faced the accusation of witchcraft. Two other women were also hauled before the authorities. One was Sarah Good, a pipe-smoking beggar, and the other was Sarah Osburne, a widow known to hold the church in contempt. Matters might have died down following their confinement, but for the admission by Tituba, implicating the other two women, of contact with Satan himself. When the child accusers were brought into their company, the youngsters fell into fits – proof, if any were needed, that these women were indeed witches.

WITCH HUNT

Now the zealous village dignitaries led a witch-hunt, convinced that the Devil's agents were lurking in their midst.

The first witch to hang was Bridget Bishop, in her late fifties and a tavern owner of dubious reputation. A field hand claimed to have seen Bishop's image stealing eggs and then transforming into a cat to run off with her plunder. Another villager said she visited him at night in spectral form to torment him. Yet others maintained that she was responsible for numerous examples of bad luck in the community.

A short excerpt from the trial of Bridget Bishop reveals how pointless it was for supposed witches to try and prove their innocence. When she was accused of being a witch, the luckless woman replied: 'I know nothing of it…I know not what a witch is.'

'How do you know then that you are not a witch?' was the response of the prosecutor. Her continuing protests were deemed unsatisfactory in law. Following her trial she was taken to Gallows Hill on 10 June 1692 and hanged.

The plight of witch-hunt victims was heart-rending. Four-year-old Dorcas Good was arrested after Salem children claimed to have been attacked by her spectre. She spent months in jail in chains, weeping continually, and then watched her mother Sarah being carried off to the gallows.

THE INNOCENT PUT TO DEATH

Rebecca Nurse, a church-goer and a pillar in the community, was found not guilty at her trial. Judge William Stoughton was so irate at the decision that he sent the jury back to re-consider and they returned with a guilty verdict. On appeal, the state governor pardoned her, but prominent Salem men compelled him to reverse the decision. Eventually, Rebecca was excommunicated from the church and sent to hang.

Deputy Constable John Willard was brought before the court after he refused to make further arrests. His fate was the same as the convicted witches. Another tavern owner, John Proctor, was denounced as a witch after pouring scorn on the trials. Robust in his own defence, he asked for the trial to be moved to Boston. His request was denied and he was hanged, although his pregnant wife was spared the noose.

Former minister Reverend George Burroughs, it was decided, led young girls into witchcraft. Before he was hanged he recited the Lord's prayer, a feat supposedly impossible for a witch, and once again maintained his innocence. When the crowd hesitated, Cotton Mather himself stepped forward to remind them of the court's authority.

After Giles Corey refused to co-operate with the court he was pressed to death – pinned out in an open field with rocks piled upon his body until all life was crushed from it. This terrible punishment, probably illegal, was never used again in America.

A GRISLY END

Within a few months the lust for witch persecution in Salem was ebbing. A change in the judicial proceedings that meant 'spectral evidence' was no longer accepted. Given that firm facts were in short supply, this effectively put an end to the string of convictions.

By May 1693, all prisoners awaiting trial or already convicted of witchcraft were released. Judges and jurors alike were largely filled with remorse and made public apologies. The notable exception was William Stoughton, one of the driving forces in the campaign, who maintained that the village had been riddled with witches. He went on to become governor of Massachusetts.

However, no fewer than twenty people had lost their lives during the witch-fever, all through public execution. A further four people died in jail where conditions were foul. Two unlucky dogs were executed as witch accomplices.

HOW COULD THIS HAPPEN?

The terrible events that took place in Salem in 1692-93 were the result of a small community riven with feuds. Suspicion and distrust were rife amongst the villagers, and the witch-trials became an opportunity for them to settle long-standing scores.

At the time there was an unshakeable belief in the existence of witches. The dangers of Satan and his faithful crones were expounded weekly from the pulpit to the God-fearing congregation. Witchcraft was an issue often hotly debated among adults, particularly after Cotton Mather's book appeared, and it was a constant worry to many.

TITUBA'S TALE

But what of Tituba, at the start of all the troubles? Ironically — having confessed her guilt — she walked free, and was ultimately sold on into another community. The effects of her story-telling there remain unknown.

Some of the unlucky women of Salem, brought to trial for witchcraft. As their former friends and neighbours denounced them, they had little chance of survival against a corrupt court intent on the harshest punishment.

Signs of the Devil

According to many religions, the Devil is the opposite of God and an enemy of mankind. Known by different names, including Satan, Beelzebub and Old Scratch, he is a difficult figure to pin down. Just as some people have devoted their lives to searching for signs of God, there are others who seek affirmation of the Devil's existence.

The idea of a devil probably first evolved as a metaphor for the flawed side of man's character, the aspect that sought money, power and carnal pleasures. Ironically, the Devil was made larger than life by clergymen in the pulpit who sought to drive their parishioners to God through fear. Naturally, some members of the congregation were intrigued and wanted to know more.

Worship of the Devil or Satanism ensued and was for centuries an underground movement or secret society that thrived through its twilight existence and elaborate rituals.

CHURCH OF SATAN

It was not until 1966 that the Church of Satan was unveiled in San Fransisco, offering a belief system up to scrutiny. The founder of this unorthodox church was Dr Anton Szandor LaVey, who explained: 'Satan is a symbol, nothing more. He's a symbol of man's carnal nature – his lust, greed, vengeance but most of all his ego.'

The idea of a devil probably first evolved as a metaphor for the flawed side of man's character that sought money, power and carnal pleasures.

Dr Edward Moody, an American social scientist, joined the Church of Satan to discover more. The churchgoers were, he discovered, society's least prepossessing members. 'The cult attracted them because it offered a simple explanation for their inadequacies: they were bewitched or under an unlucky star or not vibrating to the right rhythm. Their failure was supernatural; their remedy was supernatural. The rites and medicines of the church promised the success that had so far eluded them.'

Horrific crimes have been carried out in the name of Satan. The murders of pregnant Sharon Tate and others by the drug-addled cohorts of Charles Manson are the most notorious. Of course, these can hardly be taken as proof of the Devil's existence, since there have been many more atrocities committed in the name of God. However, an incident that occurred more than 150 years ago in rural Devon, England, is still cited today as a mystery that perhaps points to an embodiment of the Devil at work on earth.

DEVILISH COLD IN DEVON

The bitter winter of 1855 turned southern Britain into an icy wasteland. The frail froze in their beds, thousands were laid off work and bread riots erupted in towns isolated by heavy snow. This was the 'Crimean Winter' – an uncertain, fearful time.

However, on the morning of 9 February, cold and hunger were briefly forgotten, when Devon villagers awoke to a new fall of snow bearing strange tear-drop shaped tracks. The tracks defied gravity, trod impossible paths and created a trail some hundred miles long. Soon there was talk of these being the Devil's footprints.

For weeks it dominated national newspaper letters columns. *The Times* referred to 'the marks of Satan' and added: '…that great excitement has been produced among all classes may be judged from the fact that the subject has been descanted on from the pulpit.'

On 24 February the *Illustrated London News* weighed in with an attempt to explain why the 'Great Devon Mystery' could not be attributed to farm or wild animals. The marks were 10cm x 5cm, like a donkey's hoof, but whereas a donkey would have made double prints, the 'Devil's' appeared in a single line some 20cm apart. Every parish reported the same size print and stride. Struggling for a description, many witnesses said they seemed 'branded in the snow'.

The writer concluded: 'It is very easy for people to laugh at these appearances and account for them in an idle way… [but] no known animal could have traversed this extent of country in one night, beside having to cross an estuary of the sea two miles [3km] broad…'

By now south Devon was a cauldron of fear, rumour and wild speculation. Search parties armed with 'guns and bludgeons' were despatched from Dawlish to follow the trail. Fishermen spoke of prints emerging from the sea at Teignmouth. Doors were barricaded at night.

PROTESTANT REVENGE?

Some churchmen took advantage of the febrile mood, claiming that the 'Devil' had singled out followers of the priest Edward Pusey. At the time, Pusey had been trying to re-introduce Catholic ritual into the Church of England and he controlled a handful of Devon parishes.

'Some people say it is sent as a warning to the Puseyites,' the *Western Times* gleefully reported, 'hence it is that the 'phenomenon' has visited the Puseyite parishes of Woodbury, Topsham and Littleham-cum-Exmouth. In this place it has traversed the churchyard – and even to the very door of the vestibule.' Conveniently, the article ignores footprints in Protestant parishes.

The Illustrated London News *published a letter and an illustration showing how the prints appeared in a single line – not in double prints as you would expect from a four-legged animal.*

THE ILLUSTRATED LONDON NEWS

FOOT-MARKS ON THE SNOW, IN DEVON.
(From a Correspondent.)

As many of your readers have perused, I have no doubt, with much interest, the paragraph which appeared in several of the papers of last week, relative to the mysterious foot-marks left upon the snow during the night of Thursday, the 8th, in the parishes of Exmouth, Lympstone, and Woodbury, as also in Dawlish, Torquay, Totnes, and other places on the other side of the estuary of the Exe, in the county of Devon, extending over a tract of country of thirty or forty miles, or probably more; and as the paragraph I allude to does not fully detail the mysterious affair, it may probably be interesting to many to have a more particular account—which I think this unusual occurrence well deserves.

The marks which appeared on the snow (which lay very thinly on the ground at the time), and which were seen on the Friday morning, to all appearance were the perfect impression of a donkey's hoof—the length 4 inches by 2¾ inches; but, instead of progressing as that animal would have done (or indeed as any other would have done), feet right and left, it appeared that foot had followed foot, in a *single line*; the distance from each tread being eight inches, or rather more—the foot-marks in every parish being exactly the same size, and the steps the same length. This mysterious visitor generally only passed *once* down or across each garden or courtyard, and did so in nearly all the houses in many parts of the several towns above mentioned, as also in the farms scattered about; this regular track passing in some instances over the roofs of houses, and hayricks, and very high walls (one fourteen feet), without displacing the snow on either side or altering the distance between the feet, and passing on as if the wall had not been any impediment. The gardens with high fences or walls, and gates locked, were equally visited as those open and unprotected. Now, when we consider the distance that must have been gone over to have left these marks—I may say in almost every garden, on door-steps, through the extensive woods of Luscombe, upon commons, in enclosures and farms—the actual progress must have exceeded a hundred miles. It is very easy for people to laugh at these appearances, and account for them in an idle way. At present no satisfactory solution has been given. No known animal could have traversed this extent of country in one night, besides having to cross an estuary of the sea two miles broad. Neither does any known animal walk in a *line* of single footsteps, not even man.

Birds could not have left these marks, as no bird's foot leaves the impression of a hoof, or, even were there a bird capable of doing so, could it proceed in the direct manner above stated—nor would birds, even had they donkeys'

THE INVESTIGATION

The leading investigator of the prints was the Rev. H. T. Ellacombe. He concluded the following: 'There is no doubt as to the facts – that thousands of these marks were seen on the snow on the morning of the 9th extending over many miles,' he wrote. It was 'as if the snow had been branded with a hot iron – …tho' the snow in the middle part did not appear to be touched.'

The vicar sent various drawings of footprints (and a sample of 'white, grape-sized excrement') to the renowned naturalist Sir Richard Owen and the Oxford professor Dr I. A. Ogle. One of the sketches included claws, which Sir Richard believed might have belonged to a badger. The vicar's own theory was that birds' feet had become iced up, leaving single prints in the snow. But it seems unlikely that country folk would not have recognized common bird prints.

Six ewes and a ram had been herded together, strangled and laid out in what police believe may have been an occult ceremony.

Bizarrely, a kangaroo had escaped from 'Mr Fisher's private zoo' at nearby Sidmouth just before 8 February and was later shot at Teignmouth. But no reports relating to the footprints mentioned tail marks, so it seems the two events cannot have been linked.

There were attempts try and explain the prints, including the theory that they were in fact condensation marks, and claims that the cold and hungry population had become hysterical. In February 1855 the average temperature across southern England was minus 1.7 degrees and snow fell every day for six weeks.

A CONCLUSION?

Exeter University research fellow Theo Brown (now deceased) who unearthed Rev. Ellacombe's notes, scoured the evidence. She came to the conclusion that a combination of events was probably responsible. She says the trail was not continuous, the prints were not all single file and neither were they identical. Crucially, she states that the prints were laid over several days rather than just six hours. 'All the people concerned,' says Miss Brown, 'were quite content to leave the thing in the air, rather than spoil a good story.'

However, she concludes: 'To this day, no one has offered an explanation which takes account of all the available evidence…even if the single-footed track only covered a part of the distance we still have no idea what creature could possibly have made it.'

LAND OF THE UNEXPLAINED

Devon is an English county often associated with mysterious goings-on. On 3 January 2005, a walker stumbled across a gruesome scene near Sampford Spiney, just 32km west of the 1855 'visitation'. Six ewes and a ram had been herded together, strangled and laid out in what police believe may have been an occult ceremony. According to ancient belief, seven is a significant number for satanic rituals. A contract with the Devil had to contain seven paragraphs, was binding for seven years and needed seven signatures. It seems that the Devil had struck again.

The Power of Curses

Can the utterance of a few malicious words really change someone's destiny? Those who believe in the power of a curse are convinced that catastrophe will follow in its wake. And sometimes ensuing mishaps and disasters are so bizarre and numerous that all the evidence points to a jinx.

CURSE OF THE BOY KING

Perhaps the most infamous curse of all was one that protected the tomb of King Tutankhamen. When Egyptologist Howard Carter discovered the tomb in 1922, it was the culmination of a career spent scouring the desert for riches. The honour of opening the inner door, revealing the treasures of the king in all their splendour, fell to Lord Carnarvon (financier of the expedition) on 17 February 1923. Within weeks after that fateful day Carnarvon was dead, apparently from an infected mosquito bite. The bite mark on his cheek was said to resemble one borne by the boy king himself.

When Carnarvon died, the lights in Cairo flickered and failed, while miles away at home his dog fell into a fit and passed away. Tales of other expedition members dying suddenly abounded. Even the pilots who took the royal artifacts as cargo on their planes apparently met unexpected deaths. For several years the string of ill fortune continued, as museum curators associated with the exhibition of Tutankhamen's treasures keeled over.

The curse that protected the tomb was written in hieroglyphics on a clay tablet. When deciphered, it read: 'Death will slay with its wings whoever disturbs

Lord Carnarvon and Howard Carter with Carnarvon's daughter, Lady Evelyn Herbert, at the entrance to the tomb of King Tutankhamen.

'Death will slay with its wings whoever disturbs the peace of the Pharaoh.'

the peace of the Pharaoh.' Yet, despite careful cataloguing of all the tomb's contents, the dire warning has vanished. Perhaps it never existed in the first place, being the product of some sun-affected imagination. However, there is another explanation. Carter may well have hidden the tablet bearing the curse to prevent a walk-out by superstitious local workers, on whom he was reliant for his work.

Cynics have poured scorn over the curse claims, pointing out that mosquito bites were and still are frequently fatal. They say that the lights in Cairo often blacked out, and that the story of the death of Carnarvon's dog is only anecdotal. Much has recently been made of the theory that the tomb contained lethal spores that afflicted those who went inside, giving weight to the sceptics' argument. Yet when Carter died a decade later it was from natural causes. The debate on the curse continues.

Unluckiest of all, of course, was King Tutankhamen himself, who died when he was still a teenager and whose memorial was all but erased by subsequent royals.

A HISTORY OF CURSES

Belief in curses stretches back into the mists of time. Ancient verbal curses may seem comical today, but in the past they would strike terror into the heart: 'May the seven terriers of hell sit on the spool of your breast and bark in at your soul-case,' says an old Irish curse. 'She should have stones and not children,' according to a Yiddish one.

In the past people have made a profitable business out of issuing curses. The philosopher Plato (427-347BC) wrote in *The Republic*, 'If anyone wishes to injure an enemy, for a small fee they (sorcerers) will bring harm on good or bad alike, binding the gods to serve their purposes by spells and curses.'

Curses are a common Biblical theme, perhaps the most famous being issued by God against Adam and Eve in the Garden of Eden (see page 205).

THE HOPE DIAMOND

A wrathful god appears to have orchestrated fearful vengeance after the Hope diamond was plundered from a temple in Mandala, Burma in the seventeenth century. Mined in India, it was a fabulous violet-coloured specimen of the very highest quality. No one knows what happened to the thief, but it fell into the possession of a French trader, Jean-Baptiste Tavernier. Tavernier sold the diamond to French king Louis XIV, who had it made into a heart before giving it to his mistress Madame de Montespan. Shortly afterwards she was publicly disgraced in a black magic scandal. The luckless trader Tavernier met a grisly end on a trip to Russia and dogs were discovered gnawing on his bones.

The gem remained in the royal collection, and it was worn by Marie Antoinette before she was beheaded in the French Revolution. In the chaos that enveloped Paris it was stolen and its whereabouts were unknown for some three decades. Could it be that the curse of the Hope Diamond had finally lost its power?

LIVES DESTROYED

The diamond turned up in the 1830s, in the possession of Dutch diamond cutter Wilhelm Fals. Its exquisite beauty bewitched his son Hendrick, and the hapless boy ultimately committed suicide.

The dangerous gem was then bought by the banker Henry Philip Hope, who gave it his name, but suffered no harm from it. Afterwards, though, the curse appears to have gained some momentum. It was bequeathed to a relative, Lord Francis Hope, whose marriage collapsed.

By 1904 a certain Jacques Colot was the owner, until he lost his mind and committed suicide. Russian nobleman Prince Kanilovsky presented it to his lover, whom he later shot and killed before being bludgeoned to death himself. Diamond dealer Habib Bey drowned and Greek merchant Simon Montharides plunged to his death with his wife and child when their horse and carriage went over a cliff top. The Hope diamond then went to the Ottoman ruler, Abdul Hamid III, shortly before an uprising usurped the Sultanate. His favourite wife, often seen wearing the jewel, was stabbed to death.

LAST REVENGE

The last ill-fated owner was wealthy Evelyn Walsh McLean. Within a year of purchasing the diamond from jewellery impresario Pierre Cartier for $180,000, her son Vinson was killed in a car accident. Her husband Ned began drinking, left her for another woman and finally lost his mind. Then, in 1946, their daughter took an overdose of sleeping pills. After Evelyn died in 1947 the gem finally went into the Smithsonian Institute in Washington, a move that appears to have neutered its potency.

Evelyn Walsh McLean, who bought the Hope diamond from jewellery impresario Pierre Cartier for $180,000.

Evelyn had received numerous warnings about the curse of the Hope diamond, many in unsolicited letters from strangers. But she maintained that the bad luck attached to its ownership was pure chance. 'What tragedies have befallen me might have occurred had I never seen or touched the Hope Diamond. My observations have persuaded me that tragedies, for anyone who lives, are not escapable.'

From treading the sacred corridors of Tutankhamen's tomb, to plundering the exquisite jewels of Burma, many of the most potent curses seem to be released when humans tread too far into forbidden territory. And where some curses seem to lose potency over time, others retain their venom, wreaking havoc down hapless generations…

Cursed Dynasties

A family rich in fame, fortune and political power often arouses envy, but could anyone be so jealous as to invoke terrible curses, designed to bring a dynasty to its knees? Many people believe that the appalling misfortunes that befall a few well-known clans occur at a rate far beyond what could be expected under normal circumstances – and that a jinx is the obvious explanation.

Joe and Rose Kennedy, unaware of the calamities that were to befall their children, pose for a family portrait (with eight of their nine offspring) in 1934.

THE KENNEDY CURSE

Although no known curse has been sworn against the Kennedy family, a prominent political clan in the United States, the number of tragedies they have suffered far exceeds the average, and seems almost unnatural.

For Joe Kennedy, the adage that 'money can't buy happiness' must have left a sour taste. A multi-millionaire by the age of 30, and the father of nine children, Joe

appeared to have the Midas touch. But although he and his wife Rose lived long, comfortable lives, their children were famously ill-starred.

In 1944 their eldest son, also called Joe, died aged 29, when the bomber aircraft he was piloting exploded above the English Channel. He was fighting in the Second World War – a war which Joe Senior had publicly advised the US against joining. His son's body was never found.

His daughter Kathleen's husband, the Marquis of Hartington, died in the same year, and Kathleen herself perished in an aircraft accident aged 28, in 1948. Another daughter, Rosemary, was institutionalized in 1941.

In 1960, second son John Fitzgerald Kennedy became the thirty-fifth president of the US, fulfilling Joe Senior's dearest ambitions. But just three years later, the 46-year-old was shot in the head by an assassin as his motor cavalcade crawled through Dallas, Texas. He and his wife Jackie Kennedy had recently lost their son Patrick, who died at just two days old.

Now the political aspirations of the grieving Joe Kennedy lay with his son Robert. But within five years he was also dead, killed in Los Angeles while campaigning for presidency.

If all these deaths in the family were not hard enough to bear, the tragedy was compounded when youngest brother Teddy, a senator, was in a near-fatal car accident in 1969. His car plunged from a bridge and sank into the waterway at Chappaquiddick Island, and although he struggled to safety his passenger, Mary Jo Kopechne, 29, was drowned. Questions were raised about the reasons for the crash, and why Teddy had been unable to rescue his passenger. It seemed the trouble would never end.

Daughters Eunice, Patricia and Jean emerged largely unscathed from these troubled times. But the curse regained momentum with the next generation of Kennedys. John Junior died in a light plane crash in 1999. One of Robert's sons, David, died of a drugs overdose in 1984, while another was killed in a skiing accident at Aspen in 1997. Meanwhile Teddy Junior, son of Edward, was struck down with cancer and had to have a leg amputated.

Joe Kennedy senior saw only a portion of the disasters that fate had in store for his family. He died in 1969, aged 81. Were his children the pawns of a cursed fate, or were they simply the victims of aberrant behaviour or poor judgement? Perhaps the real victim of the string of tragedies was Rose, who lived until the age of 104, scarred by the misfortunes that piled upon her children and grandchildren.

MONACO MISFORTUNE

The Royal family that rules the small principality of Monaco has often hit the headlines through a succession of calamities. In 1956, a union between Monaco's Prince Rainier III and Hollywood film beauty Grace Kelly seem to augur well for the dynasty. Together they had three children and were the picture of happiness.

Unfortunately, all that ended in 1982, when a car driven by Princess Grace with her daughter Stephanie a passenger plunged down a cliff. Grace was immediately killed, aged just 52, while 17-year-old Stephanie suffered neck injuries and was emotionally scarred.

After this tragic incident, the ties that bound the close-knit family began to unravel. Stephanie had a succession of doomed relationships – she even ran away with the circus in pursuit of love. Her sister Caroline's first marriage ended after two tumultuous years, and she eventually found happiness with Italian businessman Stefano Casiraghi and had three children. But they were still infants at the time of Stefano's tragic death in a powerboat crash in 1990.

Prince Albert II of Monaco, who inherited the throne when Prince Rainier died in 2005, has shown a marked reluctance to marry and produce an heir. Perhaps he is mindful of the curse reputedly laid upon the family when one of his ancestors, Prince Rainier I, kidnapped and raped a witch. Her revenge was to curse the family with the words: 'Never will a Grimaldi find true happiness in marriage'.

And if that were not sufficient, there is talk of another curse laid in 1297, the year the first Grimaldi, Francesco the Spiteful, conquered the world's second smallest state. After he tricked his way into a fortress by dressing as a monk, he was cursed by its defeated defenders.

NOBLE DEATHS

Problems have beset the Craven family in England, since seventeenth-century baron William Craven made a servant girl pregnant and refused to wed her. She used her Romany heritage to summon a curse that seems to have had lasting effects.

Since then, the family history has been fraught with calamity. The eighth Earl, Simon Craven, died in a car crash in 1990. He had inherited the title from his

Brandon Lee was shot by a gun that should have contained blanks, but was in fact inexplicably loaded with live bullets.

older brother Thomas who, morbidly obsessed with the curse and depressed following a drugs incident, shot himself aged 26. Their father, the sixth Earl, had died of leukemia aged 47. His father had drowned after falling from a boat following a party. Indeed, from the creation of the peerage in 1801, none of the incumbents have reached the age of 60. Could the curse of the servant girl all those years ago really still have the power to cause so many untimely deaths?

A PERSONAL CURSE?

The efficacy of curses is often psychological, and has much to do with the victim's state of mind. If someone feels like a victim, in many cases they will become one. Indeed, in many parts of the world, an effigy speared with pins, such as a voodoo doll, is still a powerful and disturbing symbol of a curse. This practice has long been used in India, Iran, Egypt, Africa and Europe to provoke profound fear when witnessed by the intended victim.

This psychological aspect of curses seems to have sealed the fate of Kung Fu fighter Bruce Lee, who achieved international stardom with his films. Yet his success could not shield him from his dreadful personal conviction that demons were lying in wait for him. His greatest fear was that the curse he believed was intended for him would pass to his offspring.

In 1973, Lee collapsed in convulsions on a film set. Within two months, aged 32, he died after apparently suffering a brain haemorrhage. His son Brandon grew up in the same mould as his father, loving Kung Fu and fearing its spiritual powers. In 1993, aged just 27, he was killed following a film stunt calamity. Lee was shot by a gun that should have contained blanks, but was in fact inexplicably loaded with live bullets.

Logically, it seems impossible that supernatural forces could emanate from oaths uttered centuries ago, or from dolls pierced with pins, to blight the lives of a dynasty. Yet curses, like superstitions, have a habit of proving themselves. However ancient their origins, belief in curses stays firm even in the twenty-first century.

Bruce Lee in the 1973 martial arts classic Enter the Dragon. *His talent as a martial artist combined with his acting skills to ensure box-office success.*

GHOSTLY EXPERIENCES

We think of time as the ultimate force in life, and the reason we eventually die. But frequent sightings of ghosts suggests that after death, part of us will linger here on earth. Haunting houses, film studios and ships, and even turning up in photographs, the dead seem here to stay. Some people have even experienced timeslips, suggesting that our universe is not such a fixed quantity after all.

Celebrity Ghosts

Hollywood may seem like a place of glamour and lighthearted living, but behind the bright façade lie dark secrets. Many of the stars lured to Hollywood by fame and fortune have died untimely and mysterious deaths, and continue to haunt the luxurious settings of their success.

MARILYN MONROE
Perhaps the most famous of these Hollywood haunters is celluloid sensation Marilyn Monroe. In life, she was a tormented soul whose poignant pursuit for personal happiness touched a generation. So perhaps it is hardly surprising that she has remained a restless figure in death.

The ghost of the young Marilyn Monroe (1926-62) is said to haunt the Roosevelt Hotel on Hollywood Boulevard.

Monroe's career started at the Roosevelt Hotel on Hollywood Boulevard. It was here that she posed on a diving board for her first advertisement, for sun-tan lotion, brimming with aspiration. The starlet, blessed with stunning looks and a voluptuous figure, appeared to have the world at her feet. But later she became embroiled in studio politics and struggled through many doomed love affairs. She even developed a draining drug dependency. On 5 August 1962, she was found dead at her Brentwood home, aged just 36. She is believed to have died from a self-administered drugs overdose, although some people doubt this explanation, and conspiracy theorists have since claimed she was murdered.

Since her death, Monroe's reflection has been seen in a full-length mirror that once hung in her favourite poolside suite at the Roosevelt Hotel, where she started out years before. Could it be that her restless soul is seeking to recapture youth and happiness? The dark-framed mirror that has captured her ghostly image has been moved to the hotel basement.

HAUNTED HOTEL

And Marilyn is not the only A-list celebrity making unscheduled appearances at the 320-roomed Roosevelt. Montgomery Clift – her co-star in the 1961 film *The Misfits* – can be heard up in room 928 labouring over his lines for the 1953 movie *From Here to Eternity*.

After becoming a star, Clift, like Monroe, led a tortured existence. He became an alcoholic and a drug addict. He was also homosexual, a fact he felt compelled to hide from the public for fear of people's response. He was found dead in his New York home at the age of 45, apparently suffering from heart disease.

Staff at the Roosevelt have been alarmed after hearing loud noises while standing outside the room 928. Sometimes the telephone is found off the hook. One member of staff claimed a ghostly hand brushed her skin. It seems Clift never really checked out.

The last spooky site in the hotel lies in the Blossom Ballroom where a sizeable 'cold spot' has been noted by some visitors, management and staff. This was the setting for the first ever Academy Awards in 1929. Perhaps the phenomenon is the result of some bitter disappointment suffered by an early Hollywood hopeful.

THE SIDEWALK CAFÉ

Comedy actress Thelma Todd starred in more than forty films before her death in 1935, aged 29. She had appeared alongside the Marx brothers and Laurel and Hardy to great acclaim, and she also ran a restaurant called *Thelma Todd's Sidewalk Café* (situated on what is now known as the Pacific Coast Highway).

Her body was discovered in a car, in a garage above the café, still wearing evening clothes and a mink stole. The cause of death was presumed to be suicide through carbon monoxide poisoning. Yet there has long been speculation that it was murder, by a jealous former husband, an angry lover or perhaps even the Mafia.

If there was indeed an undetected murder, this might explain why Todd's ghost would want to return to earth. She has been seen descending a staircase at her old café, now owned by the religiously inclined TV and film company Paulist Productions. Employees have also smelled fumes in the building.

SPOOKY CEMETERY

Clifton Webb is another wandering soul, witnessed close to his burial place in the Hollywood Memorial Park Cemetery. His spirit also reportedly appears from time to time at his old home in Retford Drive, Beverley Hills. Webb was famous for his roles as 'Mr Belvedere' and for an enduring friendship with playwright Noel Coward. However, nothing in his life took precedence over his beloved mother Mabelle. The pair lived together until her death aged 91. Frustrated by Webb's excessive grief, Coward remarked with characteristic humour: 'It must be tough to be orphaned at 71.'

Another ghost has been heard in the same graveyard, that of Virginia Rappe. This ill-fated starlet died after apparently being shut in a hotel bedroom with outsized comedian 'Fatty' Arbuckle during a debauched party. Later she was discovered weeping and in pain. She died later from peritonitis brought about by a ruptured kidney. The ensuing scandal engulfed Hollywood and Arbuckle's career was ruined by it, although he was eventually cleared of wrong-doing.

STILL AT THE STUDIO

The cemetery is also the last resting place of Douglas Fairbanks and Rudolph Valentino. Although Valentino's spectre has not been seen in the cemetery itself, it is thought to haunt the costume department of the Paramount Studios on Marathon Avenue.

Not to be outdone, Universal Studios has its own celebrity ghost, since the actor Lon Chaney is alleged to be haunting Sound Stage 28. But this does not seem to be his favourite haunt, since he was most often seen on a bus stop bench at the intersection of Hollywood and Vine. The son of deaf-mutes, Chaney learned to communicate with facial expressions. During his career he acted mostly in horror films and was heavily made up, becoming known as 'the man of a thousand faces'. He died in 1930 of throat cancer, aged 47. It is not known which of the thousand faces the ghost at the bus stop used to wear. When the bus seat was removed the ghost moved on.

Not only do staff see Welles' corpulent, caped frame, but they smell the cigars he was fond of smoking and the brandy he loved to swig.

HARD TO LEAVE

Another man who has struggled to leave Hollywood behind is former bull-fighter and *War of the Worlds* broadcaster Orson Welles. Since his death in 1985 aged 70, he has been glimpsed at his favourite restaurant, Sweet Lady Jane's in Melrose Avenue. Not only do staff occasionally see his corpulent, caped frame, but they smell the cigars he was fond of smoking and the brandy he loved to swig.

Guy Gibson was a different brand of celebrity. He came to prominence during the Second World War, after leading the 1943 raid against two hydroelectric dams in industrial Germany, using specially-designed bouncing bombs. The risks were incredibly high, and only eleven of the nineteen bombers from the celebrated 617 Squadron that embarked on the Dambusters raid returned. But the ambitious raid achieved its aim and, after the exploit, Gibson was awarded the Victoria Cross for his indisputable valour. He became well-known on both sides of the Atlantic, went on a lecture tour in America and wrote a book about the raid called *Enemy Coast Ahead*. Gibson finally returned to active duty a year after the raid and was killed in a mission over Germany in September 1944.

As the fifieth anniversary of the start of the Second World War beckoned in 1989, visitors saw the ghost of Guy Gibson relaxing in his favourite armchair at the hotel that used to serve as an officer's mess for those in the Dambusters squadron. Guests also reported hearing a piano rendition of wartime songs in the hotel. The music continued to play, despite the fact that the bar containing the piano was firmly locked.

There is nothing to suggest that celebrities are more likely to return to earth in ghostly form than those with more mundane day-jobs. But it is tempting to

The actor Lon Chaney, 'the man of a thousand faces', in the 1926 film **The Road to Mandalay.** *Chaney's ghost chose to divide his time between Universal Studios and a bus stop.*

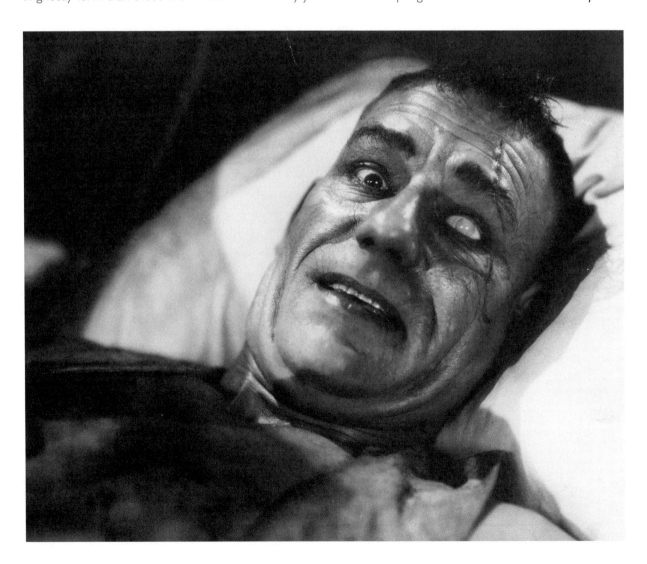

Timeslips

For the moment, time machines that transport people to the future and the past at the flick of a switch are strictly the stuff of science fiction. Yet there have been instances where people appear to stumble into a different era, and their memorable anecdotes offer serious food for thought.

In fact, time travel is probably not impossible, according to some of the greatest brains of the age. Albert Einstein left a window for it in his famous Theory of Relativity. However, although the theory is sound, we do not yet have the know-how to make time travel work.

What we do have is stories related by people who believe they have inadvertently seen a glimpse of another epoch. They can offer no explanation of how they got into this different dimension nor, by the same token, how they returned. The most compelling stories of time travel are those backed up by a number of witnesses.

A LESSON IN FRENCH HISTORY

In 1979, Len and Cynthia Gisby and their neighbours Geoff and Pauline Simpson, from North Lancashire, were driving through France on their way to Spain on a holiday. They decided to break their journey and stop for the night in the Rhone Valley near Montélimar, but the first hotel they tried was full. They were given directions to a second hotel that lay off the main road, down a bumpy track. Although the man at reception struggled to comprehend them, they finally secured two rooms for the night. They noticed the building was gas-lit, while the rooms had bedsteads with wooden bolsters and blankets rather than duvets. The windows had no glass in them and in the bathroom the soap was speared onto the wall by a metal spike.

Dinner was also a curious affair, with steak and beer. At breakfast they watched as gendarmes wearing cloaks and pillar-box hats arrived to speak with a woman in a long dress with button shoes. It seemed as if they had happened upon a theme hotel that paid particular attention to detail. And when it came to paying the bill, they discovered it was a tiny sum. Each of them had been charged only a few pence for the hospitality.

Charmed by the rustic nature of the place, the four decided to pay a return visit on their way home. However, when they returned, the hotel seemed to have completely disappeared. Stranger still, all the photos they had taken of it previously came out blank.

TURBULENT TIME

The next bizarre timeslip had only one witness, and was therefore more open to doubt. But the man concerned was to become one of the stalwarts of the Royal Air Force during the Second World War, whose reputation was impeccable.

In 1934, Wing Commander Victor Goddard was flying a Hawker Hart biplane from Scotland to Andover, in Hampshire. Turbulent weather enveloped the plane, and blinded by a deluge and dense cloud, Goddard went into a spin and only narrowly avoided crashing.

As soon as he had regained control of the rudimentary aircraft he suddenly found himself in radically different conditions. The clouds had parted and the sun was beating down. Below him, he recognized the Drem airfield he had visited the day previously, abandoned after the First World War and now derelict.

Yet the airfield was a hive of activity. Three biplanes were there, just like his own but painted yellow, and there was a fourth plane was of a type he had never seen before. Goddard saw ground crew dressed in blue overalls, although as far as he knew all RAF uniforms were brown. The men failed to notice Goddard's plane above them, and when the Drem airfield was out of sight he found himself once more in the teeth of a storm.

Goddard put the strange incident to the back of his mind, although he never forgot it. And in 1939, as Britain geared up for war, he was astonished to see bi-planes being painted yellow and mechanics' uniforms switching from brown to blue. Monoplanes like the fourth plane he had seen at Drem were finally being flown by the Royal Air Force. And after the outbreak of the Second World War, the airfield was put into use again.

Goddard, who had joined the Royal Navy in 1910 and switched to the Royal Air Force in 1918, held numerous senior posts during the Second World War and afterwards. Following his retirement in 1951 he was knighted. When he finally wrote about the eerie experience in 1966, he concluded that he must have flown into the future, and seen the airfield as it was to be during the Second World War. Goddard maintained an interest in the supernatural until his death in 1987.

A squadron of British monoplane fighters, of the type that Goddard saw at the Drem airfield. During the Second World War, these were said to be the fastest warplanes in service in any of the world's air forces.

Other timeslip witnesses have stayed rooted in the present and seen people from another age passing through.

One such incident involved two men, only ever identified as L.C. and Charlie, who were driving on Highway 167 between Abbeville and Lafayette in Louisiana in 1969. The road ahead was empty, save for a vintage car bearing the distinctive plates '1940'. Behind the wheel was a woman dressed in old-fashioned clothes to match the car, and her only passenger was a child similarly attired. What caught the attention of the two men was not only the immaculate condition of the vehicle, but also the fearful expression haunting the driver's face. As they drew alongside the slow-moving car they asked through their open window if she needed help. She indicated that she did, so the men overtook her and pulled over onto the roadside. But when they looked back to see where she was, the vintage car had vanished.

As they battled their incredulity, another car pulled in. The driver insisted he had seen the old car ahead and watched as the modern vehicle overtook it. Then the old car had simply disappeared before his eyes. Together they searched the area, but found no clues. It was tempting to believe that the car had somehow time-slipped into the year 1969, and then seamlessly returned to its own era.

Sometimes we all suspect time of playing tricks on us, when the hours race by like minutes, or drag by like days.

DISAPPEARING ACT

Sometimes we all suspect time of playing tricks on us, when the hours race by like minutes, or drag by like days. But cases of time slippage are difficult to prove in isolation, without witnesses. In some cases, though, there are witnesses, and Eula White was one of them. Born in 1912, she grew up in rural Alabama. One day she went to a local farmhouse owned by the Hawkins family to sell peas and beans from the front porch. Mr Hawkins, who had gone into town on horseback for provisions, came into view with a white sack of flour over the saddle and a brown grocery bag in the crook of his left arm. As he came up the driveway, one of the boys playing nearby ran to open the farm gate for him. Then, right before of the eyes of everybody there, Mr Hawkins simply disappeared. Astonishment soon gave way to fear, and Eula and her colleagues let out piercing screams. Eventually they calmed down and closed the farm gate again.

Alarm rose in their throats once more when, some time later, they saw Mr Hawkins with flour sack and groceries riding into view for a second time. But this time he rode up to the gate, showed no signs of vanishing, and demanded that someone open up for him. Eula's feelings were of overwhelming relief, tempered by anxiety about the initial incident. It was an experience she would never forget.

Investigation into the possibilities of time travel did not end with the death of Einstein. Indeed, some of the most able brains of the age have wrestled with the notion, knowing that success would bring fame of a magnitude hitherto unknown for a scientist. But even today, the procedure still eludes them, and time remains a tangle no one has tamed.

Ghost Photos

Debate about the existence of ghosts will continue for years. But there are pieces of persuasive evidence that leave even the most hardened sceptics scratching their heads. While a proportion of ghost photos are patent forgeries, others appear to capture a genuine spirit image, and they send a tingle down the spine.

SPIRIT IN FLIGHT

One of the most striking examples of a ghost photo is that featuring a flight unit of the Royal Air Force based at HMS Daedalus in Cranwell, Lincolnshire, in 1919. Servicemen and women gathered together and formally posed in full uniform for the photograph before they all scattered to new postings.

The close-knit flight unit had been devastated when, three days prior to the photograph being taken, one of their number had died in a horrific and tragic accident. Freddy Jackson perished on the tarmac when he stumbled into a whirling propeller. Some of those in the official picture, taken by Bassano's Photographic Company, even marched behind the coffin of their friend and colleague during the military funeral.

Yet when the photograph was pinned up alongside an order form for reprints, there was an audible gasp. The face of Freddy Jackson was clearly seen peeping out from the back row. The photograph became a cherished possession of a Wren driver at the base, Bobbie Capel. Australian-born Capel saw Jackson regularly in the course of her duties, driving to and from the Daedalus vehicle maintenance yard. She clearly recalled his death occurring shortly before the photograph was taken. 'When we lined up for that photograph to commemorate the disbanding of the transport yard, we all knew one familiar face would not be with us. Only later did we discover that, actually, he was.'

Capel met her first husband, Royal Flying Corps pilot Flt. Lt. Henry Moody MC, while serving at HMS Daedalus. He died twelve years later in a flying accident. In 1934 she married her second husband, Air Vice Marshal Arthur Capel. Like both men, she believed those present on the day of the photograph witnessed a supernatural event. 'I cannot entertain the idea that this was a deliberate fake. For one thing the photographer came from outside the base. He didn't know any of us and once he'd taken his picture he left immediately. He just would not have known about the accident. Neither can I understand how the face could have appeared by some mishap. I have thought and puzzled over it for years but I can think of no explanation other than that it is the picture of a ghost.'

Her view is supported by Air Marshal Sir Victor Goddard (See Timeslips on page 130). As a navy Flight Lieutenant at the time, Goddard also saw the photograph and wrote about it in his memoirs,

> 'When we lined up for that photograph we all knew one familiar face would not be with us. Only later did we discover that, actually, he was.'

Flight Towards Reality, 'There (Jackson) was, and no mistake, although a little fainter than the rest...Indeed he looked as though he was not altogether there, not really with that group, for he alone was capless, smiling;...Not only would Bassano's not have dared to fake it; the negative was scrutinized for faking and was found to be untouched.'

FACES OF THE DEAD

In 1924, another curious photograph was taken by Keith Tracy, captain of the oil tanker SS *Watertown*, following the death of two crew members. James Courtney and Michael Meehan were overcome by fumes while they were cleaning a cargo tank as the vessel sailed from New York towards the Panama Canal. Both were duly buried at sea.

Yet for several days afterwards both fellow crew members and the captain himself saw phantom faces resembling the dead men in the ship's Pacific wake. The tale might have been dismissed as a sailor's yarn, had Tracy not photographed the phenomenon to provide proof to those on land. When the pictures were developed, the faces of the dead men were distinct in the murky waters.

Another remarkable image was captured in November 1995, while an English

A close-up of the back row of the flight unit photograph shows the face of Freddy Jackson, fourth from the left, peeping out from behind his colleagues.

Hampton Court Palace just outside London, once home to the larger-than-life character King Henry VIII, is said to be swarming with ghosts.

town hall was burning down. Local man Tony O'Rahilly took photographs intended to record the momentous event. In fact, he discovered later, in doing so he had captured the image of a small, partially transparent girl standing in a doorway. At the time of the fire neither O'Rahilly, other onlookers or firefighters had seen any trace of the girl. After the photograph was submitted for analysis, Dr Vernon Harrison, a former president of the Royal Photographic Society, decided the negative appeared genuine. Delving into the past to explain the mystery, it was found that much of the Shropshire town had been destroyed by fire in 1677. The blaze had been accidentally started by a young girl called Jane Churm. Could it be that Jane's spirit had been roused when the town hall was once more engulfed in flames?

HAMPTON COURT MYSTERY

If legend is to be believed, Hampton Court Palace just outside London, once home to the larger-than-life character King Henry VIII, is swarming with ghosts. Only one, though, has been caught on closed circuit television cameras.

In winter 2003, security staff at the palace were alerted when alarms sounded, indicating that the fire doors of the exhibition hall had been opened. On investigation, the guards found the doors were closed, so they viewed security film to determine what had occurred. The film revealed a white-faced man in flowing clothes shutting the open doors from the inside. The alarm was set off at the same time on three consecutive days, but the figure was only caught on camera once. Although the palace does employ guides dressed in Tudor garb, it was quickly established that the figure was no ordinary employee. Although some observers claim the figure looks altogether too earthly to be a ghost, inspection of the digital film by independent experts implied it was genuine.

But the ghost did not fit the description of the usual suspects. It did not appear to be that of Jane Seymour, Henry VIII's third wife, who died giving birth to their son Edward. She is said to haunt a cobbled courtyard clutching a lighted taper. Nor was it the oft-reported screaming white lady, thought to be the ghost of Catherine Howard, Henry's fifth wife who was beheaded on a charge of adultery. Indeed the ghost has never been identified, despite choosing to haunt such grand surroundings.

FAKING IT

There are, of course, numerous ways to fake ghost pictures. Using long exposure is the most popular way to create a ghostly image on film. If a figure stands in front of the camera during part of the exposure time, then it will appear semi-transparent in the final picture. Other ghost-like images are the reflection of the

The image of one of Henry VIII's unfortunate wives haunting the corridors of Hampton Court Palace. Could this be Catherine Howard, his fifth wife, who was beheaded on a charge of adultery?

photographer and occasionally, a ghost image is created inadvertently, either by dust on the negative or by using old film. Thus every example of a ghost photo has to be treated with caution until the relevant probes have taken place. There remains a sizeable number that presently defy explanation.

SEANCE

Among them is the image of a long, lean figure apparent in a photo taken by an infrared camera. It was taken during a seance held at the Toys R Us store in Sunnyvale, California, in 1978. Following a string of complaints by store workers about ghostly goings-on, a TV show arranged to host the seance, held with psychic Sylvia Browne. The conclusion reached was that the photograph had captured the image of a preacher-cum-ranch hand of the 1880s, known as Johnny or Johan Johnstone. Johnstone was unlucky in love and his life ended when he bled to death on or near the site of today's store. Perhaps Johnstone's ghost was unable to keep away from the place, and had been excited by the forces present at the seance. Intriguingly, another photograph taken at the same moment by a neighbouring camera with a high-speed film shows nothing untoward.

Ghost photos do not provide incontrovertible proof, but they are perhaps the closest we can get to certifying the existence of unearthly phenomena. This is why ghost hunters always go armed with cameras. But by and large, ghosts remain camera shy and every determined effort to capture them on film has failed. The success stories, like those related above, are happy accidents.

Haunted Ships

The creaking timbers of a swaying ghost ship looming through swirling mists, with red warning lights on its bow, is sufficient to strike fear into any stout heart. For the phantom crew of the vessel the threat is past, but for unfortunate observers, it lies just ahead.

So goes the tale of the *Flying Dutchman*, a ship that foundered on the tip of Africa after being lashed by a ferocious storm more than three centuries ago. The ship's captain, Hendrick Vanderdecken, refused either to seek shelter or to drop anchor despite the raging tempest. Following curses made either to God or the devil, he was allegedly condemned to sail around the region forever with, quite literally, a skeleton crew. Moreover, anyone who sights the phantom vessel is also doomed.

Since the dawn of the sea-faring age, sailors have been notoriously superstitious. They are quite likely to interpret cloud formations and naturally forming prismatic effects as ghost ships haunting the high seas. Curiously, though, there have been numerous reports about the *Flying Dutchman*, some from highly reliable sources.

On 11 July 1881, a lookout on the HMS *Bacchante* rounding the Cape of Good Hope was the first to see what he believed to be the *Flying Dutchman*. Before the phantom ship vanished, no fewer than thirteen men had witnessed it first-hand. In the ship's log, the midshipman recorded: 'During the middle watch the so-called *Flying Dutchman* crossed our bows. She first appeared as a strange red light, as if a ship all aglow, in the midst of which light her spars, masts and sails, seemingly those of a normal brig, some 200 yards [183m] distant from us, stood out in strong relief as she came up. Our lookout man on the forecastle reported her close to our port bow, where also the officer of the watch from the bridge clearly saw her, as did our quarter-deck midshipman, who was sent forward at once to the forecastle to report back. But on reaching there, no vestige, nor any sign of the ship, was to be seen either near or away on the horizon.'

The writer went on to become George V of England – and he fared notably better than the lookout, who fell from the rigging and died later in the voyage.

Among other definitive sightings of the *Flying Dutchman* was one off South African shores in 1939. Bathers on Glencairn beach were united in their description of the sailing ship heading towards the sands, although few can have known details about merchant vessels of the seventeenth century. According to the *British South Africa Annual* of that year: 'Just as the excitement reached its climax, however, the mystery ship vanished into thin air as strangely as it had come.'

THE *QUEEN MARY*

Once one of the most prestigious liners afloat, the *Queen Mary*, now has the reputation of being the most haunted. The spirits that frolic in the ship's first class swimming pool area are so prolific that a 'ghost cam' is trained on it at all times.

The Queen Mary *in dry dock. This vast and sumptuous liner is said to be the portal to another realm, teeming with ghostly passengers from a long-gone era.*

Staff have seen child-sized wet footprints appear around the pool when no accompanying body is visible. Sounds of water-borne high jinks are heard from outside when the pool is empty. A medium invited aboard to investigate the sights and sounds believed one of the changing cubicles to be 'a portal to another realm'. If there are ghosts in the pool, they appear to belong to the years between the maiden voyage of the *Queen Mary* in 1936 and its war service, which began in 1940.

From the same era come accounts of the ghost of a white lady who, once spotted, disappears behind a pillar. However, some of the unearthly sounds that emanate from the ship are thought to be later in origin, stemming from the death of 17-year-old John Pedder, who perished trying to escape a fire onboard in 1966, just a year before the liner ended its service. Loud and frantic knocking sounds have been heard from behind door 13, and sometimes it feels hot to the touch. Could Pedder's ghost still be haunting the liner, condemned to relive his terrible last moments to the end of time? The *Queen Mary* is now a permanent fixture in Long Beach, California, where she is a major tourist attraction, not least for the paranormal activity rumoured to take place aboard.

> *The spirits that frolic in the ship's first class swimming pool area are so prolific that a 'ghost cam' is trained on it at all times.*

THE *LADY LOVIBOND*

Another ghostly vessel spotted off the English coast is the *Lady Lovibond*. During her last voyage, she was bound from London to Portugal, carrying not only cargo but also Captain Simon Peel's bride and fifty of their wedding guests.

On deck, first mate John Rivers was contorted with jealousy. He had hoped to make Peel's bride his own wife, but his hopes had been dashed. By way of desperate revenge, he drove the three-masted barquetine in full sail on to the treacherous Goodwin Sands. All on board were killed as the ship's woodwork splintered and smashed down.

The incident happened in February 1748, on an unlucky Friday 13th. However, that particular superstition is rooted in twentieth-century lore, so it would not have resonated with audiences of the time.

But this was not the last of the ill-fated *Lady Lovibond*. In 1798, exactly fifty years after the vessel foundered, Captain James Westlake of the Edenbridge reported seeing its apparition across his bow. The *Lady Lovibond* resurrected itself from that ship's graveyard again in 1848 and in 1898. On both occasions, it was seen in full sail by Kent fishermen. However, nothing was reported in either 1948 or 1998, despite the best efforts of ghost hunters from across Britain. They might have been thwarted because an eighteenth-century calendar switch (when England adopted the Gregorian calendar) would have the ghost ship sailing some eleven days earlier than expected.

THE SS *GREAT EASTERN*

When it was launched in 1858, the SS *Great Eastern* was the largest ship ever built, with six masts in addition to paddle and screw propulsion. It should have been heading for a bright future.

But the ship was already associated with misfortune. Building the giant vessel had put one company out of business. On its eventual grand launch day it was so big it got stuck on the runway. Proud designer Isambard Kingdom Brunel died within four days of its first sea trials.

More significantly still, it suffered a series of mishaps at sea. Perhaps the worst of these was when a boiler over-heated to such an extent that it launched a funnel of the ship into the air like a rocket, killing one crew member and injuring others. Furthermore, crew on the SS *Great Eastern* reported hearing hammering sounds loud enough to drown out any Atlantic gale.

In short, the SS *Great Eastern* was a commercial white elephant, which was eventually sold for a fraction of its building costs. It went on to lay 4,185km of transatlantic telegraph cable before being sold for scrap. During the eighteen months it took to dismantle, it is said that a skeleton or even two were found in within the double skinned hull. Although this may have been the case, skeleton stories like these are relatively commonplace in connection with cursed or haunted places. Still, there remains a chilling possibility, however slight, that workmen became entombed during the building of the ship, and hammered to call for help.

In 1975, the Edmund Fitzgerald *sank during a storm on Lake Superior, killing twenty-six crew members. But the ship has refused to sink into obscurity, and its ghost lingers on...*

THE GREAT LAKES

Ghost ships are not only found on the open sea but also in lakes and even rivers. There are two similar stories from the great lakes of North America that have fascinated seafarers and public alike. The first dates back to September 1678 when the *Griffon* vanished from Lake Michigan. Although no trace of the vessel was ever found, several sailors in ensuing years reported seeing the ship sailing on the lake. Much later, in 1975, the *Edmund Fitzgerald* sank into the waters of Lake Superior, taking twenty-six crew members with her. Once again, sailors in the region have spotted the ship afloat and untouched by disaster.

Mention should also be made of the SS *Iron Mountain*, which was not so much a ghost ship as a vanished vessel. In June 1872 it left Vicksburg, Mississippi, with its cotton and molasses cargo, towing a line of barges. Later that day, another steamship by the name of *Iroquois Chief* came across the barges floating freely down the river with the tow line apparently cut. Crew secured the barges and waited for the arrival of the SS *Iron Mountain*. It never came. Indeed, no one ever saw the ship, its crew or its cargo again. Nor was there a trace of wreckage along the river banks. The fate of the SS *Iron Mountain* remains unknown.

No one knows just how many ghost ships may be sailing the oceans and great lakes, lost in time and space. Whilst the sea swallows up some vessels and their crews without a trace, others seem condemned to return as haunting reminders of their watery fate.

Haunted Places

Ghosts can be benign or frightening, jovial or malicious. For some householders they are a blessing, while others find them a curse. While hard-edged facts about ghosts are in short supply, tales of wandering spirits and their bizarre behaviour in houses around the world are abundant.

LEGAL HAUNT

The ghosts that haunted the Ackley family home on the Hudson River in Nyack, 32km from New York, were cherished guests. Although the family had to endure the odd bump in the night, they were recompensed when silver gifts mysteriously appeared for relatives.

A female ghost in a hooded cape woke the children for school by shaking their beds. And there were at least two other ghosts in the house, both of whom sported revolutionary garb. When asked about her unusual residents, Helen Ackley said, 'They have been a delight to us.' She insisted the ghosts were 'gracious, thoughtful – only occasionally frightening – and thoroughly entertaining…'

However, the prospect of moving in with the ghosts did not please would-be buyers of the Ackley home, Jeffery and Patrice Stambovsky. They did not find out about the otherworldly squatters until after they had paid a $32,500 bond for the Victorian property. When they tried to back out of the deal, the Ackleys refused to co-operate. In 1991 the dispute ended up in the New York Supreme Court, where a judge ruled: '…as a matter of law, the house is haunted.' The Ackleys were compelled to return the money, despite winning the first legal round of the case, when a judge ruled that vendors had no duty to reveal the existence of supernatural inhabitants in a house.

DEATHLY COLD

The Ackley house is not, however, regarded as America's most haunted home. That accolade goes to the Whaley House in San Diego, California, which is apparently built on land that was once a Native American settlement and then a cemetery. It is also the site where outlaw 'Yankee Jim' James Robinson was hung from the end of a wagon. None of this deterred merchant Thomas Whaley from acquiring the land in 1856 and building a grand house. Soon after he and his family moved in, they heard heavy footfalls which they believed to be the ghostly tread of 'Yankee Jim'. Whaley family fortunes blossomed and waned, and for the first half of the twentieth century Thomas' daughter Anna lived there alone. Today, the house has been turned into a museum, where many visitors believe they can smell cigar smoke or sometimes perfume wafting through the air. Window shutters open and close at will. Curtains billow when the windows are nailed shut, electric lights flicker and body-sized dents appear in the bedding. Kitchen implements jangle together on a windless day. And 'Yankee Jim' is not the only ghost on the grounds. Other spirits are believed to be that of a young girl accidentally hanged on the property, an American Indian, Whaley's infant son and his daughter Violet who shot herself in the house. Finally, to complete the motley crew, comes Mr Whaley himself, clad in frock coat and pantaloons.

50 BERKELEY SQUARE

Some ghosts are more malevolently minded and do not let humans get away so easily. One of the most notorious haunted houses is 50 Berkeley Square in London. The ghosts who reside there are said to be that of a violent lunatic confined to an upstairs room by his brother, an eccentric recluse who was jilted at the altar and a small girl in a kilt who was cruelly treated by her nanny. Individually or together, the ghosts are believed to have caused the deaths of three unfortunate people.

A maid living in a haunted room was found gibbering with fear during the night. She died the following day after seeing 'something hideous'.

Sir Robert Warboys perished after spending the night in the property for a bet, having sneered at the ghost stories attached to it. He went to the room armed with a pistol and a bell to raise the alarm. His friends went rushing to his aid when they heard the bell ringing frantically. A shot rang out before they arrived at the room. Inside, Warboys lay dead on the bed with his face contorted by terror. There was no trace of a bullet wound.

On Christmas Eve in 1887, two sailors decided to hole up in the empty property for the night. Edward Blunden and Robert Martin, on leave from the HMS *Penelope*, chose to stay in the bedroom where Warboys had died. As they tried to sleep through the night, Blunden became increasingly agitated. Finally Martin woke to see a sinister shape entering the room and fled the house as fast as he could. When he returned soon afterwards with a policeman he discovered Blunden's body at the foot of the basement stairs, his eyes wide open and his neck snapped.

The address, once the home of British Prime Minister George Canning and one of the most desirable in London, has been empty for long periods. Now the home of a bookseller, there are still regular reports of dancing lights in an upstairs room seen from the street.

One of the grand townhouses in Berkeley Square. Perhaps not such a desirable address after all...

SINISTER VAULT

Another old and enduring ghost story from the Caribbean illustrates the freakish physical strength that restless spirits are reported to have.

A vault in Christ Church Cemetery, Barbados, was the last resting place of one Thomasina Goddard, who died in 1807. After her death, the vault was sold to the Chase family. First of the family to be added to the robust semi-subterranean vault was 2-year-old Mary Ann Chase who died in 1808. Her sister Dorcas joined her in July 1812, widely rumoured to have starved herself to death because life was so miserable with her overbearing father Colonel Thomas Chase. Ironically, the Colonel himself died in August of the same year. But when his lead casket was carried to the vault the coffins already inside were in disarray.

The scene was repaired, the Colonel buried, and the vault was sealed up again. In 1816 the vault was re-opened twice for the burial of Chase relatives and on both occasions the coffins already inside were upended. Once again the damaged coffins were laid straight and the marble doorway was sealed.

By now the vault and its flying coffins were the subject of intense local speculation. When Thomasina Clarke's body was borne there in 1819 it was once again a scene of destruction.

...the coffins appeared to have been flung against the walls with such force that at least one was chipped.

Sir Stapleton Cotton, the Governor of Barbados, decided to sprinkle sawdust on the vault floor to capture the footprints of intruders. To further deter vandals, he put his personal seal in the mortar that once more fixed the door.

In 1920 he decided to open the vault to see what had occurred. While the mortar and the sawdust were untouched, the coffins appeared to have been flung against the walls with such force that at least one was chipped.

Flooding was one possible explanation for the damage, but it seemed highly unlikely since the vault lay 30m above sea-level, and there are no reports of excessive rainfall during the era. Whatever the cause, Sir Stapleton Cotton decided to lay the matter to rest by ordering the coffins be buried elsewhere. The vault was left open.

The mystery of the vault came to an end, but it was not forgotten. On 18 April 1820 the Honourable Nathan Lucas, one of the island dignitaries accompanying Sir Stapleton, wrote: '...I examined the walls, the arch, and every part of the vault, and found every part old and similar; and a mason in my presence struck every part of the bottom with his hammer, and all was solid. I confess myself at a loss to account for the movements of these leaden coffins. Thieves certainly had no hand in it; and as for any practical wit or hoax, too many were requisite to be trusted with the secret for it to remain unknown; and as for negroes having anything to do with it, their superstitious fear of the dead and everything belonging to them precludes any idea of the kind. All I know is that it happened and that I was an eye-witness of the fact...'

Exasperated and mystified, he penned those words nearly 200 years ago. Since then technology has bounded ahead, yet today we are no closer to comprehending whether or not ghosts really exist.

Past Lives

Most of us are kept busy enjoying or enduring our everyday lives, too frantic to hear the quiet inner voice that speaks of another place, another time. But for a minority of people, details of a previous existence encroach on the present, making a strong case for the principles of reincarnation.

Several major faiths, including Hinduism, Sikhism, Jainism and others give credence to life after death. Buddhists have a similar but not identical philosophy of re-birth, although Tibetan Buddhists invest heavily in the idea of reincarnation in order to identify legitimate heirs to the role of Dalai Lama.

SEARCH FOR THE DALAI LAMA

Tenzin Gyatso, today's Dalai Lama, is believed to be the reincarnation of his predecessor. Indeed, he was born in the same year his predecessor died (1935), to a peasant family in north-eastern Tibet. A Buddhist dignitary trying to divine the identity of the new Dalai Lama had a vision in which he saw a monastery. Aides were given detailed descriptions of the monastery and dispatched across the region to find it. They discovered one that fitted the description in Taktser. There they encountered a two-year-old boy who demanded the rosary being worn by one of the party that had once belonged to the deceased Dalai Lama. When he correctly identified the men in the deputation by name and rank, it was deemed that he was the embodiment of the Dalai Lama. He was finally enthroned in 1940.

There is a growing body of evidence in the West to say that earthly life after death is a reality. Two methods have been used to gather examples of past lives: regression through hypnosis in adults and the spontaneous recollections of young children, whose previous lives remain fresh in their memories.

Psychologist Helen Wambach carried out a ten-year survey of past-life recollections among 1,088 subjects. With the exception of only eleven people, the descriptions given about minute details of past lives, including kitchen utensils, clothing and footwear, were uncannily accurate. She found that the majority of the lives described were in the lower classes, reflecting the appropriate historical distribution. She also discovered that 49.4 per cent of the past lives were female and 50.6 per cent were male, reflecting the correct biological balance. Although she started out as a sceptic, Wambach became convinced by the evidence in front of her. In 1978 she declared: 'I don't believe in reincarnation — I know it!'

CELEBRITY REINCARNATION

Among the celebrities of today are several who are convinced they have lived before. These include Sylvester Stallone, who thinks he has been here no less than four times in the past, and was on one occasion guillotined during the French Revolution. He also claims to have been a boxer who was killed by a

The Tibetan spiritual leader the Dalai Lama, who is believed to be the reincarnation of his predecessor.

knockout punch in the 1930s. Actor Martin Sheen talked of being a cruel US cavalry soldier who was trampled to death by a horse. Today he has a loathing of horses, which might be linked to his past life experiences. Singer Englebert Humperdinck thought he once ruled the Roman Empire, while pop goddess Tina Turner has been told she is a reincarnation of the Egyptian queen Hatshepsut. Shirley MacLaine also claims numerous past lives, among them a Moorish girl living along a pilgrim trail in Spain. Under hypnosis, movie star Glenn Ford was able to speak fluent French, since one of his past lives was spent as a French cavalryman in the reign of Louis XIV.

HYPNOSIS

The fact that hypnosis subjects are suddenly able to speak in a foreign language is one of the oddest and most compelling pieces of evidence about past lives. Other positive benefits such as the relief of long term illnesses, nightmares or phobias have been felt when the harm supposedly caused by past life injuries or experiences was addressed.

Opponents to hypnosis believe it is perilous and that beneficial results are unproven. They believe that symptoms people put down to past existences are more likely to be caused by inherited or suppressed memories. Hypnosis might even be making the problem worse by creating a multitude of personalities in a subject, rather than pinpointing true past life experiences.

The experience of a Colorado housewife who regressed into a supposed past life as Bridey Murphy of nineteenth-century Ireland was documented in a book.

The fact that hypnosis subjects are suddenly able to speak a foreign language is one of the oddest and most compelling pieces of evidence...

But the account was swiftly debunked when it was proved that no woman of that name was born in the year she had claimed. Nor was her death on record anywhere. Her command of the old Irish language and lifestyle was later deemed to have been learned through a close relationship with an Irish woman in her early years.

Still, the stories relating to hypnotherapy remain intriguing. In 1983, psychologist and former sceptic Peter Ramster featured in a documentary with four women who recounted their past life experiences. One woman remembered a life in Somerset, England, in the second half of the eighteenth century. When she was taken to the rural village in question – a place she had never visited before – she was able to find her way around and identify local landmarks, some of which had been long forgotten. Furthermore, it became clear that she had a thorough knowledge of local legends, dialect and families.

A CHILD'S HISTORY

For many, the coherent and cohesive descriptions of different environments recounted by very small children are altogether more persuasive. One benchmark case is that of Shanti Deva. In 1930, aged 4, Shanti told her parents that she had once lived in a place called Muttra, that she had been a mother of three who died in childbirth and that her previous name had been Ludgi.

Only when they were continually pressed by the youngster did the bewildered family from Delhi investigate. They discovered there was indeed a village called Muttra and that a woman named Ludgi had recently died there. When Shanti was taken to the village, she lapsed into local dialect and recognized her previous-life husband and children. She even gave twenty-four accurate statements that matched confirmed facts, an impressive feat for such a young child, and one that it would be impossible to hoax.

Since 1967, psychiatrist Dr Ian Stevenson has pioneered the scientific study of spontaneous past life recollections among infants. Usually a youngster is aged between two and five years old when they describe what went on in a previous existence. In most cases, although not all, recall has faded by the age of seven.

Having interviewed thousands of children from all over the world, Dr Stevenson has discovered some interesting facets to the phenomenon. In some cases, the mother had experienced a prophetic dream, announcing or implying the past life identity of the child in her womb. Meanwhile, a number of children claiming a previous existence bore birthmarks that corresponded to wounds inflicted on them when they lived before. For

> *When Shanti was taken to the village, she lapsed into local dialect and recognized her previous-life husband and children.*

example, a boy in India who was born without fingers on one hand remembered that in a prior existence he had put his hand into the blades of a fodder-chopping machine, amputating the digits. Dr Stevenson aimed to corroborate the verbal evidence of a child with relevant death certificates and interviews with witnesses to both existences.

Critics think the prophetic dreams are no more than wishful thinking. They credit Dr Stevenson with collecting anecdotal rather than scientific evidence.

Yet some of his cases are compelling and strangely thought-provoking. On one occasion, Dr Stevenson made an unannounced visit to a Druze village in Lebanon to see if any children there were subject to past life statements. He was immediately dispatched to the home of 5-year-old Imad Elawar, who had for several years been talking about another life in a different village some 40km distant. Young Imad had even stopped a former neighbour in the street to share recollections about the life he once lived. His first words as a child were Jamileh and Mahmoud, the names of his mistress and uncle in his previous life. Stevenson noted more than fifty-seven separate claims by the child about his past life, the majority of which could be supported with evidence from elsewhere.

While the study of reincarnation has leapt ahead recently, it is a subject that is by no means the preserve of the modern age. In 1824, a Japanese boy called Kastugoro recounted details of a village where he had once lived and the family that was once his own. Despite his tender age, the minutiae he recalled were sufficient to persuade investigators of the day that past lives were a reality.

Throughout the ages, belief in reincarnation has been powerful and widespread. Perhaps we are closer to history than we imagine…

DISAPPEARANCES

That people and things go missing without trace is almost beyond our comprehension. Individuals, communities, even whole cities have vanished into thin air, leaving an empty space where we would expect clues to be. Whilst theories about their fate abound, extensive efforts to solve disappearances are futile and we are left baffled. Unless new evidence comes to light, such mysteries will remain unexplained, haunting reminders of our own precarious existence.

Atlantis

When it comes to discussing the mystery of Atlantis, there are two opposing views. One view holds that it was a great civilization from long ago, known and discussed among the ancients. The other insists it is a long-standing fabrication, a fictional island that represents a lost Eden.

The most significant account of Atlantis is by the ancient philosopher Plato (427–347BC) in two stories called *Critias* and *Tinnaeus*. The sceptics claim that the entire account is a metaphor, and that Plato is using Atlantis to illustrate the disastrous fate of corrupt regimes. Yet significantly Plato says more than once that the stories he recites are true. Nowhere else in his work does he claim allegorical events to be real.

ANCIENT UTOPIA

So just what does Plato say about this utopian Atlantis? Well, it was big – larger than Asia and Libya combined. Its people were virtuous, its soldiers skillful, its kings wise. There were fertile plains backed by picturesque mountains, hot and cold springs, horse racing and elephants. A central temple was adorned with golden statues. A system of deep-water canals enabled shipping to enter the city. Likewise, a man-made irrigation system kept crops green and abundant.

Curiously, Plato makes much of a precious metal called orichalcum that was mined in Atlantis and was a familiar decoration of the buildings there. It was, he says, second only to gold in value. But even by Plato's time, this prized commodity had vanished. No one knows precisely what type of metal orichalcum is, although it is mentioned years later by the Roman commentator Josephus in relation to Solomon's Temple. But here too, evidence is scarce, and there is little archaeological data to confirm the materials used in that great temple. Whatever the physical properties of orichalcum, it seems certain that it was of great value to ancient cultures, and that Atlantis was rich in it.

According to Plato, Atlantis was an island once ruled by Poseidon, god of the sea. Poseidon fell in love with a native of Atlantis and she bore him five sets of twins. Admittedly, this part of his story does not seem to be anchored in reality, and the date is implausible. Plato dates the era of Atlantis to 9,000 years before his own day. Today, we have no knowledge of sophisticated civilizations existing so early in human history. It would have been a shining jewel in a Stone Age world.

DOOMED CIVILIZATION

But if Atlantis did exist, it was doomed to destruction. Plato's account tells how, within a single day and night, a natural disaster eradicated the entire civilization. This is entirely credible, since we know how powerful and ruthless nature can be. The island apparently disappeared into the depths of the sea, leaving only a shoal of mud that barred shipping from the area thereafter. Presumably an earthquake was to blame for the wholesale destruction, which would have extinguished the lives of countless thousands.

Initially it might sound like Plato was recycling some favourite myths that have cropped up down the ages. Atlantis bears some resemblance to a Garden of Eden (see page 205), while its destruction might be likened to a great flood similar the one in the Bible and in numerous other beliefs. But why then did Plato go into such historical detail about the civilization and the metal they mined? What if Atlantis was simply the ancient name for another culture that had been wiped out, one that we have evidence of today?

SO WHERE WAS IT?

For a long time it seemed as if Plato must have been referring to the Minoan civilization on Crete. This was named only relatively recently by an archaeologist, and no one knows what Plato's contemporaries would have called it. The Minoans had glorious palaces, paved roads and running water. A colossal volcanic eruption on the island of Thera 100km away from Crete caused wholesale destruction in the region, but it did not obliterate the Minoans immediately. Archaeological evidence indicates they survived the tsunamis and the noxious sulphur clouds that must have followed the volcanic explosion, but fared poorly in the face of the ensuing climate change. By 1450 BC the Minoan civilization had burnt out, succumbing either to starvation, insurrection or invaders.

Perhaps it was to the Minoans that Plato was referring? However, he confidently dates Atlantis to an era far earlier than that of the Minoan civilization on Crete. It leads one to speculate where the Minoans might have lived before migrating to the island.

Other sites for Atlantis have been put forward at various times throughout history, and these have been as far flung as Spain, South America, the Caribbean, Cyprus and the South China Seas. The evidence for Spain has been supported by

This seventeenth-century woodcut shows a supposed location of Atlantis. One more recent theory is that the civilization was in fact that of the Minoan people on Crete.

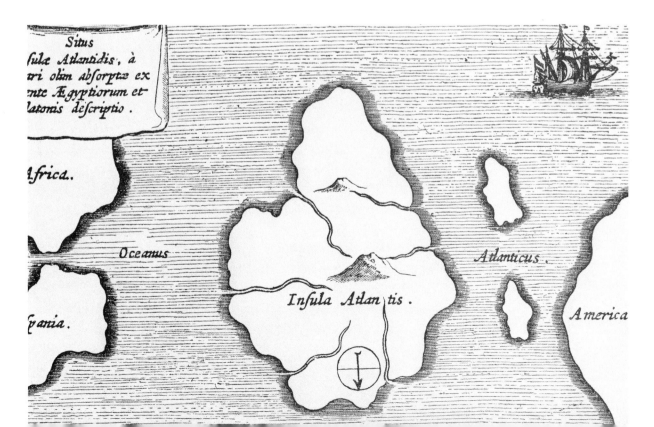

satellite photographs, which appear to show concentric circles like those described by Plato. Although the size of the circles does not exactly match the philospher's description, this might be accounted for by a mistake in translating his unit of measurement, the stade, to present day measurements. The proposed site lies in salt marshes near Cadiz.

Ancient writings contain accounts of attacks on Egypt and the eastern Mediterranean by 'the Sea People'. One theory is that the Sea People, the Atlanteans and the Iron Age residents of southern Spain, known as the Tartessos, were one and the same people.

Tiahuanaco in the Bolivian Andes of South America has been earmarked as a possible Atlantis. Satellite photography has revealed it boasted hundreds of miles of inland canals. The residents are believed to have been of the Aymara tribe, a pre-Inca civilization. Such an investment in waterways implies they were a seafaring race who probably traded with Europeans and Africans. Generally, Tianhuanaco is thought to have dated from the middle of the first millennium (c. 500AD) but one researcher, Arthur Broznansky, was certain it was significantly older.

The Nazis believed the Atlanteans were a superior race and the ancestors of the Ayrans.

Elusive in place and time, it seems impossible, even using modern technology, to pin down Atlantis to one geographical location.

BELIEVERS

Nevertheless, many beliefs have sprung from the possible existence of Atlantis. Many people believed it to be the single root of all civilization. The odd co-incidences of ancient history, like the way pyramids were built on both sides of the Atlantic and that various races chose to write in hieroglyphics, might have been explained by the existence of the great Atlantis. But there is no evidence of a linking civilization, and science has largely dismissed such claims.

The Nazis believed the Atlanteans were a superior race and the ancestors of the Ayrans, those favoured by the unsavoury fanatics for peopling the earth. Hitler's henchman Heinrich Himmler was particularly taken with the theory and invested much in a fruitless search.

There have even been claims that the Atlanteans were in fact highly advanced aliens. These assertions have proved popular, but evidence hard to come by. Edgar Cayce, the famous American psychic and healer, maintained that Atlantean existence focused on a giant crystal. This was used not only for healing but in a psychic sense for communication and teleportation. Disaster struck when the crystal exploded. Although they seem bizarre, Cayce's theories are backed by thousands of people today. He remains the inspiration behind the Association for Research and Enlightenment, based in America but present in sixty different countries.

If the mystery of Atlantis has retained its grip on human imagination for so long, it is because it remains a powerful symbol of the nature of human civilization, reminding us that however wealthy and powerful nations become, the forces of time and nature will eventually overcome them.

The Roanoke Settlers

The early history of the USA is shrouded in mystery, and the identity of those who discovered the North American continent is still in dispute. Supporters of St Brendan, the Danes, the Chinese and the earliest inhabitants of Asia all lay claim to the discovery. Another enigma is the fate of the Roanoke settlers who, some ninety years after Columbus breached the American shores, vanished without a trace.

Roanoke is an island off the North Carolina coast measuring about 19km by 3km. In the sixteenth century, the island would have been covered with untamed vegetation. In 1584, an initial expedition to Roanoke island was dispatched from England, funded by Sir Walter Raleigh. The explorer and adventurer had been awarded colonial rights by Queen Elizabeth I of England as a special prize for his ocean-going exploits against the Spanish as a privateer, or 'authorized pirate'. The expedition represented a marvellous opportunity to cash in on nature's riches. But the rewards were not to be so easily won.

FIRST FORAY

On arrival at Roanoke this first expedition, under the leadership of Sir Richard Grenville, did not get off to a promising start. Their most pressing concerns were a lack of food (since their supplies had been ruined by seawater) and the presence of local tribes in the vicinity. Even though they were strangers in a

The Roanoke settlers celebrate the baptism of Virginia Dare, the first European child to be born in the American colony.

strange land, and dependent on the Indians for food, water and information, the English chose a heavy-handed approach and antagonism between the settlers and the indigenous population soon accelerated to acts of murder.

Grenville decided to report back to England, leaving Ralph Lane and about 100 other men in a settlement that they were painstakingly hacking out of the wild landscape of Roanoke. He pledged to return in April 1586 with ships and supplies.

Short of food and water, Lane further threatened the locals to secure their co-operation. Unsurprisingly, it was a policy that largely failed. Grenville did not turn up in April 1586 as promised. When Sir Francis Drake stopped at Roanoke in June, a ragged band of Englishmen boarded his ship headed for home with him. Grenville turned up a few weeks later at the empty site. He deposited fifteen men there before he too returned to England.

PIONEERING SPIRIT

In 1587 another pioneering group set off comprising ninety-one men, seventeen women and nine children. Their leader John White, who was a veteran of the first voyage, was told to pick up the fifteen men from Roanoke and head on to Chesapeake Bay to found a new settlement, grandly entitled the 'Cittie of Ralegh'.

White decided to go back to England for assistance. He left 117 people at Roanoke, including his daughter and grand-daughter.

When they landed at Roanoke on 22 July 1587, they found the skeleton of just one of the men left there by Grenville, a poor omen for what lay ahead. But the expedition navigator Simon Fernandes claimed he could not go on to Chesapeake for fear of Autumn storms. So the colonials were compelled to stay at Roanoke and establish their settlement there.

Everything began on a note of optimism. Within a month White's daughter gave birth to a daughter and little Virginia Dare was the first English child born in the American colony. Furthermore, White was hopeful of repairing relations with local Indians and he struck up an understanding with the Croatan tribe. However, his attempts at cordiality with other tribes were rebuffed. Hostilities became as tense as before and one man, George Howe, was killed.

When it became clear to White that the long-term viability of the colony looked doubtful, he decided to go back to Britain for extra assistance. He left 117 people at Roanoke, including his daughter, grand-daughter and another new-born.

FATEFUL ABSENCE

Now international events played their part in the fate of those on Roanoke island. As White attempted to rally a return expedition, the Spanish sent its Armada against England. Every high capacity sea-going vessel was needed for the defence of Elizabeth's realm, and White found himself reduced to two small ships.

Unfortunately the captains of these vessels were more interested in picking up booty from enemy ships they encountered on the voyage to America than in reaching the stranded settlers. Eventually they were attacked themselves and the supplies earmarked for Roanoke were stolen. White and the ships returned to port in England with nothing. Conflict still raged between England and Spain, putting colonial ambitions on the back burner.

GRIM DISCOVERY

It was a further two years before White finally returned to Roanoke, landing on 18 August 1590 for what he imagined would be a happy reunion with his granddaughter on her third birthday. He found no one. The settlers had quite simply vanished, and a search of the area confirmed there was no trace of them to be found. But they had left just one clue. The name 'Croatoan' was carved into one of the posts in the Roanoke fort where the settlers had lived, while the letters 'CRO' were found on a tree. In an era when spelling was imprecise, Croatoan or Croatan was the name of both the friendly Indian tribe and of an island. It seemed to White that the settlers had departed, and had indicated their destination as Croatan Island. He pondered why the signal did not include a Maltese cross, which would have indicated that group members considered themselves in danger. But there were no signs of attack at the Roanoke site and White was confident that they must be in a safe haven.

The settlers had quite simply vanished, and a search of the area confirmed there was no trace of them to be found.

However, White's attempts to reach Croatan were repeatedly thwarted by bad weather, as though the elements were in league against him. Eventually, defeated, he returned at the bidding of his crew to England, leaving the mystery of the missing settlers unsolved.

SEARCHLIGHT ON HISTORY

To this day, there has been no proven explanation for the disappearance of all 117 people. It is possible that they were wiped out in an attack by hostile Indians or perhaps even by Spanish forces keen to colonize the region themselves. Captain John Smith, who landed at Jamestown in 1607, was certainly convinced that they had been horribly massacred. Unfortunately, there is no way of finding out the exact location of the Roanoke settlement, so archaeological probes are out of the question.

One current opinion is that a terrible drought paralyzed the area at the time. Lack of food and fresh water could have driven the settlers to another site where they later died, perhaps after turning to cannibalism. Alternatively, they might have resorted to boat construction in a desperate bid to return to England and perished at sea. In support of this theory, it was found that a pinnace or small ship left by White was missing.

Another theory maintains that the Elizabethan political subtext may have a direct bearing on the incident. While Raleigh had an admirer in Queen Elizabeth, he also had a host of enemies at court, who probably envied his success in the colonies and his colonial rights. Modern day investigation has suggested the second Roanoke expedition was sabotaged, primarily to put Raleigh in the shade. Not for the failure of the Roanoke colony but for other overseas misdemeanors, Raleigh was finally put to death at the Tower of London in 1616 by King James I.

FAMILY TREE

So the quest to uncover the truth about the vanished Roanoke settlers goes on. The prevailing theory is that the English men and women were not killed, but were absorbed amongst the Croatan Indians. The exact history of the Croatan Indians between the Roanoke settlement and the wholesale colonization of North America is indistinct. However, we do know that following lethal smallpox epidemics, the Croatans joined with the remnants of other tribes. The new group became known as the Lumbee tribe, and evidence has emerged over the years to suggest that the members of this tribe have mixed blood. Indeed, in 1719, white hunters visited Robinson (or Robeson) County, North Carolina, just 160km inland from Roanoke, where they found a tribe of unusually fair-skinned Indians who spoke English. A 1790 census of the Robinson County Indians revealed that fifty-four of the ninety-five family names mirrored those of the lost colonists. Surely this was more than just coincidence…

An engraving of one of the chieftains of Roanoke island. Could the settlers have become absorbed into the indigenous tribes?

The Mary Celeste

A ship bobbing on the open seas, its crew inexplicably missing, sails flapping aimlessly in the wind. A search aboard reveals no trace of life, and few clues as to what might have occurred. The story of the Mary Celeste *is one of history's most intriguing mysteries.*

On 7 November 1872, Captain Benjamin Spooner Briggs sailed out of New York. He was bound for Genoa, Italy on what should have been a workaday voyage. With him was his wife Sarah, 30, their two-year-old daughter Sophia Matilda, and a capable crew of two Americans, one Dane, one German and three Dutchmen. In the hold of the half-brig *Mary Celeste* was a cargo of 1,700 barrels of alcohol intended for wine fortification.

After she left New York there were no further reports of her progress until 5 December, when the ship *Dei Gratia*, loaded with petroleum, spotted her between the Azores and the Portuguese coast. As it happened, the captain of the *Dei Gratia*, David Morehouse, was one of Briggs' personal friends, and the pair had dined together shortly before Briggs left New York. Morehouse noted the erratic progress of the *Mary Celeste* and tried to make contact for some time before dispatching a boarding party.

GHOST SHIP

Led by Chief Mater Oliver Deveau, the merchant seamen climbed aboard the erring ship. But it quickly became clear that the *Mary Celeste* was completely deserted, and there were few clues as to why. The chronometer and sextant were missing but the log book was in its place. Hatches were open but the crews' oilskins were still there. The lifeboat was gone, although food and water supplies were intact, as were the barrels. The galley stove had been dislodged. Belongings aboard the ship were soaked and there was water sloshing about in the hold where one pump was not working. But the ship was, to all intents and purposes, still seaworthy. Ignoring the sinister atmosphere aboard the mystery ship, some hardy members of the crew from the *Dei Gratia* sailed her into Gibraltar.

Reading the last entry in the ship's log, Morehouse learnt that the *Mary Celeste* had passed 10km from St Mary's in the Azores at 8am on 25 November, some ten days earlier. Just what happened between that day and the discovery of the empty ship may never be discovered. Theories about the possible fate of those aboard have abounded.

PROCESS OF ELIMINATION

Suspicions that it was some manner of insurance scam have been dispelled. Briggs was a devout man with a solid reputation. Likewise, there is nothing to indicate a mutiny among the crew, who were all experienced men well used to short commercial voyages such as these.

The Mary Celeste was found floating, empty but undamaged, in the sea between the Azores and the Portuguese coast.

Some have speculated that Briggs and his crew members became drunk on the liquor they were carrying. But their cargo was lethal industrial alcohol rather than regular tipple – and the scenario would have required a sea-change in personality by the teetotaller Briggs – it seems wholly unlikely.

What about the possibility of an attack by pirates? But surely if pirates had boarded the vessel surely there would be some sign of a desperate struggle? Besides, the $35,000 cargo had not been stolen, nor had the ship's supplies.

A freak wave caused by an undersea earthquake has also been ruled out, as there are no records of such cataclysmic events occurring at the time. And although a sudden waterspout might explain why the ship was sodden, it could not account for the disappearance of those on board.

At a British Board of Inquiry in Gibraltar, Morehouse had to defend himself against charges of conspiring both with Briggs and against him to coin the salvage value of the ship. But ultimately the inquiry proved nothing, other than to assert that there was no sign of blood on the ship.

PROBING THE DEPTHS

One man, having examined the calamity in depth, felt he had touched on the correct explanation. Charles Edey Fay made a detailed study of the oddities surrounding the discovery of the *Mary Celeste*. He concluded that Briggs had probably taken advantage of unexpectedly calm conditions to ventilate the cargo. In fact, nine barrels of the alcohol had leaked, causing noxious fumes to pour out of the hold. In the chaos that ensued, perhaps it seemed as if an explosion was imminent or that the ship was sinking.

Briggs, who had never carried alcohol before and was religiously opposed to its very existence, may well have given the order to abandon ship and take to the lifeboat. His best option was to maintain contact with the ship through the halyard, a weighty rope. Once they felt the danger had passed, those in the lifeboat would have clambered back aboard the ship and resumed their voyage. What they had not anticipated was a change in the weather. Fay's theory is that they were surprised by a squall, and the halyard was severed, leaving the lifeboat adrift in the open. The lifeboat would then either have sunk, or drifted in a south-easterly direction away from the land and the shipping route. Either way, its hapless occupants were doomed either to drown or to die of thirst, starvation or exposure.

> *The hapless occupants of the lifeboat were doomed either to drown or to die of thirst, starvation or exposure.*

A letter from the Servico Meteorolgico dos Acores confirmed that a period of calm gave way to gale force winds during that fateful night of 25 November 1872. The halyard upon which the lives of those in the lifeboat depended was found frayed over the side of the ship.

ONE FOR SHERLOCK HOLMES

Fay's findings are outlined in *The Story of the Mary Celeste*, which he had published in 1942. His account, rooted in fact, was very different from many of the more fanciful stories inspired by the empty ship. One fictional account, published in 1883, was written by a certain Arthur Conan Doyle. He changed the name of the ship to *Marie Celeste* and asserted that everyone aboard the fated vessel came to a violent end.

The waters were further muddied by the claims of Abel Fosdyk. He claimed to have been a stowaway aboard the *Mary Celeste*, and recounted how he had watched the captain and some crew members being eaten by sharks during a swimming race. As the others rushed to witness the tragedy they all fell overboard and met the same end. Fosdyk said he clung to driftwood until being washed up on African shores. But Fosdyk wrongly identified the nationalities of all the crew, so it seems his account was also made up.

Fictional though their accounts may be, Conan Doyle and Fosdyk both helped to keep the memory of *Mary Celeste* alive. Intriguingly, she was not the only ship found abandoned at sea. In 1849, the Dutch Schooner *Hermania* was discovered dismasted and deserted. Six years later, the *Marathon* was found in a similar state, yet neither of these ships became household names.

WHAT BECAME OF THE *MARY CELESTE*?

The infamous ship was built in Nova Scotia in 1860, and was to have a brief but dramatic existence. Some accounts allude to her being an unlucky ship prior to 1872, although there are no details to support this notion. But, as the sole survivor of the 1872 disaster, she was not destined for a long life. Just a dozen years after limping into Gibraltar, she was wrecked on the rocks at Haiti. Her captain on that occasion was later punished for attempting insurance fraud.

In 2001, the coral-covered wreck of the *Mary Celeste* was located. The discovery caused ripples of excitement worldwide, but the ship's skeleton gave up no secrets, and eventually the hype subsided. The mystery of the *Mary Celeste* proved as impenetrable as it was 130 years ago.

Abel Fosdyk claimed that during a swimming race, some members of the crew were attacked by sharks. When the others rushed to see what was happening, they fell overboard and met the same fate...

Mysterious Disappearances

Every year, thousands of people are reported missing. Usually the person involved has meticulously planned his/her own disappearance for personal reasons. Sometimes it is the result of foul play or an unfortunate accident. But there are some people who randomly vanish into thin air, with no reasonable explanation to account for it.

THE MYSTERY OF JERROLD POTTER

Jerrold Potter is perhaps the most mysterious of these cases, since he disappeared from an aircraft in mid-flight. He was one of twenty-three passengers aboard a DC-3 flight between Kankakee, Illinois, and Dallas, Texas. The plane had been chartered from the Purdue Aviation Corporation to transport local members of the Lion's Club to a national convention.

The weather on 29 June 1968 was clear, the skies azure blue. Potter's wife had no reason to suspect anything was amiss when he got up to use the lavatory on the plane. She saw him make his way to the rear of the aircraft, stopping en route to chat briefly to a fellow Lion. Moments later a shudder shot through the plane, but it seemed to be nothing more serious than a spot of turbulence. But after a short while Potter's wife became anxious when he failed to return and asked a stewardess for help.

At about this time, in the nose of the plane, pilot Miguel Raul Cabeza noticed a 'door open' indicator and asked his co-pilot Roy Bacus to investigate. At this point, the stewardess alerted Bacus about a missing passenger.

The door nearest to the lavatory was indeed ajar, but this had not caused any undue difficulty in flight since the plane was not pressurized. A safety chain used to secure the door was lying on the floor. It appeared that Potter must have fallen against the door and it had opened, causing him to plummet to his death. The plane put down in Springfield, Missouri, where it was established that Potter was no longer aboard.

Although it seemed that the tragic accident had been explained, a later report pointed out that it was not the safety chain alone that kept the door closed. The handle would have to be turned 180 degrees before it could open. This would be a difficult manoeuvre on the ground, let alone in mid-air, thousands of feet high. No one in the plane heard a scream or any sound of struggling. Moreover, Potter was not likely to have committed suicide. He was, according to family and friends, a happy man with everything to live for.

What is more mysterious still is that his body was never found, despite an extensive search along the route taken by the flight. On that sunny afternoon, he quite simply vanished from the face of the earth.

> *It appeared that Potter must have fallen against the door and it had opened, causing him to plummet to his death.*

THE BENNINGTON TRIANGLE

Potter is not alone in disappearing without trace. An area in southern Vermont, America, known as the Bennington triangle, was blamed for numerous disappearances. On 12 November 1945, Middie Rivers was leading four hunters on an expedition through the wilderness surrounding Glastenbury Mountain. An experienced guide who knew the area well, 74-year old Rivers went ahead of the others and simply vanished. During an extensive search no trace of him was found, save for a bullet lying at the side of a stream. It is presumed that it fell from his pocket, perhaps as he was taking a drink.

Hiker Paula Welden, just 18 years old, vanished from the Long Trail on Glastenbury Mountain on 1 December 1946. A middle-aged couple travelling behind her had seen the young girl round a bend in the path without apparently encountering any problems. But when they turned the corner, there was no trace of her ahead. A huge manhunt was launched that included the police, Paula's fellow students from Bennington College, the FBI and even a clairvoyant, but to no avail.

Three years to the day after this mysterious occurrence, James Tetford vanished from a bus. He was spotted dozing in his seat between Bennington, where he lived in the Old Soldiers' home, and St Albans. Yet when the bus reached its destination, there was no sign of Tetford. His baggage remained on the vehicle and a bus timetable lay open on his seat.

In 1950 an eight-year-old boy, Paul Jepson, was left playing near a pigsty by his mother when she went to tend other animals on a family smallholding. By the time she returned he had gone and was never seen again. According to local lore, bloodhounds followed his trail up Glastenbury Mountain to a point where the scent suddenly stopped, with no apparent explanation.

When Jerrold Potter inexplicably disappeared from a plane in mid-flight, it seemed he had literally vanished into thin air.

Just sixteen days later, the last and perhaps the most mysterious of this string of disappearances occurred, once again in the immediate vicinity of Glastenbury Mountain. The victim was again a hiker, 53-year-old Freida Langer, who dissolved into thin air on a wooded track as she returned to a campsite to change wet

clothes. A search of the area yielded no clues. Yet seven months later her body was discovered in the exact place where she is presumed to have disappeared, wearing the same clothes. There was no obvious cause of death.

Various theories have been put forward to explain the Glastenbury disappearances. Maybe Rivers was murdered and possibly Welden eloped to Canada with a lover. A serial murderer might have killed them all, although it is more usual for a multiple killer to pick off particular types. The victims in the Bennington triangle covered both sexes and many different ages. Bigfoot – who is blamed for all kinds of evils in remote areas – was another suspect.

It is perhaps worth noting that native Americans have long been wary of the area, using it only for a burial ground. It is, they claim, where the four winds meet and therefore subject to strange goings-on.

One day Diderici began to fade away before the eyes of the other prisoners. The process continued until the chains binding him fell empty to the ground.

HISTORICAL VANISHINGS

Weird occurrences such as these are not confined to the twentieth century. In 1809, British diplomat Benjamin Bathurst was returning by coach and horses to Hamburg in Germany. Following a visit to an inn at Perelbery, his companion watched him step forward to examine the horses and then he seemed to evaporate on the spot. Six years later a valet called Diderici was imprisoned in the Prussian jail at Weichselmunde after assuming the identity of his dead employer. One day Diderici began to fade away before the eyes of other prisoners. The process continued until the chains binding him to other men fell empty to the ground. He, like Bathurst, was never seen again.

There remains a degree of doubt as to whether another infamous disappearance really occurred at all. According to the legend, shoe-maker James Worson made a wager with friends that he could run between his home town of Leamington Spa in England to the neighbouring town of Coventry, a distance of some 24km. The challenge began on 3 September 1873 in fair weather, with Worson setting the pace and his friends following in a horse-drawn carriage. A short way along the route they saw Worson stumble – and vanish.

The tale may be rooted in truth, or it could have emerged from a short story by American author Ambrose Bierce, who enjoyed spinning yarns with a paranormal angle. Ironically, Bierce himself disappeared from public view and the circumstances of his death remain a cause for speculation.

Unexplained disappearances continue to baffle and to fascinate us, although for the families and friends involved they can be harrowing. Whilst none of us expect to live forever, these mysterious vanishings do not favour the elderly or the unwell, but choose people of all ages and types, seemingly at random.

Amelia Earhart

When aviator Amelia Earhart vanished during a round-the-world flight in 1937, the US mobilized one of history's biggest search and rescue operations. It failed to find any trace of Earhart, her navigator or their aircraft. Seventy years on, a luckless quest to solve the disappearance of Amelia Earhart continues.

Even as a child, Amelia Earhart set herself apart from her peers. Growing up in Atchison, Kansas, she spent her spare time shooting rats with a rifle, climbing trees and riding. After completing her schooling she worked as a nurse's aide in a Canadian military hospital before beginning a career in aviation. Thrilled at the prospect of a newly emerging civilian aircraft industry, she persuaded her father to pay for a first flying lesson on 28 December 1920. A year later she bought an aircraft of her own, a bright yellow bi-plane nick-named 'Canary'. Before long she was achieving aviation records.

RECORD-BREAKER

In 1922 she was the first woman to reach 4,270m. In 1928 she became the first woman to cross the Atlantic. She made this audacious flight with two men in a Fokker F7, which departed from Trepassey Harbour in Newfoundland and arrived at Burry Port in Wales some 21 hours later.

Four years later, she became the first woman to fly solo across the Atlantic. Bad conditions meant she had to put down in Londonderry, Northern Ireland, rather than Paris as planned. Nevertheless she was hailed a national hero, becoming the first woman to be awarded the 'Distinguished Flying Cross'. An international celebrity, she rubbed shoulders with royalty, received roses from Italian dictator Mussolini and had an audience with the pope. The public was enthralled by her continuing adventures, like the solo flight across the Pacific from Honolulu to Oakland, California, in 1935.

In 1931 she married publisher and publicist George Putnam who managed her career. Although Earhart had already satisfied her dearest ambition – to prove that women were equal to men in jobs that required 'intelligence, co-ordination, speed, coolness and willpower' – she yearned to undertake one more spectacular exploit. As her fortieth birthday loomed, she determined to fly around the world.

She yearned to undertake one more spectacular exploit. As her fortieth birthday loomed, she determined to fly around the world.

THE WORLD ATTEMPT

In 1937, a first attempt at a round-the-world flight was aborted after Earhart's aircraft crashed on take-off in Hawaii. But when she took off from Miami on 1 June that year, accompanied by navigator Fred Noonan, all went according to plan. The two commenced their 46,670km odyssey in favourable conditions.

By the end of the month, all but 11,265km of the marathon had been completed. However, the hardest leg lay ahead. Earhart had to fly from Papua New Guinea to a tiny, uninhabited atoll called Howland Island that was just a pinprick in the ocean.

A runway was constructed especially for the event, and the US Navy coast guard cutter *Itasca* was standing by to provide radio guidance. Despite all the preparations made for the tricky journey, it ended in disaster. Radio contact between Earhart and *Itasca* was at first patchy and then became non-existent.

On 2 July 1937, the *Itasca* headed north-west in a bid to find the missing aircraft. There were distorted radio signals, and wild speculation that the missing pair was marooned on any one of numerous deserted islands in the region. However, some sixteen days later, the huge search and rescue operation was called off, having drawn a blank.

The spirited aviatrix had achieved everything she wanted in life, but she yearned to take on one more big challenge.

US SPY?

Before long there were a host of conspiracy theories about her disappearance. Even with the passing of time, these have not abated.

A 1943 film called *Flight for Freedom* suggested Earhart had been employed by the US government on a spying mission over Japanese-held territory. Although the fateful flight was prior to the Second World War, tensions were already running high in the Pacific as Japan, having invaded China, sought to strengthen its grip on the region. This theory might have been dismissed as Hollywood hype, were it not for a series of perplexing events that occurred during the ensuing world conflict.

In 1944, after the Americans captured Saipan from the Japanese, soldiers found a photograph album containing pictures of Earhart. There were reports by the Saipanese of sightings of a white woman on the island. Could it mean that the missing aviatrix was on Saipan? An army sergeant claimed to have seen US marines on the island guarding a hangar housing Earhart's plane, which was later burned, according to him.

A map of Earhart's route shows how she may have ended up on the island of Saipan. Could she have been a US agent, spying on the Japanese?

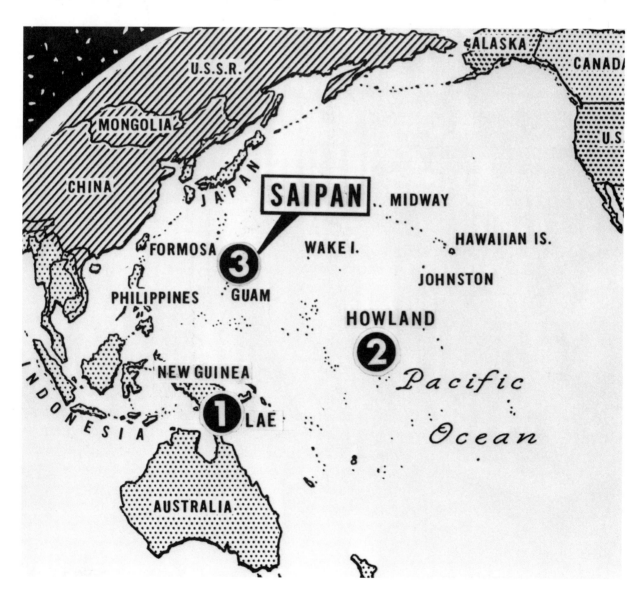

On the adjoining island, Tinian, a marine gunner from the US believes he was shown the graves of Earhart and Noonan in 1944. He was told they had been executed as spies.

The collective implication of these accounts is that Earhart was indeed a US government spy, who was captured by the Japanese and killed. Rather than admit the truth and risk the embarrassment of causing the death of this popular figure, US authorities decided to cover up the scandal.

A marine gunner from the US believes he was shown the graves of Earhart and Noonan in 1944. He was told they had been executed as spies.

MAROONED?

However, this is not the only theory about Earhart's disappearance. Another says that, with the plane running short of fuel, she and Noonan landed on or near the uninhabited island of Nikumaroro, where they ultimately perished.

If this was indeed the case, then they might have discovered a stash of supplies on Nikumaroro, left by a ship's captain and some of his crew who were shipwrecked there in 1929. After being rescued, Captain Daniel Hamer explained: 'Before leaving camp, all provisions etc were placed in the shelter but I sincerely hope that no one will ever be so unfortunate as to need them.'

When the island was searched in 1940, there was evidence of recent habitation. But there was a marked absence of plane wreckage and, indeed, bodies. Skeleton parts discovered on the island were later said to be that of a man, possibly one of the victims of the SS *Norwich City* shipwreck. The analysis could have been incorrect, but unfortunately re-examination is now impossible since the bones are missing. Nevertheless, one devoted group, The International Group for Historic Aircraft Recovery, felt the evidence for Earhart on Nikumaroro was so compelling that it mounted a series of expeditions to search for clues. Nothing it has found to date puts the theory beyond doubt. But expedition members have discovered the remains of a shoe that might have fitted the aviatrix and some items that possibly came from the plane. Although it still favours the Nikumaroro theory, TIGHAR investigators have been to other islands in pursuit of the truth about Amelia Earhart.

LIVING MYSTERY

Yet another theory in existence is that Earhart was kept prisoner throughout the war and released when her prison camp was liberated, returning incognito to live under an assumed name in America. Unfortunately, the proof to support this notion is sparse indeed.

Science will almost certainly answer the Earhart mystery after appropriate evidence is brought forth. But at the moment that remains elusive and the hunt for clues continues.

MIRACLES

Miracles may seem out of sync wtih our largely sceptical and consumer-driven society, yet millions of faithful still believe they occur. For those who experience them directly, miracles are an unforgettable and life-changing event. Whether it is statues that appear to be crying, visions of the Virgin Mary or angels coming to our rescue in the nick of time, miracles may come in all shapes and sizes, from all corners of the globe. And, contrary to what we might expect, our belief in awesome, unexplained phenomena seems to be growing.

Stigmata

The grievous injuries suffered by Jesus on the cross included bloodied hands and feet, a spear wound in the side and sharp scratches around the brow from his crown of thorns. Followers of Christ have been known to exhibit some of the same wounds, a mysterious phenomenon known as stigmata.

The wounds, although not necessarily permanent, tend to defy treatment by doctors and are never prone to infection. Often, they do not have the same odour that might emanate from other long-running sores, and there are even some reports of them radiating a perfume. The belief, as yet unproven, is that the holy wounds allow Christ's blood to come forth rather than that of the sufferer.

In addition to the bloodied patches, there might be lash marks and shoulder scars. These seem to mimic the wounds inflicted on Jesus when he was whipped and beaten before hauling his cross-beam to Golgotha. And the pain endured by stigmatics is not confined to external injuries. They also suffer acute feelings of hopelessness, desperation and sorrow.

A HISTORY OF SUFFERING

About three hundred cases of stigmata are on record, a staggering ninety per cent of which occurred in women. Sixty-two saints have been afflicted. The first stigmatic on record is Stephen Langton who, in 1222, appeared to suffer all the hallmark injuries. No one knows how his condition was investigated, but his claims were swiftly dismissed as a hoax. It is surely not coincidence that the iconic emblem of Jesus on the cross had just become widespread in Europe at this time.

Just two years later, St Francis of Assisi (1181/2-1226) was revealing signs of the crucifixion on his withering body. The son of a merchant, St Francis had turned his back on a comfortable middle class existence to champion the poor, following a series of dreams that beckoned him to his faith. He went on to live a Spartan existence in Italy in prayer and solitude. Not only did he bear the wounds of Christ, but he also exhibited the strangest of stigmatic symptoms: his hands and feet appeared to be pierced with black nails of flesh, bent backwards.

In the following centuries a number of holy figures were stigmatics, including St Catherine of Siena in the fourteenth century, St John of God in the sixteenth century and St Mary Frances of the Five Wounds in the eighteenth century.

His hands and feet appeared to be pierced with black nails of flesh, bent backwards.

PADRE PIO

The most famous stigmatic of the twentieth century was Saint Pio of Pietrelcina, better known simply as Padre Pio. Born in Italy in 1887, he became a Capuchin monk called Brother Pio at the age of 15. In 1910, a year after his ordination as a priest, he noticed the first signs of the condition that would come to dominate his existence. A red mark about the size of a penny appeared on each of his palms, causing him some pain. The left hand, he reported, hurt more than his right, and he felt the same sensation in his feet.

But it not until 1918 that the full-blown symptoms of stigmata afflicted Padre Pio. He wrote to his mentor about the experience, which occurred just after he had celebrated a mass. 'I yielded to a drowsiness similar to a sweet sleep. All the internal and external senses and even the very faculties of my soul were immersed in indescribable stillness. Absolute silence surrounded and invaded me. I was suddenly filled with great peace and abandonment which effaced everything else and caused a lull in the turmoil. All this happened in a flash.'

He described how a man whose hands, feet and side were dripping with blood appeared before him. When the vision disappeared Pio discovered he had similar wounds, with blood pouring forth. For the next fifty years he bore the injuries that imitated those of Christ, and bleeding from the side wound was especially severe between Thursday and Saturday, the days that led up to the crucifixion of Jesus.

Padre Pio won a reputation as someone who could read souls, foretell the future and heal the sick. Thousands of people flocked to see him, convinced that he possessed divine gifts passed on from Christ himself. Their faith was further confirmed when, on his death in 1968, all signs of stigmata had vanished. Flesh in the affected parts had healed without leaving scars. Padre Pio had predicted this would occur.

Therese Neumann, a stigmatic who apparently lived for thirty-six years on nothing more than a daily communion wafer.

FRUGAL FERVOUR

Stigmatics, including Padre Pio, are renowned for their frugal lifestyle. Therese Neumann, (1898-1962), another twentieth-century stigmatic, apparently lived for thirty-six years on nothing more than a daily communion wafer. She also eschewed sleep for most of her life, concentrating instead on her visions. Despite significant blood loss, St Pio also managed to survive on minimum sustenance.

A QUESTION OF FAITH

In 2002 Pope John Paul II elevated Padre Pio to sainthood. All doubt about the authenticity of his wounds was officially banished by this decision. Yet, for the impartial observer, there is an obvious difficulty in believing the accounts of stigmatics. How do we know the wounds were not self-inflicted? Only 24-hour surveillance could eliminate doubts about that possibility. Self-inflicted stigmata could be an attempt to attract attention, or an example of what is known as a 'pious hoax', one carried out with the sole intention of shoring up people's faith.

There have been numerous examples of frauds, notably Magdalena de la Cruz (1487-1560) who confessed before death that she had injured herself in order to duplicate Jesus' wounds. Many people believe injuries like this could be incurred through self-hypnosis.

Padre Pio was seen with Pope Pius XI at the Vatican at the same time he was reportedly taking mass in his church at San Giovanni Rotundo.

The issue has been further complicated by the enduring enigma of the Turin Shroud (see page 175). The shroud clearly indicates that the body supposedly wrapped in it suffered wounds to the arm rather than the hands. Indeed, modern research into ancient execution methods tells us that those who were crucified were pinioned between the radial and ulna, two wrist bones, rather than nailed through the palms. This distinction is not made in the depiction of traditional crucifixes. If the stigmata signs were a heavenly miracle, ask sceptics, why do puncture marks not appear on the wrist?

Whatever questions are raised, mystery still surrounds stigmata, which is often accompanied by other mysterious phenomena. Padre Pio was seen with Pope Pius XI at the Vatican at the same time he was reportedly taking mass in his church in San Giovanni Rotondo. He later explained that bi-locution (being in two places at once), was an extension of his personality. What is more, images of Padre Pio in the sky allegedly deterred pilots in the Second World War from emptying their bombs on his home town. The bodies of stigmatics are frequently found to be incorruptible after death, that is, they do not deteriorate in the usual way. Four days after Therese Neumann died, for example, there was no sign of rigor mortis. It seems that the bloody signs of stigmata are parts of a much larger puzzle, divine or otherwise, that has yet to be solved.

The Turin Shroud

For countless thousands, the Turin shroud is the holiest of relics. They believe it is the shroud in which Jesus was wrapped following his death, and that the image of a face and body imprinted in the cloth are those of the Saviour himself. But others dispute the age of the shroud, and believe it is the work of an artful medieval hoaxer. Conclusive proof of its authenticity has been hard to come by.

THE FACTS

There are some things we know for certain about the shroud. Today, it is housed in the Cathedral of St John the Baptist in the Italian city of Turin. The cloth measures 4.4m in length and is 1m wide. The first reliable records of it appeared in France in 1357, and we know that in 1532 it was damaged in a fire. The markings – which appear to be a man's face with shoulder-length hair, a middle parting and a beard and moustache – are etched into the cloth. The image is both three dimensional and photonegative, although no one knows exactly how it was made.

These few facts are probably the sum total of what can be said with certainty about the Turin Shroud. Almost everything else concerning it is the subject of conjecture and controversy.

CRUCIFIED EVIDENCE

There is visual evidence on the shroud of bodily wounds consistent with a crown of thorns and with the torture of crucifixion. Yet while some scientists have said that there is blood on the shroud others have disagreed, pointing out that the fragile quantities of DNA have brought forth inconclusive results.

The cynics have insisted that the features on the shroud were painted on by a talented artist in the Middle Ages. This was a time when the church badly wanted to focus the faithful on convincing relics and deflect their attention from rampant disease and poverty. But in turn, their opponents have claimed that there is not a trace of paint in evidence.

Some scholars of the shroud – known as sindonologists – have recently come to believe that coins once covered the eyes of the dead man and are still visible on the imprint. At least one of the coins is said to be a lepton, produced in the Roman Empire at the time of Christ. But others have been unable to identify the coin marks at all. They point out that, in any case, it was not the Jewish custom to cover the eyes of the dead with coins at that time.

Even the height of the body supposedly kept within the shroud is a source of disagreement. One study claims he stood at 1.8m while another puts him closer to 1.9m tall.

Modern scientific methods might well clarify some of these hotly debated issues if only they were applied to the shroud. But its great age and sacred value mean that the Catholic church is reluctant to permit wide-ranging experiments.

CARBON DATING

Sceptics thought the long-running debate was nailed in their favour when radio carbon testing carried out in 1988 put the age of this intriguing cloth firmly in the Middle Ages. To be precise, the findings of researchers at Oxford University, the University of Arizona and the Swiss Federal Institute of Technology put its creation at somewhere between 1260 and 1390, some twelve centuries after the

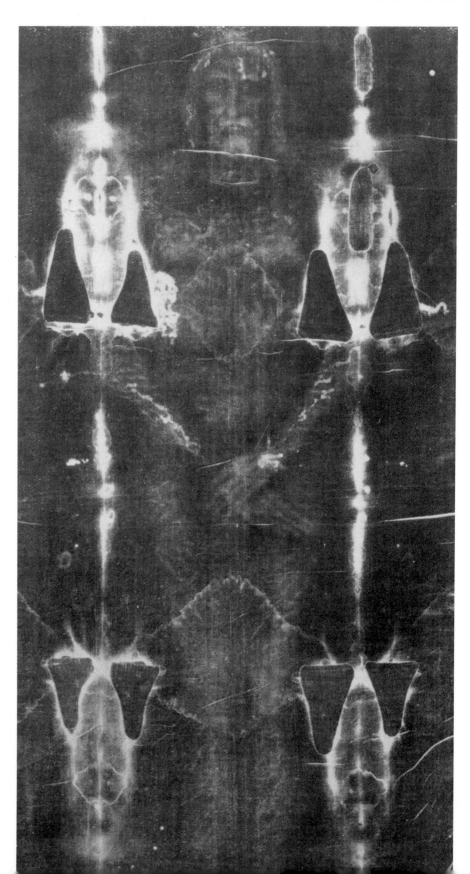

In this photograph of the Turin shroud, the image of a head and body appears clearly, surrounded by water stains and fold marks.

era of Christ. The revelation led the Cardinal of Turin, Anastasio Alberto Ballestrero, to admit publicly that the shroud was a hoax. This was particularly embarrassing for the Catholic Church given that, eight years earlier, Pope John Paul II had reverently kissed it, clearly believing it to be genuine.

However, two factors now point to the carbon test result being flawed. The material taken for testing was from the corner of the shroud where repairs were evidently made following a blaze. For the purposes of scientific analysis, the repaired material would not yield accurate results.

TEXTILE DETECTION

Perhaps more significant still were the findings of Swedish textiles expert Dr Mechthild Flury-Lemberg who announced the seams on the shroud were of a style used in the first century AD or before. She caught sight of the seam during a restoration project that took place in 2002.

The findings of a botany professor just prior to the millennium have lent greater weight to the argument for the authenticity of the shroud. Avinoam Danin, of the Hebrew University in Jerusalem, looked not at the cloth but into the minute evidence of plant life upon it. The pollen and the imprints of thorns, said Professor Danin, indicated that the shroud originated in the Middle East. Together with colleagues, he identified the bean caper plant, the Rock rose and Goundelia Tournefortii tumbleweed, an unlikely combination anywhere else in the world other than the Holy Land.

WHOSE FACE?

There are several theories in existence that claim the face belongs to someone other than Jesus. Jacques de Molay, the leader of the powerful Knights Templar, is one name in the frame. The Knights Templar were persecuted after 1307 by the French king who sought to control their mighty wealth and De Molay was tortured before being burnt at the stake. The contention is that his badly battered body was kept in the shroud before his execution and that chemical reactions caused the imprint.

Leonardo da Vinci is another possible contender for the face of the shroud. The

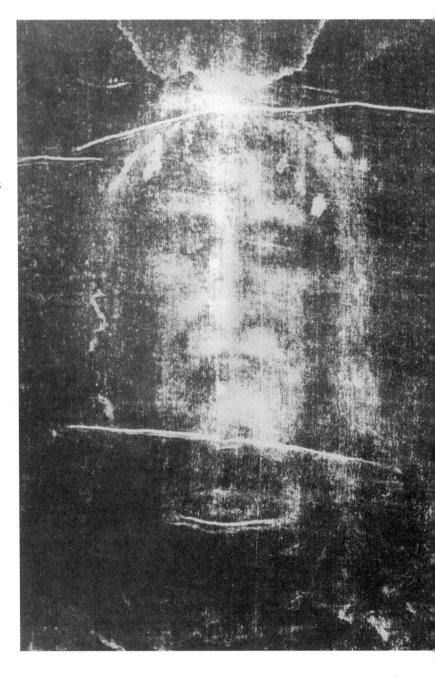

A close-up of the shroud shows the face at the centre of the debate. Could this be the face of Jesus himself?

artist and inventor may have been attempting photography using a *camera obscura*, the most rudimentary instrument upon which to secure an image. But, quite apart from the fact that the kind of camera necessary has proved difficult to construct even now, the shroud was reportedly in existence before da Vinci. There is no doubt that if da Vinci could have imprinted his image on the shroud he would have done so, and enormously enjoyed the ensuing furore, but the theory is tenuous.

SHROUDED JOURNEY

If the shroud is genuine, the presumption is that it was taken by one of Jesus' disciples and presented to King Abgar V, who ruled from Edessa (in present day Iraq) and was in correspondence with Jesus. Much later it would have found its way to Constantinople – known today as Istanbul – and was stolen when the city was ransacked in the Fourth Crusade early in the thirteenth century. Following this, the French knight Geoffrey de Charny put the relic on display in Lirey, France, and pilgrims flocked to see it. In 1578 it moved to Turin, and it has been there ever since. Surprisingly, the shroud was owned by the House of Savoy (European royalty) as recently as 1983, when it finally became the property of the Vatican.

Nails through the two major bones above the wrist kept the victim vertical, and denied them a quick death on the cross.

WRINGING OUT THE TRUTH

There is one credible indicator to suggest the shroud is not history's greatest art forgery, and this is the twin wrist wounds visible on the cloth. The bloody spots are definitely visible on the wrists rather than the palms. In the Middle Ages it was assumed that the crucifixion of Christ entailed his hands being nailed into position and so presumably, any belated (fake) representation would have been made that way. But recent research has revealed that nailing through the hands would not be sufficient to keep the human body upright during crucifixion and the victim would have died relatively quickly from suffocation via a collapsed chest. Nails through the two major bones above the wrist would have kept the victim vertical, and denied them such a quick death. It is these grisly details that constitute the best proof of the shroud's authenticity.

In 2004 researchers discovered a second, much fainter face on the opposite side of the shroud, which corresponds exactly to the face on the front. This second image is superficial, meaning that it has not soaked through from paint or some other substance on the front. This finding lends weight to the theory that a chemical reaction between body and cloth implanted the image on the shroud, and it makes the idea of a faked image implausible. Of course, it tells us no more about whether the body in question belonged to Jesus.

Expect a respite in the Turin shroud debate for a few years. The elusive garment is not scheduled to be seen again in public until 2025, when the controversy will surely be ignited once more.

The Miracle of Fatima

In 1917, three Portuguese children playing in a wooded glade were suddenly struck by a vision of a woman in white, emanating a startling light. This was to be the first of six visitations to the children by the Virgin Mary and became known as the Miracle of Fatima.

The Miracle of Fatima has earned a place as one of the most famous stories of a religious vision, because the final apparition of the Virgin Mary was, to some extent, witnessed by thousands. Furthermore, the prophecies that the Virgin is said to have imparted became a source of mystery and intrigue during the twentieth century.

JACINTA   FRANCISCO   LUCIA

Jacinta, Francisco and Lucia were unexpectedly propelled into the limelight by their mysterious rendezvous with the Virgin Mary.

In February 2005, the death of a modest Portuguese nun at the age of 97 finally put the events at Fatima into the context of history. For Sister Lucia was the last surviving member of the trio who had witnessed the now famous apparition in her childhood.

A MIRACULOUS CHILDHOOD

Lucia grew up in humble circumstances in the village of Aljustrel in Portugal, the youngest of seven children. As a young girl, she believed she had encountered an angel on two occasions in the year 1916. On 13 May the following year, she was playing with her cousins Jacinta and Francisco Marto among their sheep when they claimed to see the Madonna at close quarters. In the conversation that ensued, it was ten-year-old Lucia who spoke for her cousins. They were told to meet at the same spot on the 13th of each month until October.

Lucia wanted to keep the strange events of the day a secret but Jacinta, aged just seven years old, blurted out what had happened to her family.

Lucia wanted to keep the strange events of the day a secret but Jacinta, aged just seven years old, blurted out what had happened to her family. It became the talk of the neighbourhood and when the children next went to meet the Virgin Mary a month later, they found themselves in company. Onlookers at this and subsequent assignations were unable to make out the heavenly visitor, although the children could see and talk to her.

SUNDANCE

A few months later, on 13 October, a 50,000-strong crowd had gathered to witness the meeting. As before, none of the hopeful throng saw the Virgin as the children had done. But as they watched with baited breath, the driving rain suddenly gave way to sunshine. The sun then appeared to dance in the sky, inspiring fear and adulation in equal measure. The *O Dia* newspaper reported the miraculous events like this:

'The sky had a certain greyish tint of pearl and a strange clearness filled the gloomy landscape, every moment getting gloomier. The sun seemed to be veiled with transparent gauze to enable us to look at it without difficulty. The greyish tint of mother of pearl began changing as if into a shining silver disc, that was growing slowly until it broke through the clouds. And the silvery sun, still shrouded in the same greyish lightness of gauze, was seen to rotate and wander within the circle of receded clouds! The people cried out with one voice, the thousands of the creatures of God whom faith raised up to heaven, fell to their knees upon the muddy ground.'

Two years later, Jacinta and Francisco died in the influenza pandemic that gripped Europe. Now, Lucia alone could offer a first-hand account of the marvellous events of 1917 that had inspired her own decision to enter a convent. It was not until the 1940s that Sister Lucia noted down the prophecies imparted by the vision that had appeared to her and her cousins. Two of the three prophecies were made public. They appeared to relate firstly to the Second World War and then to the evils of Soviet Russia, particularly with regard to Catholicism. At least, those were the Vatican-approved interpretations of the Madonna's messages.

THE FINAL PROPHECY

The last of the prophecies was apparently given to the Vatican in a sealed envelope, with instructions that it should be opened in the 1960s. The presiding pope of the era did so and, having read the contents of the envelope, declined to make a statement and returned it to secret safe-keeping.

Debate about the content of this last prophecy began to rage. Did it predict a nuclear holocaust? Was mankind doomed to extinction in the short-term? Just what could the vision of the Madonna have said that was so potentially explosive it could not be made public? One man was so tormented at the thought of it that he hijacked a jet in an attempt to force the Vatican to speak up.

So it was something of an anti-climax when, in 2000, Pope John Paul II decided to reveal the nature of the prophecy. It referred to the assassination

The last of the prophecies imparted to the children by the Virgin Mary apparently referred to the assassination attempt against Pope John Paul II in 1981.

attempt made against him in 1981 in St Peter's Square. Indeed, the date of the shooting (13 May) coincided with the anniversary of the Fatima visions and the Turkish gunman, Mehmet Ali Agca, maintained that his actions were connected with the events of that distant Portuguese summer.

It seemed the mystery was solved. Pope John Paul II proceeded to beatify Jacinta and Francisco Marto, putting them on the road to sainthood. He revealed his confirmed belief that the 'motherly' hand of the Madonna had guided the bullet's course, saving him from serious harm. As a mark of his gratitude he placed the bullet upon the Virgin's statue at Fatima.

BITING THE BULLET

The only remaining mystery seemed to be why the Catholic Church kept the text of the prophecy under wraps for so long. Eventually the wording transmitted by Sister Lucia – who attended the beatification service and heard the prophecy revealed – came under closer scrutiny. It spoke of the Holy Father passing through a big, ruined city, and continued like this;

The Medjugorje prophecies are said to predict grim repercussions for those who do not undergo religious conversion.

' …half trembling with halting step, afflicted with pain and sorrow, he prayed for the souls of the corpses he met on his way; having reached the top of the mountain, on his knees at the foot of the big cross he was killed by a group of soldiers who fired bullets and arrows at him, and in the same way there died one after another the other bishops, priests, men and women religious, and various lay people of different ranks and positions.'

By any standards, this relates a greatly exaggerated version of what went on in St Peter's Square in 1981. The third prophecy seemed to be discussing Armageddon, although both Pope John Paul II and Sister Lucia were content to uphold the official interpretation referring to the assassination attempt.

THREAT OR PROPHECY?

The same dramatic tenor characterizes the prophecies coming out of Medjugorje in Bosnia-Herzegovina where the Virgin Mary has reportedly made regular appearances since 24 June 1981. She is said to have imparted ten secrets to six young visionaries, only one of which has been revealed. But some information on the prophecies has leaked into the public domain, and they are said to predict grim repercussions for those who do not undergo religious conversion.

Although stories of visions like those at Fatima and Medjugorje play well to a Catholic audience, they are often greeted with a measure of scepticism. Many Christians and even Catholics believe that such stories are grounded in superstition and hallucination, not in authentic religious phenomena. The Vatican is cautious of reported sightings of the Madonna and rarely endorses them. However, the vision of the three children at Fatima, and the thousands of faithful who shared the miraculous experience with them, has earned the Papal seal of approval and is famous with Catholics and others the world over.

Angels

When a crisis is looming, panic sets in and the heartbeat starts to race out of control. But suddenly a stranger appears out of nowhere to offer a helping hand, and disaster is averted. A coincidence, perhaps, but many believe such timely intervention is the work of angels sent to guide and protect us.

All the major faiths embrace the existence of angels. Indeed, the Koran, the Bible and the Torah are littered with references to them.

Nor has belief in angels waned in recent times. Eight out of ten Americans questioned for a Fox News poll in 2005 admitted to believing in angels. (The precise breakdown was 86 per cent of women and 72 per cent of men.) A different survey concluded that as many as one third of Americans had actually seen an angel. So what proof is out there for such widespread conviction?

SAVED FROM A COLD FATE

Author Joan Wester Anderson relates one compelling story concerning her son Tim. On Christmas Eve, 1983, he and two friends were making their way back from college in Connecticut to her Chicago home. Weather conditions were atrocious and there was a widespread freeze. Having dropped one friend off in Indiana, Tim was driving on a rural road when his car spluttered to a halt. Tim and his friend Jim looked at each other in terror as the voice of the radio announcer – warning against anyone stepping outside into a dangerously icy wind – echoed between them. There was not a house or another car within sight and all around the countryside was cloaked in darkness. As they battled to stay calm and ward off the cold, they suddenly became aware of headlights flashing in the rear view mirror. There was a knock on the window, followed by a cry: 'Need to be pulled?' The voice belonged to a tow truck driver who set about hitching up the car so they could return to their friend's home.

When they arrived at their destination, Tim dashed into the house, asking for cash to repay the debt they surely owed to their rescuer. But outside the truck had vanished, along with its driver. Even more mysteriously, they could find only one set of tyre marks in the snow on the road, those belonging to Tim's vehicle.

If the truck had not arrived and towed them, the two young men would undoubtedly have frozen to death. Tim and his mother Joan remain convinced that an angel heard his prayers for help on that Christmas Eve of 1983, and intervened to prevent disaster. The story is among many featured in Joan's book *Where Angels Walk*.

WIDESPREAD BELIEF

Tales of angel encounters are by no means rare. One magazine entitled *Angels on Earth*, which has a 600,000 circulation, receives about a thousand

If the truck had not arrived and towed them, the two young men would have frozen to death.

submissions a month, mostly from Americans. Nor is interest in angels solely a North American phenomenon. Theology graduate Emma Heathcote-James was intrigued by the strong presence of angels perceived among Americans and wondered if the same was true in Britain.

After putting out a plea for personal stories in the media, she was overwhelmed with the response. She received more than a thousand written testimonies from UK residents who believed they had had some kind of angelic encounter, and set about analyzing the data. She found that 'people from all cultures, backgrounds and faiths were relating the same types of experience, so (angelic encounter) has a multi-faith and cross cultural element.' The results were published in 2001 in her book, *Seeing Angels*, which is one of numerous publications on the subject.

ANGEL DATA

Angel reports claim that the heavenly visitors are tall, clad in black or white, male, female or without gender, and are often bathed in light. Apparently they can be cherubic, jovial or serious. Some talk while others are silent. Occasionally, their presence is sensed rather than seen. Often, witnesses feel able to draw a distinction between different types of angels, including archangels, messenger and guardian angels.

Children seem particularly prone to seeing angels and there are numerous reports from bewildered parents about angel incidents.

So anecdotal evidence about the existence of angels is not hard to come across. Pinning that evidence down to specific events poses a harder challenge. The response from cynics is that belief in angels represents a comfort zone that is frequently lacking in the stressful lives of today's citizens. Encounters may have occurred because a generation largely brought up without religion is now urgently seeking spiritual fulfilment. The onset of a new millennium may also have revived long-buried religious feelings in a secular society. Alternatively, events can be explained away as intuition or co-incidence. Angelic encounters often take place in hospital and therefore, say some observers, they could simply be a side-effect of prescribed drugs.

ON PRESCRIPTION

In Birmingham England, Muslim accountant Anver Hajee was in hospital suffering from chest pains. His mind was centred on his father and brother, both of whom had died prematurely from heart disease, and on his disabled daughter. Then, Anver saw a figure that he has since presumed to be his guardian angel. 'He was tall, about 7ft [over 2m tall], with very good cheekbones and pink cheeks. I felt a warmth coming off him. He touched me and said something like, "You'll be fine".'

The Angel of Mons (see over) was witnessed by scores of British soldiers facing annihilation during the First World War. He arrived in the nick of time...

Anver insists the incident had nothing to do with the medication he had been prescribed. He kept the experience quiet until he heard a radio programme about angels. Only then did he feel sufficiently confident to make his spiritual experience public.

Children seem especially prone to seeing angels and there are numerous reports from bewildered parents about angel incidents. This is believed to be because children's minds are uncluttered by pre-conceived notions and are consequently more open to extraordinary sights and sounds. It is tempting to believe that childrens' reports of encounters with fairy godmothers and invisible friends are in fact all about guardian angels.

The following account provides a poignant example of a child's encounter with angels. When his grandfather was admitted to hospital suffering from terminal cancer, five-year-old Bryan Simmerman, from New Jersey, told him: 'It's ok Pop-Pop, you can rest now. The angels are with you.' The dying man responded: 'I know, I can see them.' The story is remarkable as the pair came from a non-religious family. And joint testimony about a single incident is all the more persuasive. It is for this reason that the story of an angel appearing before scores of witnesses during the Battle of Mons in the First World War has maintained currency for so long.

THE ANGEL OF MONS

On 23 August 1914, British forces were facing annihilation by the Germans in Belgium. As the outlook grew ever more bleak, the soldiers began to lose all hope of survival. But at this point, the skies allegedly opened up to reveal a winged figure with two others, witnessed by scores of soldiers on the battlefield. Together the figures appeared to hold back the Kaiser's men while the British escaped the onslaught. The combined testimony of those present was so convincing that eminent historian A.J.P. Taylor accepted the account as fact even as late as 1963.

The skies allegedly opened up to reveal a winged figure with two others, witnessed by scores of soldiers on the battlefield.

Since then a shadow of doubt has been cast upon the tale. It was, some scoff, an illusion inspired by fear, which was exaggerated by the authorities to put a favourable spin on the conflict at home. The angelic figure was even taken to be Saint George of England accompanied by armoured figures or a row of bowmen. Furthermore, the story is similar to a fictional one written by Arthur Machen and published in September 1914. It was this, sceptics claim, that seeped into the consciousness of many, influencing their experience at the crucial moment. Curiously, though, there are a few letters home from the front which appear to verify the story, pre-dating Arthur Machen's story. And other sources have been found to support the angel accounts. The following paragraph appeared in The *Observer* of 22 August 1915.

'The Rev. A.A. Boddy, Vicar of All Saints' Sunderland, who has just returned home after two months ministerial work at the front, says he had several opportunities of investigating the story of the vision at Mons. The evidence, he says, though not always direct, was remarkably cumulative, and came through channels which were entitled to respect.'

However, as the veteran soldiers from the terrible conflict aged and died during the twentieth century, the potency of the story seemed to ebb away. While angel sightings by individuals appear to be many and frequent in the twenty-first century, it seems that mass visions belong to a different era. But perhaps it is mankind who is changing, not our guardian angels...

Weeping Statues

When a ceramic statue brings forth tears, bleeds, or even appears to sweat, it is baffling and awe-inspiring for those who witness it. When the statue in question has religious significance, the display of human characteristics seems to represent a divine message.

WORLDWIDE WEEPING

Stories of weeping statues are more frequent than one might imagine. In 1992, in the home of Olga Rodriguez in La Cisterna, a poor neighbourhood in Santiago, Chile, a porcelain statue standing just 15cm high cried tears of blood. An investigation by the coroner's office decided the drops were human blood, type 0-4.

On 31 May 1993, a 1.2m-tall statue began to weep in a domestic shrine in Las Vegas. The owner Pablo Covarrubias had imported the green-robed figure two years previously, where it had been manufactured along with thousands of others to mark the appearance of the Guadalupe Madonna in Mexico City in the sixteenth century. The tears, first witnessed by Pablo's daughter Martha as she meditated and prayed, were filmed by a TV station. On 12 December that year – the feast day of Our Lady of Guadalupe – the statue wept again. A police officer surreptitiously took a sample of the liquid cascading down the cheeks of the statue. Scientific analysis proved it comprised human tears. Moreover, swabs soaked in the tears were later reputed to possess healing powers. Today, scores of pilgrims flock to the Covarrubias house to see for themselves how the Madonna is moved to tears. The miraculous statue has not become a backyard money-spinner, since the family will not accept money from the faithful.

In 1994 a 30cm-high statue in Grangecon, County Wicklow, Ireland, cried tears of blood and, during the next year, a Madonna brought back from the shrine at Medjugorje in Bosnia-Herzegovinia similarly wept in Civitavecchia, Italy. Tests in that case proved it was human blood from a male. In 1996, an egg-shaped plaster Madonna began to cry in a trailer in Lewis, Kansas. Once again the event marked the feast day of Our Lady of Guadalupe. In April the following year a statue belonging to a religious community in Gebegamey, Benin, Africa, began weeping tears of blood.

> *An investigation by the coroner's office decided the drops were human blood, type 0-4.*

OFFICIAL BLOOD AND TEARS

The first recorded instance of a weeping statue was in 1953 in Syracuse, Sicily. Antonietta Januso was in bed with a rare illness she contracted after giving birth. When she opened her eyes on 29 August she saw the little Madonna on the wall with tears streaming from her eyes. The miracle continued for four days and attracted thousands of spectators. After a swift investigation, the bishops of Sicily unanimously agreed the tears were 'authentic'. The *Osservatore Romano* stated: '(The bishops) have expressed the sincere desire that this manifestation of our heavenly Mother may inspire the whole world with a true spirit of penance, and more fervent devotion to the Immaculate Heart of Mary.'

A weeping Mary in Akita, Japan, in 1973 was viewed as equally persuasive. Having cried blood and apparently sweated, the Virgin Mary imparted three messages to Sister Agnes Sasagawa. The statue subsequently continued to weep over a period of years, notching up 101 recorded occasions.

THE MECHANICS

A number of other crying statues during this era were proven fakes. How is it possible to make an inanimate object like a statue cry? Well, a system of pumps and tubes is easily exposed. But a report drawn up Dr Luigi Garlaschelli puts forward a more convincing scenario. Take one statue made of porous but glazed material, like a ceramic. Fill the statue with liquid until it is absorbed. Then make minute pinholes around the eyes or cheeks that will permit small amounts of the liquid soaked inside the statue to seep out.

Dr Garlaschelli has carried out an experiment along these lines that has produced compelling results, sufficient to convince an audience that the Madonna statue he used was really crying. It might be possible to soak the inside of a

This ceramic statue appears to be crying tears of blood. Is this a divine message, or a hoax made using a system of tubes and pinholes?

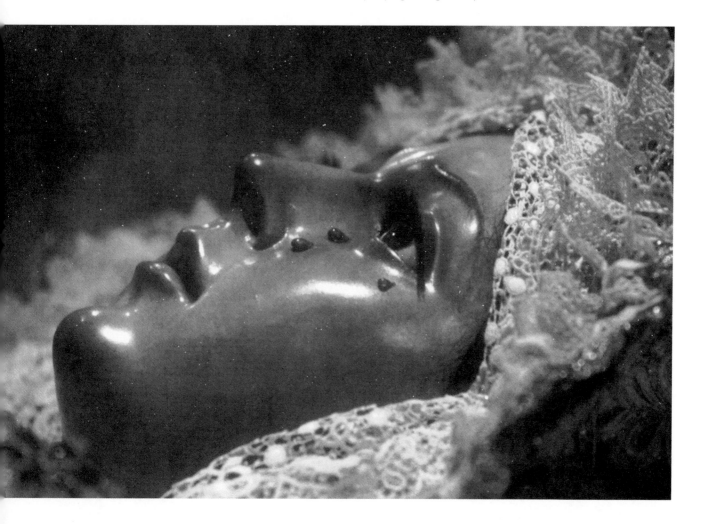

Religious pictures have also been known to cry, while angels and Madonnas sometimes exude the scent of roses or 'sweat' rose-scented oil.

glazed statue using a syringe, leaving no visible entry point. Another suggestion is that oil-soaked sponges are fixed behind the pinholes. The crying begins when the weather warms up, as the oil becomes more fluid.

Other ideas have been put forward, including that of condensation, humidity or a leaching out of the adhesive used to secure the eyes on the statues.

In 2004, two statues in the Vietnamese Community Church in Brisbane, Australia, were seen to bleed and weep. After the sightings began, the church attracted thousands of worshippers who hoped to witness a miracle. But the Catholic Church concluded that they were fakes. According to the Brisbane Catholic Archbishop John Bathersby, the red substance oozing from the statues was synthetic. 'The substance that seeped from the artifacts is very like one that is commercially available and it is possible that the substance was applied to them by human hands,' he told a news conference. After an official investigation, the Archbishop ordered that statues should be removed from display.

These arguments more than satisfy the sceptics, who point out that virtually all cases of weeping statues have religious significance and most, although not all, outbreaks are in fervently Catholic countries. The vast majority of cases involve statues of the Madonna rather than Christ or other saints. Perhaps the desire for a miracle among some of the faithful is such that they may be subject to psychological delusions.

The sight of crying statues has been potent enough to bring some lapsed Catholics back into the fold. And that might be a sufficiently powerful motive to forge the phenomenon. However, there are also obvious opportunities to cash in on such religious events, which attract the faithful in large numbers. Given all this in their armoury, the sceptics might feel they have right on their side.

JURY OUT

But the fact is that there is practically no peer-reviewed research about weeping statues. So the answer, for the moment, does not lie with the scientific community.

As for the Church, officials these days are more cautious when it comes to weeping statues. While some awe-struck witnesses hail the enigma as a sign from God, the Vatican keeps its own counsel on the issue. The current opinion of the Catholic Church is that Churchmen look for God in people rather than artifacts. Secretly, they must be baffled as to how some statues can weep so convincingly after the rudimentary searches for fraud have been carried out. What is even more perplexing is that religious pictures have also been known to cry, while angels and Madonnas sometimes exude the scent of roses or 'sweat' rose-scented oil. Pictures and statues taken into police custody overnight have continued to weep in isolation. Crying, sweating and bleeding are all distinctly

BIBLICAL MYSTERIES

For centuries, the words of the Bible were taken literally, and to heart. To question its wisdom exposed one to inquisition, torture and even death. But today the shackles that bound Bible critics are off, and many have relished the opportunity to probe the enduring mysteries of biblical history. The results have been spellbinding, shedding a bright new light on a time-honoured subject.

The Ark of the Covenant

The discovery of the Ark of the Covenant, considered the greatest of all hidden treasures, would provide indisputable proof that the Old Testament is hard fact rather than embellished fable. Its recovery remains the goal of every modern archaeologist and adventurer but, despite having pieces of the Ark puzzle readily to hand, this great prize has so far eluded everyone.

Although no one is sure where the Ark is, there is plenty of information about its physical appearance in the pages of the Bible, where it is called the Ark of the Testimony, the Ark of the Testament, the Ark of God and the Ark of the Lord. It is better known these days, though, as the Ark of the Covenant.

The purpose of the Ark was as a container for the ten commandments given on stone tablets by God to Moses on Mount Sinai. These were the laws by which the Israelites would live, having escaped from servitude in Egypt and headed for the Promised Land.

In Exodus, the second of the Old Testament books, a description of the Ark reveals that it was made of shittim wood (something similar to acacia), that it was gold-covered inside and out and was topped by a mercy seat comprising two cherubs, also made of gold. It was carried by parallel shittim wood staves, coloured in gold. So it would have been a valuable and extremely distinctive construction.

The size of the Ark was considerable, at two and a half cubits in length and a cubit and a half in width. A cubit reflected a half-arm length, from the tip of the middle finger to the elbow. It is better expressed today as between 43cm and 56cm, which would make the Ark itself about 0.75m by 1.25m.

HEAVY DUTY

However, the Ark was more than just a receptacle for God's laws. It was intended to be a symbol of God's presence in Israel among his chosen people. It was even believed to have supernatural powers, not least because it appeared to have caused the death of one ill-fated man by the name of Uzza. He died when he attempted to steady the Ark, as the oxen hauling the cart that held it stumbled.

Just a single touch of the sacred object was enough to arouse God's anger, according to the account of Uzza's death given in the Chronicles.

The Ark was credited with bringing down the walls of Jericho during one battle and showering misfortunes upon the Philistines after they captured it in another.

There is no shortage of references to the Ark on the pages of the Bible until the time of Solomon. After that, word of the sacred vessel and its whereabouts is sparing, which has fuelled

The Ark was even believed to have supernatural powers, not least because it appeared to have caused the death of one ill-fated man by the name of Uzza.

speculation that it was taken from Jerusalem during the rule of Solomon. The prime suspect for taking the Ark at this point is Menelik I, by tradition the son of Solomon and the Queen of Sheba, who took charge of it following a visit to his father's kingdom.

ETHIOPIAN TREASURE

If this were the case, then it lends credibility to one theory concerning the present day whereabouts of the Ark. For Menelik I was reputedly the founder of Ethiopia, and it is in this unlikely corner of Africa that some believe the Ark resides. The precise location is Axum, a city holy to the enduring Ethiopian Orthodox faith.

Today, the Chapel of the Tablet, where the Ark is allegedly closeted, has a somewhat shabby appearance. Local clergy who have access to the room that houses the Ark (known to them as the Tablet of Moses) are unable to give a full description to curious westerners, as it is veiled at all times. Its power is respected, if not feared. Legend has it that a seventeenth century ruler of Ethiopia called Iyasu was so wise and good that he could peer inside the Ark and seek wisdom from it. Iyasu could, it is said, trace his lineage back to King David. The implication is that others less worthy will perish if they try to handle the venerated artefact. Unfortunately, all attempts to establish a scientific examination of the object have so far been rebuffed.

TIME WARP

But it is possible that this is not the real Ark. Solomon lived and died in the latter half of the tenth century BC. If his son Menelik I really made off with the Ark, he cannot have taken it directly to Axum, since the city did not come into existence

The supernatural powers of the Ark are reputed to have brought the walls of Jericho tumbling down.

The Ark is ornate and covered in gold, but its material value pales into insignificance next to its religious and spiritual importance.

until the third century AD. In another region of Ethiopia, locals insist the Ark remained in a tent on the banks of a lake for 800 years, until the first Christian king of Axum commandeered it. But even if this were true, there is still a chronological gap in the story that remains unexplained.

THE TEMPLE OF SOLOMON

Solomon is also the starting point for a rival theory that places the Ark firmly in Jerusalem. He is supposed to have built a marvellous temple there that became the home of the Ark. All was well until 587BC, when Nebuchadnezzar's marauders destroyed the temple and perhaps everything in it. The assumption is that the second temple, existing in Herod's time and destroyed by the Romans in 70AD, was built on top of the site of the first. So if the lost Ark was placed in the bowels of the first building, then there is plenty of stonework lying on top. Or perhaps Jewish authorities managed to hide this exceptionally significant item elsewhere in Jerusalem, maintaining the secrecy of its whereabouts to their deaths.

While some heavyweight scholars think Jerusalem the most likely site for finding the Ark, its existence cannot be proven until extensive excavations have been carried out. Given the city's sensitive political balance and religious divisions, this kind of work is unlikely to occur in the foreseeable future.

ENTOMBED

One claim says the Ark is housed in Jesus' burial chamber, although this notion is fraught with uncertain scholarship. The whereabouts of the Ark prior to the crucifixion and how or why it was transported to the site are entirely unknown.

Another possibility is that Jordan is the modern home of the Ark. This has obviously been inspired by the discovery of the Dead Sea Scrolls in Jordanian caves during the 1940s and 1950s (see Secret Gospels on page 202). If items of religious value like the scrolls were placed there for security, is it not possible that the Ark would have been hidden there too? But scrutiny of the caves has not turned up the Ark which, given its size, could hardly be overlooked.

So the hunt for the Ark continues. The prospect of finding God's words carved in ancient Hebrew is certainly an alluring one. Yet while it will take a shrewd operator to find the Ark, it will need a brave or even foolhardy person to open it, challenging centuries of superstition concerning its mysterious powers.

The Holy Grail

It may take the form of a chalice, a stone, a herb or even a woman. The Holy Grail has been the subject of treasure hunts, violent quests and detective work down the centuries since the death of Christ. Yet even today, no one knows its true identity or the extent of the spiritual powers it possesses.

BODY OF CHRIST

For many years the Holy Grail was thought to be the cup used by Jesus at the Last Supper. It was allegedly taken by Joseph of Arimithea to the crucifixion and was used to catch the blood spilling from Jesus' wounds. He later retrieved Jesus' body, and for that he was apparently imprisoned for a number of years. Only the chalice kept him alive during those harsh times, as it had life-giving properties.

Later he travelled to England and put the prized chalice into a well at Glastonbury, where he had started one of the early Christian churches. Even today, this well is a place of pilgrimage for the faithful.

The story sounds feasible and it has obvious significance as regards the Eucharist (Holy Communion), one of the foundation stones of today's Christian

Joseph of Arimithea, having travelled to England to found a church, is said to have secreted the legendary Grail at the bottom of this well in Glastonbury.

practice. But in reality, this is only one of many tales surrounding the Holy Grail. No one knows which, if any, is true.

Prior to the era when Christianity dominated, there were similar tales about an object – usually a cauldron – that was imbued with life-giving properties linked to a named hero. Like so many pagan traditions, it was appropriated by Christians and duly tweaked to suit the faith.

CAMELOT CUP

Grail stories that emerged in the Middle Ages frequently had an Arthurian angle to them. Among the most eminent authors of such stories are Chretien de Troyes and Robert de Boron in the twelfth century and Wolfram von Eschenbach who wrote slightly later. It is not known if they were acquainted with a single source or legend regarding the grail, or if they were party to different inspirations. It was Wolfram who lent the interpretation of the grail as a stone, although he may have been speaking allegorically.

The Grail is also sometimes thought to be a herb, mandrake, which is a member of the nightshade plant family. Some believe this herb was administered to Jesus on the cross so he could feign death and 'return' to life some time later. Until the later twentieth century, however, it was the cup theory that prevailed.

If the Grail really was an artefact directly linked to Jesus, could it have survived to the present day? Archaeology has produced numerous vessels of that age or older. There are even Grail claims attached to some cups on display today, including one in Valencia cathedral. Another in Genoa was also highly regarded until, after being dropped two centuries ago, it was found to be decorated with glass rather than emeralds.

Perhaps the Grail was kept in the safe hands of guardians to ensure its survival. One popular current theory is that it was in the possession of the Knights Templar, chivalrous warriors of the twelfth and thirteenth centuries and a somewhat perplexing sect, finally destroyed by an envious French king and a manipulated pope in the early years of the fourteenth century.

Critics argue that a true relic from the time of Christ could never have survived centuries of religious war.

Before then, it might have been in the hands of the Cathars, a heretical group living in France who, by the fourteenth century, had also been eradicated. But the location of the Grail in the centuries prior to the Middle Ages is entirely unknown. The medieval period was marked by a roaring trade in religious relics throughout Europe and the Holy Land and it is fair to imagine that many of these were forged.

THE TITULUS

Critics argue that a true relic from the time of Christ could never have survived centuries of religious war and pillage. Yet there is a good case for the existence today of part of the Titulus, the inscription that was pinned to the cross upon which Jesus died. Indeed, it is said the entire cross was rescued from the execution site firstly by early Christians and then, in 326AD, by the Empress

Helena, mother of the Christian emperor Constantine the Great (280-337AD). It was Constantine, of course, who did much to ensure that the entire Roman Empire converted to Christianity, in accordance with his own beliefs.

Faced with three similar crosses, Helena watched as a gravely ill woman was placed on each. When the woman showed signs of recovery after a spell on the third cross, it was deemed to be the relevant one. Helena, later made a saint, brought the cross to Rome and during the Crusades it was carried with Christian armies. Much later it was apparently captured by a Muslim army and dragged by a horse through the streets of Jerusalem, splintering along the way.

However, part of the Titulus was apparently secreted in the Church of Santa Croce Gerusalemme built by Helena in the grounds of her palace – probably at a time when Rome was enveloped in riots – to be discovered during renovations in 1492. The lettering running from right to left in Hebrew, Greek and Latin lends it credibility, although it could nevertheless be a clever forgery.

If this section of the Titulus is genuine, then it seems more likely that a durable relic such as a gem-encrusted chalice would survive. But there is yet another rival theory that has recently gained ground, which claims that the Holy Grail is not a cup, but a woman.

> *There is yet another rival theory that has recently gained ground, which claims that the Holy Grail is not a cup, but a woman.*

CONTROVERSIAL CLAIMS

In short, the theory maintains that Jesus did not die on the cross but lived, married Mary Magdalene and fathered at least one daughter and possibly other children. Both the womb that carried Jesus' offspring and the bloodline descended from him are known as the Holy Grail.

This highly controversial notion has been explored at length in *The Holy Blood and the Holy Grail* by Michael Baigent, Richard Leigh and Henry Lincoln, first published in 1982, when its conclusion was so radical it caused the suicide of at least one monk. The theme was further popularized in a recent novel called *The Da Vinci Code* by Dan Brown, which has been made into a film. Acres of newsprint have been devoted to this debate and yet still we are no nearer to uncovering the truth.

SANGREAL

The clues are tantalizing, among them the fact that the word grail appears to come from the adaptation from Old French and Latin for plate, *graal*. Remarkably, the translation for Holy Grail is *san grial* while the phrase for royal blood is *sang rial*. One alternative name for the Holy Grail that has endured down the centuries is the *Sangreal*, implying a close relationship with the blood of Jesus. So what is the real meaning, plate or blood? It is all inspirational material for the conspiracy theorists, who believe that the real intention of Jesus was to revive a royal house in Jerusalem and that eventually the bloodline went to France with Mary Magdalene.

The recent controversy surrounding the Holy Grail has centred on the figure of Mary Magdalene. Could she have the been the mother of Christ's children?

The time when religious bigots could pick a theology that best suited their needs, and tell the populace what to believe, is hopefully far behind us. To accept that the Holy Grail might be a person turns hundreds of years of received wisdom on its head and dislodges the cornerstone of a widely-held faith. The edifice of the Christian faith is holding firm in the face of this onslaught, with its supporters calmly refuting what once would have been branded heretical notions. However, until the Holy Grail – in whatever form – is presented for public scrutiny, speculation will abound.

Bible Codes

When author Dan Brown sought to add intrigue to a claim that the bloodline of Jesus continued today, he looked towards another of history's most enigmatic figures to flesh out the tale – Leonardo da Vinci (1452-1519), artist, scientist and visionary. But did da Vinci really include compelling clues in his work about great strategic truths that would affect the faith of millions?

INTO THE FRAY

Dan Brown would have us believe that the truth about Jesus is concealed in da Vinci's great religious works. He states, for example, that in *The Last Supper*, painted in the late fifteenth century, the figure generally taken to be John the Evangelist is in fact Mary Magdalene. She and Jesus are dressed in mirror image colours and appear to be joined at the hip, perhaps a clue from da Vinci that they were a couple. As they lean away from one another they produce a V-shape representative of the chalice or holy grail (see page 195) so closely connected with stories of the Last Supper, but absent from the table. The symbol-seeking protagonists of Brown's book uphold that this was da Vinci's way of saying the chalice was Mary's womb. Furthermore, Peter's hostile hand illustrates his antipathy to Mary as Jesus' chosen successor. Brown was inspired to this controversial theory about the painting by Lynn Picknett and Clive Prince's book *The Templar Revelation*.

But facts about *The Last Supper* stop far short of establishing the code that Brown and his millions of readers long to see. Da Vinci was experimenting with an oil and tempera mix, which meant he could make swift changes as he worked. He did not realize that the colours would degenerate quickly, and despite several renovations, it remains difficult to say how the Mary/John figure originally appeared.

Critics of the novel's assertion of a true-life da Vinci code believe the artist had chosen to depict the last supper according to the gospel of St John, which did not mention a chalice at all. What is more, there was an artistic convention that frequently saw John painted in feminine form.

COMPLEX ARTIST

Other paintings by da Vinci, including the *Virgin of the Rocks*, are said to be littered with clues that in essence debunk some aspects of biblical history. Defenders of the faith point to the fact that many of da Vinci's original scenes have vanished under subsequent layers of paint.

Da Vinci was certainly a complex and intelligent man, more than capable of threading themes into his work for the benefit of future generations. He enjoyed mirror-writing and often indulged in riddles and wordplay to keep messages hidden. Like other artists, he worked with the threat of heresy looming large. It is surely possible that he used encrypted messages to convey his own point of view at a time when he was unable to speak freely about his thoughts and beliefs for fear of hideous punishment by the Church.

CODED BELIEF

But belief in the possibility of a da Vinci code is also fuelled by mankind's enduring fascination with codes and their use to convey esoteric knowledge. The theory that codes exist within the Bible is a topic that perplexes biblical scholars and mathematicians alike.

The words handed down from God via Moses have always been sacred to the Jewish people. If the ancient texts such as the Torah possessed hidden words and phrases it would make them even more potent than previously imagined.

In medieval times, students of the Torah began looking at it in a new light. Within the words they saw codes that brought forth new messages, which they believed issued directly from God. Among the most prominent of the scholars was Bachya ben Asher, a fourteenth century Spanish Rabbi, who became the first on record to announce that a code lay within the words of the Torah. However, it was not until the twentieth century that serious study of messages embedded in the Torah began again.

This time it was Rabbi Michael Dov Weissmandl (1903-1957) probing the theory of Torah codes. In short, he discovered that the Hebrew spelling of Torah could be found in at least three books of the Torah by using a particular formula. Inspired by his findings, Israeli schoolteacher Avraham Oren toyed with the codes until his work attracted the attention of the Hebrew University of Jerusalem.

PUBLIC INTEREST

Three men are credited with more in-depth work on the Torah codes. Eliyahu Rips, Doron Witztum and Yoav Rosenberg succeeded in uncovering the names and dates of thirty-four great Rabbi sages within the confines of Genesis. There was, they believed, only a remote possibility that the names and dates occurred by chance. They had their study published in the peer-reviewed *Statistical Science Journal*, lending it significant credibility. This fostered international interest – and a degree of sensationalism – at a time when computers meant Torah investigation was a simpler process than ever before.

Soon everybody was using code-breaking techniques to find hidden messages in both the Hebrew text of the Torah and in the Bible. There was rumour of predictions that had come to pass and prophecies as yet unfulfilled. Supposedly encoded warnings about the advent of Hitler and the assassination of Israeli premier Yitzhak Rabin were just two of the topical subjects that made banner headlines around the world.

Soon everybody was using code-breaking techniques to find hidden messages in both the Hebrew text of the Torah and in the Bible.

In terms of faith, it was deemed proof that God existed and that his words to Moses revealed a pre-planned scheme for human existence that is still unfolding.

So what is the key to the Torah code? It is a fundamentally simple system called Equidistant Letter Sequencing, or ELS. First the code-breaker runs all the sentences of the literature together so there are no spaces for punctuation and no

significance for capital letters. The code begins with a given letter, skips a certain number of letters then alights on another before making the same skip forwards to the third letter.

To find the word 'codes' in the phrase 'can you endorse this?', take a letter and miss three until the word 'codes' emerges.

C A N Y O U E N D O R S E T H I S

Da Vinci's famous painting of the Last Supper is now the subject of a heated debate. Did the artist include symbolism that could change the course of history?

Code breaking takes another leap ahead when the words are arranged in matrices. Messages can be picked out by reading forwards, backwards, up or down.

MEANINGLESS WORD PLAY?

While the biblical word searches presented an intriguing puzzle, there were many Jews, Christians and secular academics who doubted the premise that God had hidden messages to mankind in this way. After all, there are different versions of both the Hebrew Torah and the English Bible. Witztum and company used the Koren version. But had the Codex edition been selected as an example, then entirely different results would have been yielded. Idiosyncracies surrounding the Hebrew language further complicate the issue. During the thousands of years they have been in existence, both the Torah and the Bible have evolved and do not mirror the original words allegedly delivered by God to Moses.

Yet despite the difficulties, biblical codes are back in fashion. Enthusiasts the world over are working to decrypt divine mysteries, inspired by such theories as the da Vinci code. The complex abundance of holy texts and revered artwork will surely keep them busy for a long time to come.

Secret Gospels

The names of the four gospels trip from the tongue, as familiar as the names of our children or the first lines of our address. But recently, biblical archaeology has unearthed new documents and fragmented manuscripts that are throwing shadows over long-accepted doctrines.

THE JUDAS GOSPEL

One of the latest and most remarkable finds has been the Gospel of Judas. That a book was devoted to this biblical black sheep at all is enough to raise eyebrows. The four gospels attributed to the apostles Matthew, Mark, Luke and John, all concur that it was Judas who betrayed Jesus, so directly leading to the crucifixion. When Roman guards appeared after the last supper, Judas identified Jesus by kissing him, a symbolic and treacherous act. For this infamy, he was paid thirty pieces of silver. The gospel writers imply that he went on to meet a miserable end and, what is more, he became the most reviled man in Christendom.

However, an ancient manuscript that has only recently been translated from Coptic – the language of Egyptian Christians – puts a different slant on events. Crucially, it says Judas was hand-picked by Jesus for the task of betrayal. 'You will exceed all of them. For you will sacrifice the man that clothes me,' Jesus tells him, meaning that Judas will liberate Christ from his body, so that his true destiny (to die to save mankind) can be fulfilled. So it is revealed that in fact Jesus held Judas in high esteem, knowing that he alone among the disciples fully understood the ordeal that lay ahead – and the spiritual meaning behind it. According to the codex, Jesus was also aware that his friend would be scorned for generations, although still he encouraged Judas to embrace the task. 'It is an act of sacrifice,' Jesus said. 'It is good and pious.'

MOMENTOUS DISCOVERY

The Judas gospel was discovered sometime during the 1970s, near the Nile city of Al Minya in a limestone cave. There followed a mysterious series of deals which led to the flaking manuscript being left in an American safe-deposit box, as the owner failed to secure the price he hoped for. It was not until 2000 that the gospel was finally bought, and the process of translation and restoration began in earnest. The manuscript by now comprised twenty-seven main pieces and scores of much smaller ones. Prominent in the painstaking process was Professor Rudolphe Kasser, 79, one of the few people in the world capable of understanding the ancient phrasing of the text.

The results, announced in April 2006 to a worldwide audience, cast Judas in a fresh light, although findings do not alter the thrust of the

Maybe Judas was a radical trying to plot a revolution against the occupying Romans and was finally frustrated with Christ's lack of action.

Easter story. Judas was something of an outsider amongst the apostles, as he was from Judea, while the rest were from Galilee. In the past, conjecture about why he betrayed Jesus has focused on his political ambitions. Maybe Judas was a radical trying to plot a revolution against the occupying Romans and was finally frustrated with Jesus' lack of action. Or perhaps he was concerned that the troubles stirred up by Jesus would result in long-term problems for Jews. However, if the recently translated gospel is to be believed, all this is nothing but idle speculation, as he was actually acting with Jesus' best intentions at heart.

The kiss of Judas has traditionally been depicted as a heinous act of betrayal that condemned Jesus to death. But was the situation in fact more complex?

MYSTICAL BELIEF

Thanks to another cache of manuscripts found at Nag Hammadi in Egypt in 1945, we know that the Gospel of Judas was not the only one on the black list. The Gospel of Mary, the Exegesis on the Soul and the Acts of Peter are among many religious writings that have an unaccustomed ring. Again in Coptic, they were almost certainly translations of Greek originals. Today they are known as the Gnostic Gospels, discarded from mainstream Christian study for being outside orthodox thinking, and little known except among a devout few.

Gnosis comes from the Greek word for knowledge, and gnostic worshippers have long sought a mysterious, almost magical knowledge that would bring them closer to God. But as Christianity sought to define itself in the first few centuries of its evolution, Gnosticism was one of a number of concepts and ideologies that was erased from the mainstream. Gnostic beliefs may not even be rooted in Christianity, but owe more to other faiths in the region, such as Zoroastrianism.

DEAD SEA SCROLLS

Another important find in biblical archaeology was the Dead Sea Scrolls, discovered in Jordan in 1947. A Bedouin shepherd seeking animals lost from his flock tossed a stone into a cave, to frighten the animals out into the open. Instead of the expected bleating, he heard the crash of a shattering pot. On further investigation, he found a collection of vessels containing religious scripts.

By 1956, eleven more caves at the site, some lying 400m below sea level, had yielded a startling number of documents written in Aramaic, Greek and Hebrew. Among them were the lyrically titled Book of Secrets, the Book of Giants and the Divine Throne Chariot. Tests proved they were written between the third century BC and 68AD, which means that Jesus would have been alive when some were inscribed, although apparently he is not mentioned. The most impressive of these finds was the Great Isaiah Scroll, 8.5m long and at least 1,000 years older than any other known copy.

A Bedouin shepherd tossed a stone into a cave to frighten his animals out into the open. Instead of bleating, he heard the crash of a shattering pot.

But perhaps the most significant were the items that were closely linked to the Old Testament, that do not appear in modern versions. These include psalms attributed to King David and previously unknown prophecies by Ezekiel, Jeremiah and Daniel. Unfortunately, the scrolls were mostly in a woeful condition, literally scattered on cave floors in scores of pieces, which left them difficult to transcribe. The task to re-assemble them continues, six decades after they were first discovered. These were Jewish rather than Gnostic documents, probably the work of a sect unpopular with both the orthodox Jewish faith in the region and the Romans. It is likely that these, and the other scripts already discussed, were secreted in the wake of a Jewish uprising against the Romans. Vengeance would surely include the destruction of valued religious items, as the Romans demonstrated when they destroyed the Temple of Solomon in 70AD.

Religious scholars looking for answers about Jesus and God have long found them on the pages of the four best known gospels. But for those outside the confines of faith, the questions continue, and those students who quest for historical or philosophical rather than religious knowledge relish the chance to resolve their issues with new, previously unknown material as well as old.

The Garden of Eden

In our mind's eye, the Garden of Eden is a paradise inhabited by exotic creatures and lush foliage, God's idyllic chosen spot, threatened only by the presence of man. For years it has been accepted as an imaginative figment that perhaps illustrates mankind's despoilment of the planet. But the latest evidence turned up by archaeologists points to where it might actually have existed.

Genesis, the biblical book that tells the story of the Garden of Eden, contains a few clues about its location. It is marked by four rivers, for example, and its comfortable climate makes it suitable for every kind of fruit tree. Numerous people have suggested places that fit the bill down the years, often inspired by devout faith to give credence to stories of the Bible. But many felt that the Old Testament amounted to little more than allegorical fables and believed the Garden of Eden was mythical in the same way that the gold-embellished El Dorado supposedly lies in South America.

However, there is another approach, that pays heed not only to the Bible, but to other stories from various religions, cultures and legends. It brings new breath to an ancient theory that says the Garden of Eden really existed. This idea was first fashioned by Reginald Walker, a little-known academic who flew in the face of accepted notions by saying that the Garden of Eden was a place existing where the borders of Iran, Iraq and Turkey converge. Although Walker never made the trip there to encounter the region's intense heat and occasionally

The Garden of Eden is reputed to have been a haven for plants and wildlife, threatened only by the presence of mankind.

inhospitable terrain, his linguistic journey proved vital, for he claimed to have identified the four rivers in Genesis.

The Euphrates river was named, while the Hiddekel is a straightforward Hebrew translation of the Tigris. The remaining two, the Gihon and the Pishon, were more of a challenge. But Walker discovered the river today known as the Aras was once called the Gaihun, prior to the Islamic invasion of the area in the eighth century. It is a short jump from that to Gihon and is even tagged precisely as that in one Victorian book. Meanwhile, the River Uizon, said Walker, was a linguistic corruption of Pishon. To the east, Walker noted the village of Noqdi which he felt might be a candidate for Nod, where Cain was exiled following the murder of his brother Abel. Walker died in the late 1980s without adding further evidence for his theories.

JOURNEY TO PARADISE

David Rohl picked up Walker's baton and mounted several expeditions to the region in question, certain that this was the correct geographic locale for the Garden of Eden. Among the ugly industry in the vicinity of the Iranian city of Tabriz, he found verdant fields, vineyards and productive orchards in a fertile plain trapped between mountain ranges and the great lakes of Urmia and Van. Adam means 'man of red earth' and God allegedly made him from local dust. Looming over the plain at one end was a mountain apparently made of red ochre, which now seems to have added significance.

From there, Rohl plotted a logical route around the region for the offspring and descendants of Adam and Eve, in much the same way as the Bible described. He fitted a convincing chronology to this course, and published a book entitled *The Genesis of Civilization* recording his findings.

Rohl also turned up archaeological evidence for a major flood. He maintains that Noah's Ark stalled on Mount Judi Gargh, about 160km from his designated Garden of Eden, in about 3,100BC, and that humanity largely survived and thrived through Noah's ingenuity. Intriguingly, Christians in about 500AD built a monastery atop the same mountain and called it the Cloister of the Ark. Noah's sons, Rohl thinks, became the Sumerians, the builders of mighty cities with sophisticated technology and a literary culture. Controversially, he thinks other descendants of Noah set off around the Arabian peninsular and into the Red Sea, and ultimately began the high-achieving Egyptian dynasties.

Rohl believes that Adam is man's oldest ancestor, as recorded in the Jewish tradition. Indeed, all long-standing civilizations have in common a patriarch who is celebrated by subsequent generations. In Assyrian culture this is Adamu, by Babylonian tradition it is Amuta, while the Sumerian counterpart is Adapa. These cultures feature other characters who are remarkably similar in name as those in the Bible. All were largely oral traditions.

Why has no one identified the Garden of Eden before? Put simply, Rohl believes that no one – with the exception of Walker – was interested in

In 2006, an international team of scientists uncovered a 'lost world' in the Indonesian jungle.

A type of honeyeater bird was one of the many new species discovered in a remote corner of Indonesia in 2006, dubbed the 'modern Eden'.

looking. What he has done is to take the threads of existing and well-established traditions and weave them together as one. In an era when the Bible has oft been debunked by historians, Rohl has been working to bolster up the original mysteries that, perhaps rightly, held sway for centuries.

MODERN EDEN

The good news is that a Garden of Eden-style paradise has not been entirely lost to the human race. Even in the twenty-first century it still exists, albeit outside the public gaze. In 2006, an international team of scientists uncovered a 'lost world' in the Indonesian jungle, and with it dozens of new animal and plant species. They discovered a new species of honeyeater bird; a new large mammal for Indonesia, the golden-mantled tree kangaroo (*Dendrolagus pulcherrimus*); and more than twenty new species of frogs, including a tiny microhylid frog less than 14mm long, and four new butterfly species. There were also unknown plants, including five new species of palms and a rhododendron with flowers of 15cm across.

The researchers spent a month in this earthly paradise, detailing the wildlife and foliage on the lower hills right up to near the summit of the Foja range, which reaches to 2,000m high. The place is so remote that no tracks lead to it, and the team had to be dropped in by helicopter. Even local tribes, the Kwerba and the Papasena, had no idea that it existed at all. 'It's as close to the Garden of Eden as you're going to find on earth,' said Bruce Beehler, co-leader of the group.

The idea of a Garden of Eden, real or allegorical, has served as potent reminder down the centuries of the fragile balance of man's natural environment.

Acknowledgements

Image copyright © Arcturus Publishing pp. 2, 8, 17 ; Phyllis Budinger p. 15;
Annette Martin p. 93; George Phillips p. 136; Corbis pp. 5 (centre, bottom),
6 (top, centre bottom, bottom), 7 (all),13, 19, 27, 29, 35, 38, 39, 41, 46, 49,
51, 52, 57, 59, 67, 72, 77, 79, 91, 104, 112, 119, 121, 122, 125, 128, 131, 133,
142, 144, 147, 150, 153, 155, 158, 164, 167, 168, 170, 177, 181, 188, 193, 195,
198, 203, 205, 207; Hulton Archive pp. 24, 31, 44, 82, 140, 160, 184;
Mary Evans pp; 16, 18, 33, 63, 65, 68, 71, 74, 87, 106, 111, 115, 117, 126,
138, 162, 173, 176, 179, 194, 201; Rex Features pp. 5 (top), 6 (centre top),
11, 61, 88, 97, 98, 100, 102; Shutterstock pp. 84, 108, 190

The author would like to thank the following sources:

pp.10-13, Phyllis A. Budinger for access to her informative
paper *Angel Hair Analyses*;

pp. 48-50, *The Jersey Devil* by James F. McGloy and
Ray Miller (The Middle Atlantic Press, 1976) for
Nelson Evans' description of the Jersey Devil;

pp.116-118, The University of Exeter Library (Special Collections)
and the Theo Brown Estate, for access to original documents,
and the Met. Office library for unearthing weather records for 1855.